KU-660-663

Making The Ball Roll

A Complete Guide to Youth Football for the Aspiring Soccer Coach

Ray Power

BENNION
KEARNY

Published in 2014 by Bennion Kearny Limited.

Copyright © Bennion Kearny Ltd 2014

Ray Power has asserted his right under the Copyright, Designs and Patents Act, 1988 to be identified as the author of this book.

ISBN: 978-1-909125-52-0

All Rights Reserved. No part of this publication may be reproduced, stored in a retrieval system, or transmitted in any form or by any means, electronic, mechanical, photocopying, recording or otherwise, without the prior permission of the publisher.

This book is sold subject to the condition that it shall not, by way of trade or otherwise, be lent, re-sold, hired out or otherwise circulated without the publisher's prior consent in any form of binding or cover other than that it which it is published and without a similar condition including this condition being imposed on the subsequent purchaser.

Bennion Kearny has endeavoured to provide trademark information about all the companies and products mentioned in this book by the appropriate use of capitals. However, Bennion Kearny cannot guarantee the accuracy of this information.

Published by Bennion Kearny Limited
6 Woodside
Churnet View Road
Oakamoor
ST10 3AE

www.BennionKearny.com

Cover image: ©Shutterstock/somkku

Acknowledgements

To Lisa – for having the patience to put up with endless days, evenings and weekends of me locked away reading, researching, sourcing and writing. Thank you for also proof-reading every single word of *Making the Ball Roll*, even though you care little for the beautiful game!

To James – thank you for supporting me on this journey and for indulging my ideas and ultimately believing in *Making the Ball Roll*. May we work on many more projects together.

To Helen and Peter – mam and dad – I hope this makes you proud. That is all I have ever wanted.

Thank you to all my **colleagues, friends in soccer** and **coach educators** who have challenged my views on soccer and not allowed me to settle and go stale in my own coaching.

Thank you to **Kevin** and **James** for adding their weight of expertise to their relevant areas, namely psychology and communication.

Finally, thank you to those, both **anonymous and named, who contributed their *Real Coach Experiences*** to each chapter and to other areas of the book. Your stories have truly brought the lessons of this book to life.

About the Author

Ray Power is a 33-year-old coach with over a decade of experience in soccer, youth development and teaching - across three different continents.

Ray is currently the Technical Director in Tanzania, working in association with the Tanzanian Football Federation and Premier League club Sunderland AFC. He is qualified to UEFA A Licence and has extensive experience as an Academy Coach and a freelance and FA coach educator.

Table of Contents

Foreword

"There is so much information out there at the touch of a button. The difficulty today's coaches have is sorting the useful from the not so useful ideas. *Making The Ball Roll* does this for you!"

(The Coaching Family)

Youth soccer has changed dramatically in the last twenty years. Two decades ago, if you went to any local park on a Saturday or Sunday morning you would see the same sights wherever you went; muddy pitches, muddy players, parents shouting to their child and his or her team, managers shouting instructions to their players, as if they were in Sir Alex Ferguson or Arrigo Sacchi's first teams. You would see children, some as young as nine years old, running around, confused and overwhelmed on huge adult-sized pitches.

Imagine playing in those games! No doubt most of you can relate to that picture. I can remember coming home after games on Saturday mornings, at 10 or 11 years old, feeling utterly confused and thinking I was a terrible soccer player. Our coach would shout at us if we made mistakes, training sessions consisted of a couple of line drills and then a kick-around. I very nearly walked away – some of my friends actually did. I truly believe it was nothing to do with my coach as a person. He was a good guy. I believe it was his lack of education as a youth coach that meant he knew no other way of dealing with young soccer players, treating us instead as 'mini-adults'.

Youth soccer, and particularly the coaching, needed some direction and guidance. Youth clubs and their team managers were basically doing as they saw fit. Anyone could run a kid's team. There were no obvious best practice guidelines or required qualifications. If you were a coach, qualified or otherwise, you were in a difficult place. Qualifications existed but local courses were difficult to find, and that's if coaches could afford to attend them. Coaching books were poor and would only inadequately suggest rigid drills to improve your team. Grassroots clubs, youth coaches, and managers, needed a vision and some guidance.

When Ray approached us and presented his ideas for *Making The Ball Roll*, we were delighted to throw our support behind the book's intent. When we received the end product, his ideas had transformed into a fantastic book and coaching resource for coaches at any level of the game. For those who wish to immerse themselves in soccer and the discipline of coaching, the following pages will revolutionize the way you work with youth soccer players – whether they are eight or 18.

Ray has been an active participant in presenting his ideas on Twitter for a couple of years. He is open and honest, not to mention very knowledgeable about the game and the many different levels it is played at. He has shared lots of resources with fellow coaches – including session plans, development models and best-practice documents – but felt it needed more.

Coaches nowadays are hungry for ideas, hungry for education and hungry to improve themselves to benefit their young players. We see this all the time on our Twitter feed. There is so much information out there at the touch of a button. The difficulty today's coaches have is sorting the useful from the not so useful ideas. *Making The Ball Roll* does this for you!

99% of the soccer coaching community do not get a lot of free time – whether you are a busy parent, a student at university, or you are working in a full-time job. Even full-time academy coaches can have very limited time to truly study the game. *Making The Ball Roll* will save coaches time as Ray has put an abundance of knowledge and study all in one place. He himself admits that the concept for the book was what he wanted to read ten years ago!

Each chapter contains a distinct theme and topic, allowing the coach to dip in and out of specific learning – whether that is communication, skill acquisition, or talent identification. Ensure you read every page, however, as virtually every section gives you, the coach, something to consider, ponder over, and even questions your coaching habits! The illustrations are thought provoking, and best of all, Ray backs up his opinions with examples from the top level of soccer. Getting to the end of each chapter and reading the Real Coach Experience section was a particular favourite of ours.

We are positive that reading this book will better prepare you as a youth coach in the modern era. We hope you enjoy reading through, and putting into practice, the various ideas and solutions presented in *Making The Ball Roll.*

Ben Trinder and Liam Donovan

'The Coaching Family'

www.coachingfamily.com | @coachingfamily

Introduction

"Success is no accident. It is hard work, perseverance, learning, study, sacrifice and most of all, love of what you are doing or learning to do." (Pelé)

It seems appropriate to begin this book with such an inspiring quote from one of the greatest players in soccer's history. The dedication of such a naturally gifted player to work and learning can and should be an inspiration to us all.

We normally reserve these types of quotes for our players. It is the players that should be working hard, persevering, and learning. *We, as coaches however, must do the same.* Regardless of the level of soccer you played at, or how many years you have been coaching, this hard work and learning must be a constant.

A few years back, on a coach education course, the tutor began by introducing us to *The Kubler-Ross Change Curve*. The *Kubler-Ross* model suggests that when we are faced with change, or are challenged with new ideas, our initial reaction can be negative. Emotions can range from disbelief to anger and a rejection of the information provided. The tutor challenged us to race through, or even past, these initial reactions and settle quickly into the more positive emotions of open-mindedness and learning. My suggestion then, as you read this book, is to be open-minded and willing to learn.

Making the Ball Roll will challenge your opinions of soccer coaching – some of them may be long-standing norms that you have used for years. You will not accept all of the information and advice provided – that is okay! A big part of individual learning is rejecting as well as accepting opinions.

Enjoy the read, hopefully even the bits you disagree with will, at the very least, provoke thought! There is no 'one size fits all' when it comes to coaching styles, opinions, or ways of working. What there is, however, is a huge amount of good practice and poor practice.

Each of the 15 chapters that follow deals with a specific and distinct area of youth soccer development. Within these chapters I have included lots of theory, detail, study, visuals and references. One of my frustrations when I was learning my trade as a coach was that I had to consult ten different books to learn about the ten different aspects of coaching I wanted to pursue. Many of the references I have included throughout are freely available – either online or in other publications. If you want to learn more, these are great 'go-to' resources. Some documents and resources I have consulted are not referenced however. Most of these are from clubs, friends, or trusted sources in the game that I would not like to divulge.

At the end of each chapter I include a *Real Coach Experience* section that intends to bring the theory and statements of the chapter 'to life'. These stories come from all corners of the game – from top-level elite Academy coaches and ex-professionals to part-time dads involved in the game. Some of the contributors have chosen to remain anonymous.

Introduction

For ease of writing, I have used 'he', 'him', 'his', etc., rather than adding or interspersing the feminine equivalent throughout the book. This book, though, is for coaches and players of both sexes.

Enjoy the read. This book is written and influenced by youth soccer coaches *for* youth soccer coaches.

Understanding the Argument for Development Over Results

"As a kid they teach you not to play to win, but to grow in ability as a player. At Barca, we trained every day with the ball, I hardly ever ran without a ball at my feet. It was a form of training aimed very clearly at developing your skills." (Lionel Messi)

There is no better starting point to becoming a better coach than to scrutinise the most fervent argument that surrounds soccer coaching today – prioritizing development over results.

Succinctly, this means that the coach will put the *short-term* result of the game to one side, and prioritize the *long-term* development of his players. A coach's unrelenting desire to win games, leagues and medals is replaced by a more narrow focus on how his players play, how they are developing, and where they need to improve. Lionel Messi, above, notes how this was achieved at Barcelona, the world's most renowned football development academy.

This can be a very difficult concept to understand at first. Surely the whole point of sport is to win? Surely if you win games it means that you have the best players? We will analyse why that may not be the case.

Athlete First, Winning Second

The 'Athlete First, Winning Second' philosophy is concisely summarized by Rainer Martens in his comprehensive book *Successful Coaching*. He boldly states that *every* decision made by a coach should have the player at its core, and in doing so, it should put winning into second place, and firmly into perspective.

This does not mean that winning is unimportant. Everyone likes to win. Everyone wants to win. Everyone feels better when they win. Winning and competing are an innate part of the human psyche. After all, adults use competition to motivate children to do anything ("See who can pick up the most toys"; "I will time how long it takes you to tidy your room!").[1]

By prioritizing winning in youth soccer, however, we can lose focus of the long-term development of players in terms of tactics, technique, physical relevance and psychology. It may well also affect them socially. When winning and the focus on results are given less importance, however, it creates an environment that focuses on improvement and excellence. The English Football Association's Development Manager for Youth and Mini-Soccer, Nick Levett, sums it up excellently:

"It's not non-Competitive. It's child-centred competition... Non-competitive implies everything is a friendly, like the game doesn't matter. That's simply not the case. All games matter to the kids, for some adults it matters too much and therein lies a lot of the problems."

---

[1] At times, winning *may* be what is best for the group – especially if the coach wants players to buy into his methods or philosophy. Maybe the next stage for an older youth player is to find ways of winning a game. The development coach must carefully and honestly choose when this is appropriate.

But How Do We Know Who Wins?

The scoreline is not the only measure of success. There are alternative ways to measure performance that are much more productive during the journey of young players. An ex-colleague of mine, who worked with 8 to 11 year olds, was a master at it. He, and the players and parents, measured the score of the game in terms of 'good goals' the team scored ('good' goals were scored by playing out from the back, a clever pass, individual pieces of skill, etc.). They discounted 'bad goals' scored against them (goals from overtly direct play, long throws, brute force, etc.).

This took enormous strength of character from the coach and a complete buy-in, not only from players, but also from parents (on one occasion, I actually witnessed parents calculating the phantom score to see how the game had gone!). This way, winning was given a back-seat role, but the players still had the opportunity to develop their winning mentality, which is crucial in their progress as soccer players.

Winning at All Costs

In *A Cultured Left Foot*, Musa Okwonga poses the question of whether the emphasis on youth competition is perversely affecting young players. He states that an early emphasis on competition negatively impacts imagination, creative freedom, and fun for soccer players.

The issue of an over-emphasis on competition is further constructed by Terry Michler in his article *Fun or Fear? What Motivates Young Players?* He traces the way that adults have taken the concept of 'play' (i.e. activity for fun and enjoyment, which young players learn from as a consequence) and positively changed it. Adults organized it, adding discipline and skill development into the equation. However, as it has evolved into a world dominated by competition and winning, the key elements of 'play' have been taken out of the equation. So, while adding genuine value to youth soccer, adults have also extracted a vital part of youth development by placing too much focus on competition and results, and not enough on the concept of play.

The win at all costs mentality of soccer coaches is nothing new. Up and down the land it exists. The desire to win is present on every green grass pitch and on every not-so-green grass patch of every team and every club you would care to visit. This stretches from Champions League soccer right down to junior teams playing in small-sided games. From Barcelona, Manchester United and Inter Milan to Village Panthers and Manor Primary School. Winning feels good, winning produces confidence and winning allows coaches and players to have a certain prestige in the community. Every single one of us would choose winning over losing any day.

But at what cost?

The Changing Face of Soccer

Soccer has changed considerably over the past two decades. Tactics have evolved and are constantly evolving, often in reaction to previous tactical changes.[2] Technically, there has been a shift towards a more possession-based game where keeping the ball for long sequences is emphasized. Physically, club scouts are now prizing speed rather than size and strength. More value, though arguably not enough, is being placed on the psychological element of the game.

These changes have real and serious implications for the coach who is working to develop the youth soccer player. It is a necessity that coaches working within youth development are preparing their players effectively for a game that has changed significantly in recent decades, and which will continue to change. Given the game's rapid transformation, the coach is arguably

---

[2] For those interested in tracing the evolution of soccer tactics, read Jonathan Wilson's *Inverting the Pyramid*. It is also a book that poses serious questions about the tactical shifts of the future.

preparing players for a kind of game that does not yet exist. It is therefore imperative that the coach remains up-to-date with the evolution of the game to keep their players up-to-speed.

As a result, we need to examine how a 'win at all costs' mentality affects the development of players in terms of their tactical, technical and physical development, within the context of how the game is evolving. We also need to inspect the implications of our coaching on the psychological and social growth of our players. We will find that all these changes are inextricably linked.

Tactical Changes

Tactical Changes in Recent Decades
Increased tactical variety
More teams playing variants of 4-3-3 and 4-2-3-1
A recent resurgence of the back 3, especially in Italy
An increased emphasis on counter-attack and 'counter-pressing'[3]
More teams defending deep and compactly
Ability to defend against counter-attacks and 'countering the counter'
Teams attack centrally through defences, rather than around them – less crossing and increased importance of 'zone 14'[4]
Attacking full-backs[5] - even both attacking simultaneously
Full-backs often used as a team's attacking width, and more recently as extra central midfielders when in possession
Positional rotations (midfield and attacking positions)
Use of deep-lying 'holding' midfield player - soccer's quarter-back
The number '10' as 'inside wingers'
Use of just one central striker - or sometimes no striker at all!
'Half positions' - The 'False 9' (Messi); inverted wingers[6]
Wingers that play 'on the wrong side'
The death of the strike partnership, and its recent rebirth

The pressure to perform to win, on both players and coaches, impacts the tactics adopted by teams. Strategies devised to win games tend to be conservative and less flamboyant. Michler takes up this argument again:

---

[3] For further information on counter-attacking and counter-pressing, please see chapter 10.

[4] Zone 14 is the central area outside of the penalty box, also known as 'the hole'

[5] As of March 2013, only 4 players in Europe's top 5 divisions (England, France, Germany, Italy and Spain) had more assists than Philippe Lahm, Bayern Munich's German right-back who had 9 (source: whoscored.com). During the 2013-14 season, the full-backs at Bayern Munich have been joining attacks centrally, as if they were extra midfield players.

[6] There is a new breed of attacking player that is virtually position-less. Under Roberto Di Matteo, Chelsea's three attacking midfielders, Mata, Hazard and Oscar virtually played wherever they wanted in advanced midfield positions.

"Creativity, imagination, risk-taking and personal expression are compromised to play in a safe and effective way. The greatest players in the world of soccer today grew up playing in the streets without adult coaching and supervision, and learned to play by freely trying things without the consequence of making a mistake. Learning becomes greatly impeded when mistakes are not tolerated."

Will your under-10 team learn more by 'chasing' a game and bombarding the opponent's goal area with Alamo-style attacks and Rory Delap-esque throw-ins? Or by remaining calm and trying to penetrate the opposition's defence with creative passes or a flamboyant individual pieces of skill? Will the players gain more in the long-term by forcing a crude equalizing goal or by problem-solving more creative ways of scoring a goal? Both questions are clearly rhetorical, but they appear frequently on youth pitches the world over.

A pet hate of mine is the simplicity of the pre-match team formation screens shown before televised games. It depicts, to the wider world, that tactics and movements are performed in straight lines when, in reality, they are free flowing and chaotic. I will accept that these simplistic visuals help the viewer quickly understand their favourite team's formation, but basing our understanding of tactics in this way is very misleading. Soccer is not chess. The variables of a game are unending.

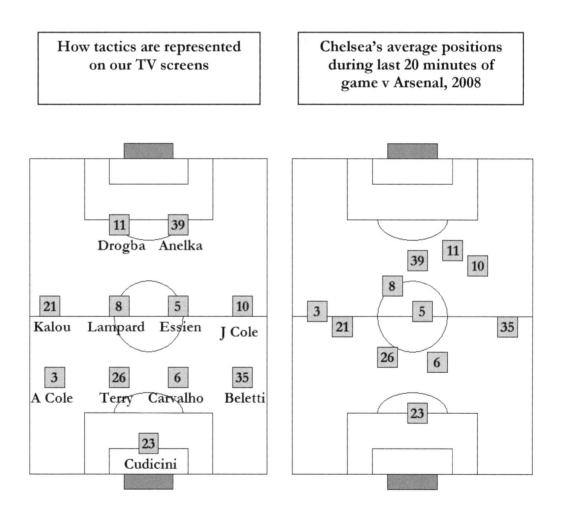

In *Bounce – The Myth of Talent and the Power of Practice*, Matthew Syed points this out in an explicit manner, noting that the complexity of predicting soccer is virtually impossible, unlike the predefined moves of pieces on a chessboard.[7] Syed tells a story of a group who were attempting to create a computer program that simulated the complex combination of combinations and variables involved in a soccer game – and found it impossible. We therefore need to produce players who can deal with these variables and chaotically unpredictable occurrences, rather than teach them to become tactical robots as represented to us on our television screens.

The role of the forward player is changing immeasurably. There has been a huge tactical shift towards playing with one striker, and indeed, with the success of Pep Guardiola's Barcelona from 2008 to 2012 and the Spanish national team's European Championship victory in 2012, more teams are willing to consider playing with no natural striker at all. Playing with no recognized striker (or 4-6-0) is expected to be the next revolutionary tactical shift in the game over the next decade.

As a consequence, strikers are becoming a dying breed, or at least those that are *only* goalscorers are. Jonathan Wilson sums this up concisely in his excellent book on the history of football tactics, *Inverting the Pyramid*: "The modern forward… is far more than a goalscorer, and it may even be that a modern forward can be successful without scoring goals." Wilson traces the career of Michael Owen. Midway through his career, with the impact of teams prioritizing one multi-functional striker, a 25 year old Owen, with an international goal-scoring rate of almost one in every two games, was unable to find a Champions League club to invest in his services, and ended up joining (and being relegated with) Newcastle United.[8]

Winner of the Ballon d'Or (the award for being the best player in Europe) in 2001, Owen himself admitted that he needed to evolve his game by adding skills such as link up play, dropping off the front, and holding the ball up. He felt he could no longer just be a goalscorer that made runs off the shoulder of the last defender. Had soccer tactics not evolved to prioritizing the use of just one main striker, there is a strong argument that the careers of goalscorers like Michael Owen and Jermain Defoe may have been even more prolific.

The tactics or strategies that coaches adopt and implement need to reflect footballing chaos and variables, and allow players to survive in these types of scenarios.[9] Players also need to be taught the technical skills required to thrive in this environment.

Technical – 'Getting Rid' v Taking Risks

Technical Changes in Recent Decades

Goalkeepers use their feet seven times more than they did prior to 1992[10]
Defenders are required to be technically more advanced rather than just able to 'kick it and head it'
Full-backs need to have attacking *and* defending qualities
(continued)
Passing and the ability to keep possession is now prioritized more – 80% of teams with the majority of possession avoid defeat, 52% win
Focus on passing and receiving below head height in tight or defensive areas
Longer passing sequences

---

[7] Some may argue that set-plays or 'restarts' are predictable as they can be rehearsed and staged. This argument, however, is only partly true as a successful set-play still hinges on the correct technique and decision-making of players, and also on the ability and reactions of the opposition.

[8] Owen later joined Manchester United where he arguably became the club's fourth or fifth choice forward, making an average of ten appearances a season for three seasons.

[9] Later in the book we will tackle ways of coaching your players to deal with the 'chaos' and variables of soccer.

[10] The back-pass rule was introduced in 1992, dramatically changing the position of the goalkeeper.

Increase in running with the ball and dribbles
Clever, unpredictable, off the ball movement
Ability to move ball at speed
Reliance on midfielders to score goals
Technical training becoming more position-specific and also individualized

Due to the variables involved in a soccer game, a coach must encourage technical creativity and risk-taking in his players. How else can they learn to deal with the diverse situations that are thrown up by the game? The same coach, however, must accept that if you facilitate this creativity, players *will* make mistakes, and the team may lose games as a consequence. FC Barcelona's risk-taking in possession, and their ultimate effectiveness of 'possessioning' the opposition into submission, is a direct product of players being allowed an abundance of trial and error as they evolved as youngsters. The club and its coaches had the foresight, during these early years, to allow this risk-taking to flourish and allowed players to develop into the adult footballers they are. Taking risks, being creative, and ultimately making mistakes are true learning curves for players. It is vitally important to foster this. Ensure players know that it is okay to lose, so long as they learn the lessons from defeat.

Technically, defenders and goalkeepers must now have the skills in possession that are at least comparable to their midfield team-mates. It is therefore exceptionally important that, during the full pressure of match days, these players are allowed to test and develop their technical skills in 'real' situations. Asking a goalkeeper to whack it down the other end of the pitch any time he is in possession does not develop any type of skill. It stunts their ability to play out from the back and stunts the development of receiving players.

Defenders are also required to have the technical traits to be able to manipulate and move the ball. The modern defender no longer just kicks and heads it. He receives possession from the goalkeeper and is the starter of attacks. He relieves pressure from midfield players and advances up the pitch in possession. Take defender Jamie Carragher as an example. Carragher is not a player who is especially renowned for his technical qualities. Despite this, the Liverpool centre-back had a somewhat surprising pass completion rate of 92% from 24 games in his last Premier League season at the club (2012/13) (source: Squawka.) In addition to this, of the 10 players with the best pass completion rates in Europe in the 2012/13 season, three of them were centre-backs (Dante 90.8%; Gerard Pique 91%; Per Mertesacker 92.2%).[11]

If your young defender is taught to 'get rid' (an often heard term to clear the ball as far away as possible), the coach is doing him a great long-term disservice. A young defender needs to be taught passing and receiving skills, as well as the key movements needed to be able to play his position in a modern way. Once again, it is only by allowing players to trial and error this within competition that you can affect real improvement, tolerating a mistake and a lost goal along the way.

The technical qualities required by the modern midfield player are vast given the different types of midfielders that exist. They vary from those who sit deep and distribute, to those who 'carry' and run with the ball, to those who score and provide goals. Midfielders need to be expert in terms of passing and receiving, taking the ball in defensive areas, and controlling and manipulating the ball in tight attacking situations. They need the ability to score goals, intercept passes, cross, dribble, and more. If these players spend their youth watching their defenders 'getting rid of the ball', and goalkeepers thumping goal-kicks as far as they physically can, it is unlikely that they will develop their skills sufficiently to move their game on.

---

[11] Players must have played at least 20 games and completed at least 1,000 passes. The unsurprising number one on the list was Barcelona's Xavi Hernandez, with almost a 3% higher pass success rate than the list's number 2, Mikel Arteta (source: givemesport.com)

The rate of change in the role occupied by strikers has huge implications for youth coaching. During their development of young strikers, coaches need to add more and more traits to their forwards' repertoire. José Mourinho is quite clear about the need for "multifunctional strikers". He noted, "To them (English youth coaches) a striker is a striker and that's it. For me, a striker is not just a striker. He's somebody who has to move, who has to cross…"

The changing role of forward players has had knock-on implications in other areas of the pitch. More and more midfield players are given greater freedom and license to get forward, score goals, provide assists and bridge the goalscoring gap that not playing with a natural goalscorer leaves. These attacking midfield players 'play between the lines' and are constantly searching for pockets of space between the opponent's midfield and defence. They have excellent receiving skills and make penetrative passes between defenders. Plus, they score goals.

Certainly in England, this type of player is rarely produced. Arguably the most prominent player of this ilk produced in England in recent decades has been Joe Cole. Cole, however, spent a career being asked to play in more stringent wide positions rather than his natural position playing 'in the hole'. As a teenager he was constantly summed up as a player with lots of quality, but someone who needed to eradicate maverick-type flamboyancy from his game. It is possible that had Joe Cole been born ten years later, this flamboyant nature may have been prized more highly.

With the prominence of these types of creative players, and a future reliance on them, it is imperative that youth coaches work to produce attacking midfield players that encompass these skills. In the English Premier League (2012/13) the top five players to play passes in the final third were all foreign imports: The Belgian Eden Hazard, Spaniards Santi Carzola, Juan Mata and David Silva, and South Africa's Steven Pienaar (source: English Premier League Index), all of whom could be considered physically diminutive.

Physical – Understanding Big and Small

Physical Changes in Recent Decades
Players at the highest level cover longer distances during games: 10-13 kilometres
More high intensity runs (short, sharp bursts)
Increased emphasis on players with pace
More changes of direction demanding greater agility
Physical training becoming more individualized
Technical changes have given the small, technically gifted player increased value

The most effective players in kids' football teams are often those that are physically more developed. Because of greater leg power they can run faster and cover more ground. Because of their height they win more aerial duels. Because of their mass and weight they win more tackles. They can kick the ball higher and further than their peers. In 1v1 situations their strength helps them to come out on top. It is tempting and virtually guaranteed that the 'win at all costs' coach will give these types of players central and pivotal roles in their team, letting the squad revolve around the performances of these 'big' players.

I recently befriended a chairman of a local football club in Nottingham. At the Under-11 age group they had enough players for two teams. As a club, a decision was made not to divide or 'band' players into an "A" and a "B" squad. Players would instead be divided into two without bias and take part in a games program appropriate for them. This caused quite a bit of consternation with the head coach of the age group. He wanted the best players to play in the A team, where they would compete to win games and leagues and trophies.

As an experiment, we asked the head coach to pick the players he would choose for his "A" team. Sure enough the result was as expected. The overwhelming majority of the "A" team were the most developed physically, with the smaller players predominantly making the "B" team. (Just consider for a moment if Lionel Messi, Andreas Iniesta and Xavi Hernandez, three of the modern game's greatest and most decorated players, were left out of their under-11 team because they were too small...)

Over the longer term, players that develop physically earlier and who dominate games purely because of size can, in fact, see a huge reversal in their influence on games as they age and their peers begin to catch them up physically. Big players need to be taught other skills involving ball manipulation, vision and fundamental movements so that they have the tools to adapt their game as their physical advantage diminishes.

Likewise, those that develop late physically need to be trusted by coaches and be given ample playing time to learn the game, rather than being cast aside as ineffective in the short-term. With this trust and foresight, their long-term development is secured and the moral fibre of the coach remains intact. If these late developers can learn, on a regular basis, how to affect games through technique and individual traits, they will possess a very accomplished armoury once they hit their growth spurt and will able to match other players physically. Because they lack relative size and power initially, maybe they will inherently adapt their game and start to play in-between players, rather than in close combat against them? Maybe they will learn to receive more quickly and move the ball on more quickly before the big guy gets too close? Maybe this will produce more Carzolas and Pienaars that have spent a childhood playing in tight areas and pockets of space? They would have the physical, technical and tactical skills to bypass their peers. Not to mention the ability of taking and dealing with physical contests where they are disadvantaged.

Psychological and Social – Pressure and Praise

When winning becomes the be-all and end-all at a young age, players take less risks. The fear of making mistakes gets hold of young minds and works to destroy them. If a player makes a mistake and their team concedes a losing goal as a result, it will be his fault. If young players are entering our soccer pitches on a weekly basis carrying this mental baggage, it will have a huge effect on their development.

Quite alarmingly, one of the biggest reasons for young players dropping out of sport, and indeed soccer, is pressure. Pressure? Such is the power of the previous sentence it deserves to be repeated with emphasis. *One of the biggest reasons for young players dropping out of soccer is pressure.*

In any walk of life, children and adolescents should not feel pressure, let alone in sport, which is, for the majority of young players, a recreational, social activity. Yet, pressure is felt throughout the game both at grassroots and at academy level. At the grassroots level, the pressure of winning leagues and trophies, the pressure to please adults, be they coaches or parents or neighbours, results in many young players leaving the game. They no longer enjoy it, have fun, or look forward to it - all the implicit traits of motivated young players. With pressure affecting motivation, players walk away.

Players within academies, meanwhile, feel the pressure of being constantly judged, being released, having their dreams dashed by the opinions of coaches and the system that is professional soccer. This can transform a talented, confident player into one that is handicapped by fear. They take fewer risks and dwell on mistakes, leading to a potential crumbling of their game. Some may argue that it is their ability to deal with pressure that will ultimately separate them from the rest when entering the real pressure cooker that is the professional game. I would debate that players facing these challenges need to be taught the mechanisms of coping with this pressure, or at least be given a chance to reach a mature stage when they can deal with it.

The pressure and anxiety that an over-emphasis on competition brings, will affect players' performance not just mentally, but technically and tactically also. Players can resort to kick-and-rush type soccer, where in one touch they will happily kick it as hard and as far as they can away from their own goal. Young players will not have the chance to express themselves with the ball. They will spend so little time with the ball at their feet that they will not grow to be able to use it sufficiently. We will simply produce narrow-minded players that will only be able to resort to kicking the ball as hard and as high as it's possible. And what is worse, this type of play is often praised!

Consider the implications that praise has on a child in any walk of life. The more praise you give, the more children want to receive it. This is why we praise toddlers heavily for saying "please" and "thank you". So let's put praise in the context of our impressionable, developing youth soccer player. If they are praised constantly for smashing the ball aimlessly up-field and putting the ball out of play unnecessarily, they will continue to do so as they will crave the praise given for that. Will this type of player develop the skills of a modern footballer? It certainly will not produce an Iniesta, Hazard or Messi.

In *The Meaning of Sport*, Simon Barnes points out the oft-used phrase of television pundits and commentators – "It is now about who wants it more". Although this statement is factually flawed (what if both teams "want it" in equal measure? How do you measure this "want"? What if only five or six of your team really want it, and five or six from the opposition) it has seeped into the psyche and team-talks of coaches. In reality, however, we find that the opposite can often be true. It may be that the players who can take competition in their stride, without being enveloped by the pressure of the win at all costs mentality, come out on top. US international Freddy Adu, himself a player who bore extremely high expectations as a young soccer player, summed it up nicely: "…if you have fun doing what you do, if you have fun playing soccer, the creativity is just going to come…"

Conclusion

At the highest levels of professional soccer, winning is what the game is all about. Coaches and managers spend hours, on a daily and weekly basis, and with a considerable backroom staff, trying to find ways to beat the upcoming opposition. Videos will be watched, performance analysis software will be utilized, scouts will sit in stands watching games, and coaches will pore over the strengths, weaknesses and restarts that the opposition will use. All of this is for three league points or a cup victory at the weekend. Those three points carry so much weight: Champions League qualification, the difference between promotion and relegation, and often the future job stability of the club's head coach.

We, as development coaches working in youth football development, however, need to take a step back from that ideology. *That is not our soccer world.*

In chapter 2 we will focus on the world of the youth development soccer coach, by analysing the characteristics of a modern coach.

Summary

- 'Athlete First, Winning Second' – prioritize the long-term development of your players, over the short-term allure of winning games.

- Adopting a 'win at all costs mentality' will inextricably affect the holistic long-term development of youth players.

- Soccer has changed radically in recent decades, which has implications for how coaches approach the game and produce young players. Ensure you are teaching an up-to-date version of the game!

- Tactically the game has evolved in terms of formations and the roles played by players.

- The game is now loaded with lone and multi-purpose strikers (or no strikers at all), interchangeable attacking midfielders, 'holding' midfield players, attacking full-backs, ball-playing centre-backs and goalkeepers that use their feet seven times more often than in 1992.

- Soccer is not played like chess. It is chaotic with an infinite number of variables involved. Coaches need to produce players capable of dealing with this chaos.

- Creativity and risk-taking must be encouraged to maximize a player's potential. Accept that this may lead to errors. Taking risks, being creative, and ultimately making mistakes are true learning curves for players.

- The most physically developed players in kids' football will be the most dominant and will often stand out as being the team's best players. This can have long-term implications for any player as he and his peers age, and his physical advantage diminishes.

- Have patience with physically less developed players – they may become the quick, clever, spatially aware players that thrive in the modern game.

- Pressure is one of the biggest causes of young players leaving the game.

- Consider the anxiety you may be causing a player and be careful what you praise them for.

- A game is rarely won just because a team "wants it more".

Real Coach Experience
Choosing Development over Results
(English Academy Coach - Anonymous)

Having completed the FA Youth Award in 2006, I decided upon pushing the boundaries with regards to focusing on the development of players rather than their results. My new focus was upon developing the whole player, by making sessions player-centred and using a more "guided discovery" approach. The players would be encouraged to take risks, be creative and play based on instinct.

It was with the under-10 age group at a Centre of Excellence club. Having "only lost one game all year", the previous coach lauded the squad. On face value, they did seem strong, but the worrying thing was that they were in tears having lost a game at the end of the season. It was all about winning, even if it meant 'goal hanging', staying in the same position, and not looking at the bigger picture.

The players enjoyed the new responsibilities and their technical development went through the roof. However, it was clear the some of the parents were not happy as "they were not winning" and because they were run very close by the development squad. There also seemed to be a real fear of trialists coming in and taking the places of their children, which was then transmitted subconsciously to the players. This led to quite a toxic, suspicious environment.

However, I would not change my decision to prioritize the players' technical development over initial results. If I could do it all again I would hold an induction meeting and explain everything. I would have explained that we were going to prioritize development, even if results dipped from the previous season. I would also have held focus group meetings for me to get on top of any problems this may have led to.

I am still in touch with players from that age group and they have always been very positive about the structure of what they did. One has even asked me when I will be moving back to work with them, as they are sick of "old school" sessions.

It is those types of comments, eight years later, which shows the long-term impact of this approach.

2

Understanding the Modern Youth Development Coach

"Modern day players are different. Their expectations are different. Players these days are expecting preparation to be good, they are expecting sessions to be planned, and they're expecting detail…" (Chris Hughton)

Being a soccer coach is hard work. It's all encompassing. It's time-consuming. It's challenging. It's brilliant. The role of the coach is broad in scope. He makes phone calls, plays taxi, completes admin work, buys equipment, takes courses, appeases parents - all before a ball is kicked, or a team and their strategy is selected!

Most people believe that being a successful coach is about an in-depth understanding of technique and tactics, and to an extent this is true. This is, after all, what lots of coaches focus on and even obsess about. A lot of coaches reading this very book will probably skip straight to the section related to technical coaching practices and tactical opinions. The traditional coach will probably read that section only. However, the modern coach will understand that tactical and technical know-how, on their own, are not enough.

The premise and motivation for this book, as a whole, is to offer an understanding that being an outstanding, well-rounded coach is more than just possessing soccer knowledge. We will certainly talk about the tactical and technical aspects of the game later, but first we *must* understand the countless traits a modern coach must have to get the best out of this knowledge. Think of the technical and tactical stuff as the furnishings in a house - the colour of the walls and the detail of the decor, furniture and fixings. The other disciplines are the foundations of the house, without which nothing else will function correctly.

Along with the huge amount of change that has taken place in soccer, as discussed in chapter 1, the role of the coach and the expectations of coaches have also evolved immeasurably. Much work has been done on the many and various roles of the coach by coaching organizations, the national governing bodies of a wide range of sports, and football-specific books such as *Focused for Soccer* by former Manchester United, Middlesbrough FC and England national team psychologist, Bill Beswick. There are certain aspects that we will not go into here. I will take it for granted that any coach forward thinking enough to pick up this book will already understand the more well-documented characteristics of a good coach – he is reliable, a communicator, a role model, a leader, a hard worker and a motivator (indeed, we will look deeply at how to enhance and maximize some of these characteristics later). We will instead, however, focus on what a *modern, progressive coach* looks like, what skills he possesses, and how he uses those skills.

The 'Traditional' Coach

From the outset it is important to point out that the use of the term 'traditional' is not meant to be derogatory. I have met many coaches that I have learned an astonishing amount from, who would openly admit to being traditional in their methods.

Being traditional does not mean that these coaches are working incorrectly. It may be that they have studied the game but picked and chosen the parts that suit them, their teams and their players. David Moyes, having just been named successor to Sir Alex Ferguson at Manchester

United, was accused of being outdated in his pre-season methods in a radio interview by Dutch coach Raymond Verheijen, before Verheijen went on to compliment the Scot's overall performance as manager of Everton.[1]

Many internationally renowned and long sought-after coaches could also be considered traditional, but it does not necessarily mean that they are ineffective. Fabio Capello, for example, uses disciplines such as orderliness and organization. Giovanni Trapattoni's powers of motivation and enthusiasm are second to none. Sir Alex Ferguson is famed for his 'hairdryer' treatment of players when they fall below the high standards he insists upon. However, Fergie's willingness to learn new things and adapt to the modern game is without question, and something he freely admits to.

The 'Modern' Coach…

The modern coach possesses some of the traits of his traditional counterpart, and makes a concerted effort to adopt many more. If the traditional coach can be described as a systematic and dictator-like organizer, the modern coach can be, as described poignantly by Beswick, "…as a smart, democratic, player-centred teacher who plans carefully and focuses on the excellence of performance…" If the traditional coach has a narrow, strict focus and views players as a cog in a machine, the modern coach is analytical, emotionally controlled and has a holistic outlook.

…is Open-minded

Being open-minded shows the real strength of a soccer coach. A willingness to listen, adapt, learn new ideas and absorb information with the goal of improving and evolving as a coach, and with the development of players in mind, is vital. The characteristics outlined below are a fantastic start-point, and the fact that you have picked up this book, and invested time and money in reading it, is already testament to your open-mindedness.

Having an open-mind is not about accepting everything. It is about looking and learning and ultimately taking the ideas that you have found, and using them as you see fit. I have a library bulging with books about soccer. From technical studies to tactical opinions. From physical sessions to psychological articles. From talent identification to communication skills. I have club and national association documents from around the world, all with many different angles on how to develop the youth soccer player. It is impossible to embrace them all. Some contradict each other, some contradict my vision of the developmental process and some are even outdated. But being open-minded about all of them allows you to create the optimal learning environment for you and your players, in your circumstances.

…is a Coach, Not a Supporter

Soccer supporters are notorious beings. They are full of almost bi-polar emotion. A win is a joyous celebratory occasion; a defeat is felt hard and has ruined a lot of weekends. Supporters are boisterous, opinionated, are overly critical and most possess wonderful pairs of rose-tinted spectacles. The place for supporters is in the stands, on a supporters' bus and milling around the streets in exuberant or sombre mood before or after games. The place for a supporter is not on the touchline. That place is reserved for the coach.

There is a terrific video on *YouTube* that I come back to, time and time again. It is of a Serbian grassroots coach living and dying by his team. I cannot understand one word of what he is screaming to his players (although a kind contributor to YouTube has offered some suggestions in the comments section!), but I have seen it occur so many times across youth soccer pitches.

---

[1] Indeed David Moyes spends every summer polishing his coaching in an attempt to learn something new, either from a course, tournament, or by visiting other clubs. "I believe in going to find out if there's anything new out there. You might see a new training drill, a different style of play or maybe just a routine from a corner kick. The corner kick might be the thing that gets you a point one Saturday and stops you being relegated."

This is not the behaviour of a modern coach. It is something you expect to see in the stands of an ill-heated derby match.

The modern coach masters his emotional control, maintaining an objective view on the game or session he is watching, without descending into the extreme behaviours that can be found in the stadiums across world soccer. Players need their coach to be rational and intelligent. They need to know that they can perform without overly-emotional reactions from the coach. Players will, after all, mimic and react to the behaviour of the coach so it is something that must be considered at all times.

A wonderful example of this is from Rafael Benitez. When trailing 3-0 at half-time in the 2005 Champions League Final against the very accomplished AC Milan, Benitez chose to be calm. Rather than rant, rave and disgrace a group of players that had just spent 45 minutes being humiliated on worldwide television, he *chose* calm. It is often easy, too easy, for a coach to hide his own failings or weakness by apportioning all the blame onto the players.[2] Maybe over-reactions to mistakes and crude touchline behaviour are designed to show everyone that you care. Maybe it is designed to show everyone that the team's poor performance is not down to the coach. Being calm, however, shows that you are thoughtful and are focused on coming up with a solution to a problem. It shows the players that you are not anxious and there *is* a remedy.

Benitez himself has stated: "You learn to be calm. You learn to analyse things in a different way. Sometimes you put yourself under pressure and put your players under pressure, they need you to relax…"

"They need you to relax…" *They*. Benitez made a decision to put the players and their welfare to the forefront. He made a decision not to blow his cool and accuse others of failing. He got on with his job of preparing his team for what was to be an extraordinary night where Liverpool fought back to win the final on penalties.

…is Player-Centred Rather than Coach-Centred

The prominence of the 'coach-centred' approach that has traditionally engulfed soccer is now being challenged more and more. Due to overwhelming research, coaching is becoming more 'player-centred'. This is not about the coach losing control or what the cynic may see as another example of young people being pampered to. What it is about is doing something that coaches are often frightened of – *letting go*. It is about using a style that assists players to develop their autonomy and decision-making skills, independent of, but facilitated by, the coach.

Youth soccer players that excel make *real* decisions in *real* games, rather than try to follow a soccer script prescribed by adults. It is quite likely that young players do not understand this script, and because of this, are unable to follow such orders. They may even blindly follow the instruction without a true understanding of what it actually means, making any long-term benefits quite futile. Don Tricker produces a fantastic summary of this approach in an article in the Auckland Football Coaches Network (AFCN) Newsletter in August 2008: "It is the athlete that makes the decision in real time; therefore you must trust the athlete to make the smart decisions under pressure. If I don't trust my athletes to make the smart decision then I would consider that I have failed them."

Adopting 'player-centred' coaching *will influence not just what you coach, but also how you coach*, and the type of practices you use. Offering players problems that need to be solved within game-related situations or using *Teaching Games for Understanding (TGfU)* practices are important in offering players the opportunity to make these real decisions. If players struggle with finding the answers

---

[2] Benitez may have had every right to be angry with his players. In his book *Champions League Dreams*, Benitez explains that his instructions were that the first pass of the game should be a long one to get his team off on a positive footing and force Milan back physically and psychologically. The first pass however went short and within the first minute Liverpool had conceded a free-kick that resulted in AC Milan's opening goal.

to the problems posed, the coach can then offer his expertise. The key is to let the player make his own decisions, and gain his own experiences. Learning is most effective when answers are found and worked out, rather than given. If the player gets it wrong, be patient. The player may well work it out, but if not, he will then need your help.

Being player-centred also means understanding the person, as well as the athlete. What motivates the individual player? What is their background? Why do they attend *your* soccer club? Understanding the person helps the coach tailor how he works with players as a group and also as individuals. I always tell young coaches that your players will never forget you, in the same way that we all remember our school teachers – some with love and fondness, others with apathy and regret. Ensure you do right by them along the way, help them learn, be a positive memory and ensure your coaching style is appropriate.

Coach-Centred Approach	Player-Centred Approach
The game revolves exclusively around the coach ("pass here", "dribble there", "run here", etc.)	Players are encouraged to make their own decisions
Treats youth players like 'mini-adults'	Recognizes the age considerations of young players
Plays his best team with the purpose of winning games	Gives all his players equal playing time with the purpose of development
Criticizes players who struggle, and substitutes players after mistakes	Is patient with players and guides them through difficult periods
Uses command coaching style only	Uses a range of coaching styles, selecting which one is appropriate in any given circumstance
Focuses on team performances	Focuses on individual development, within a team context
Sets goals for the players	Allows players to set their own goals, offering guidance when required
Produces players that are robotic, lack decision-making skills, are defensive, easy to anger, and prone to frustration	Produces players that make their own decisions and are open-minded to new ideas
Produces players that may lack enthusiasm	Produces players that are enthusiastic and show a commitment to excellence
Rarely listens to opinions or advice from players	Listens to players opinions, producing a 'buy in' to the project

...uses a Variety of Styles

The subject of coaching styles has been much discussed in recent years. See, below, a visual (*The Coaching Continuum*) which details different styles that stretch from being autocratic to being democratic. Coach education bodies (in their literature and as part of coaching courses) use this continuum, or variants of it, globally. It is perceived that traditional coaches favour the 'command' style, whereas modern coaches offer styles like *Guided Discovery* and use lots of *Question and Answer*. This does not mean that a command style does not have a place in modern coaching. Sometimes players need clear instruction detailing what you, as the coach and leader, wants. Remember, the modern coach is open-minded, so will use command, but it will not be his *only* style. The trick is being able to strike a balance between all these styles at different times, selecting the most appropriate one to use given the circumstances.

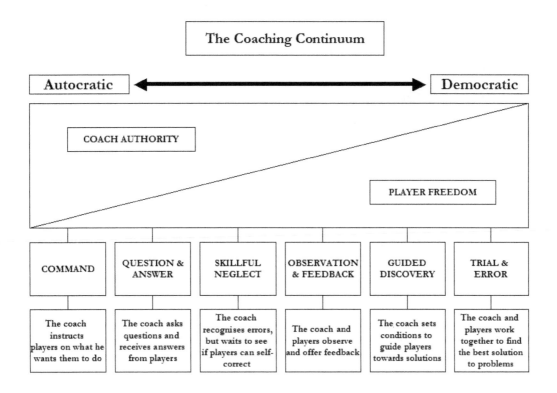

...has Presence and 'Performs'

Presence is a very difficult trait to achieve. At times it can be known as having an 'aura', an almost mystical force field generated by a person that draws the attention of a whole room towards them. One of the most impressive cases of this I have witnessed, in a soccer context, was an old colleague and boss of mine. He would walk into a dressing room and the whole place would fall silent, and once he spoke, players would be transfixed on him[3]. I witnessed these 'performances' time and time again. In *Will You Manage? The Necessary Skills to be a Great Gaffer*, Musa Okwonga describes meeting Aidey Boothroyd and drawing many of the same conclusions:

"...Boothroyd swept into the dressing room, armed with a whiteboard on which he'd scribbled a series of notes in firm and insistent capitals. His performance – for there's no better word for it – was hypnotic."

People often suggest that this presence is impossible to acquire – it is something you have or you do not. This may be true. Maybe it comes down to personality, experience, knowledge, or the role and reputation of the coach. There are however some subtle ways that presence can be developed on the training field:

- Know the names of all your players. Greet all of them with enthusiasm, as if there is nowhere else in the world you would rather be!

- Make eye contact with all of them when you speak. It feels like you are talking to them individually.

---

[3] When I quizzed him about this, the coach in question suggested that presence it is something that comes with experience, knowledge and an understanding of what motivates your group of players.

- Dress well and professionally – perceptions are huge. If you are outdated in the way you appear, you will seem outdated to players.[4]

- Consider your body language – be purposeful and energetic.

- Take 'centre-stage' – I learnt this from a friend who had a background in acting. He spoke about drawing your audience in by using eye contact, gestures and altering your tone of voice. Act as if you are on stage and need to captivate an audience.

...is Original and Innovative

Coaches love nothing more than a presentation, a DVD, or book full of session plans, 'drills', exercises and practices, particularly from top clubs and famous coaches. I myself have session plans from the top level of the game that must stretch into the thousands. Coaches, like myself, are drawn to them like a moth to a flame.

We gravitate to these sessions because they come from the best, which is perfectly acceptable. An important trait in the new breed of soccer coach, however, is the ability to be original and innovative. When these session plans are acquired, the true skill lies in *interpreting* practices, rather than simply rote learning and copying them. After all, every group of players is different, every age group is different, and every coach is different. By interpreting and altering plans as necessary, the coach is then adding his relevance to them so that his players can work appropriately.

There is a very popular document available online that details José Mourinho's 39 favourite practices. As a resource this is excellent and invaluable to coaches across the spectrum. However, the innovative coach will understand that these are practices used by the first team at Chelsea FC, so may not be quite as free-flowing or intense with youth players. The outcomes may be totally different. Becoming an innovative, modern coach means studying and questioning the practices you produce.

With the evolution of the Internet, session plans from top coaches and top academies are available for soccer coaches the world over. Use them wisely.

...uses Technology

Technology and the Internet have revolutionized soccer coaching. Some of you may fear that statement, assuming a good coach *needs* to use all sorts of wild and wonderful gadgets to be effective. This is not true, but it may well enhance the productivity of what you do. It is worth remembering that the young players you coach have *never lived in an era without mobile phones, the worldwide web or satellite TV*. It is *their* world, *their* life experience, and *their* language.

The Internet offers a wide range of useful club and player management tools, some of which will allow you to contact players and parents, provide them with feedback and allow you to create electronic practices.

As a starting point, however, I would recommend that every coach should set up a *Twitter* account. Social networking is much more than flicking through people's memories or nosing through pictures. There are thousands of coaches sharing thousands of resources through Twitter. Simply search and follow @coachingfamily and your computer will be flooded with opinions, articles, documents, session plans and videos from coaches working with youth players from all over the world. On a daily basis there will always be something new, exciting or different that I acquire from fellow coaches and Twitter users.

The power of video analysis has also become very accessible. There is software available that will assist with performance analysis and generate statistics and patterns. If that is too complicated or

---

[4] I once mentored a very well intentioned coach who wore a humorous Disney t-shirt when coaching. His players saw him as a joke.

time-consuming, high-resolution hand-held cameras are now freely available that can be used to video games and provide players with valuable feedback (young players love watching themselves play on video). It may not be Sky Sports or Fox Soccer, but it is a hugely worthwhile tool. It also assists the coach to analyse games in his own time (it is amazing what you miss in the heat of the action, and how much your opinion on performances can change once you have watched a game back).

Young people use video in some capacity virtually every hour of the day. This is a great opportunity for the coach to teach. Using videos will help the coach get on a level with players and help him speak *their* language. You may email them a clip of an outstanding piece of play, show them a motivational video or set them a post-training challenge[5] to find snippets of a player they relate to. The opportunities are endless…

If the thought of using technology truly frightens you, *get some help*. Every town and city has a college or university with young experts in many disciplines that love nothing more than volunteering, as part of their degree, portfolio, or to beef up their résumé. Your players may even be the ones to help, and some will love the responsibility of assisting you.

…has Self-Belief

We normally reserve discussions around self-belief for our players, noting its importance for performing at a peak level. Having self-belief and being self-assured is vital for the coach too. Having been given a role of responsibility in coaching a youth soccer team, a coach can feel pressure and self-doubt. This pressure can come from colleagues, parents and even the players themselves. It may be a pressure on you to get results for the team, play a player in a certain position, or to use certain team tactics.

The pressure may even be as a result of the coach's modern vision. A coach may receive criticism for doing things correctly and being up-to-date in his methods! This can come from a source that does not understand the modern game (e.g. "My son is left-footed. Why is he playing on the right? He needs to play on the left of a 4-4-2".)

Having self-belief is about making and sticking to the decisions and philosophies that the coach believes are correct, even in the face of adversity. Some may call this being headstrong, others unapproachable or even pig-headed. Be wary of striking the balance between having self-belief and being blatantly stubborn. A modern coach will review his performances and change aspects if they are not working.

…sells a Vision

Having appropriate self-belief allows you to influence your players. It is also a great opportunity for you to *sell* them a vision, rather than imposing your vision on them. By selling a vision to players, the coach adds considerable value to what he is trying to achieve, as there is a buy-in from everyone involved. If the players are on-board with the ideas of the coach then you have an extremely strong base with which to work from. If a coach inflicts his ideas on the group, players may respond well or they may also reject his intentions.

One of my proudest, most memorable moments as a coach was when I was working with an English U19 college team. Very early in the season we got together and established a set of common objectives. I told the players what I believed our team could achieve, and asked them for their input until, as a group, we came up with a shared vision. As a result, the players took ownership of everything we did. They ensured that the approach of new members to training was appropriate, and understood why we were working on certain exercises. They accepted the failings of others in the group (for example, mistakes made by players due to risk-taking, or being

---

[5] Use this term instead of 'homework'. Young people hate the term due to its association with schoolwork and losing their free time.

caught out of position when attempting to be unpredictable in possession), once they aligned with the vision of the team. On the morning before an important game, I received information that several players would be unable to take part in the fixture – and all of them were full-backs! I explained to the players that we would have to change the way we play and do some work on playing 3-5-2 instead. Before I could finish my sentence, our striker had offered to play right-back. Soon after, a midfield player offered to play left-back. The players understood our vision and wanted to protect it, even if it meant sacrificing themselves for that vision.

A great way of achieving this is through goal-setting and understanding what everyone in the group is seeking. The coach can facilitate the setting of goals that excite and are challenging, but critically, are realistic. Each player may have a different idea of what goals to set, so ultimately the coach must pull them together and persuade the group that this is the way forward. Goals need to be flexible, and if possible, tiered.

Take a new team that gets promoted to the Premier League for example. How many times do we see teams set a goal of simply "staying up"? When they reach their goal early, they tend to enter a subconscious mood of having achieved all they can accomplish and finish the season quite poorly. In *Focused for Soccer*, Beswick outlined a four-tiered goal that they set at Derby County when they were promoted to the Premier League:

1. Finish 17th (places 18, 19 and 20 incur relegation)

2. Finish in the top half of the division

3. Finish in a qualification spot for European competition

4. Compete for the Championship

This is a very clever way of selling an idea and enthusing players. Once goal one is secured, they can move on to goal two and so on. They will not rest on what they have already accomplished and are always striving for excellence.

…is a Hard AND a Smart Worker

The concept of working hard is nothing new to coaches. Whether the coach works full-time in the game, or is an unpaid volunteer with a local club, the level of time and effort put into the role goes far beyond the hours of any job description. It can involve meetings, taking phone calls, completing forms, watching other games, reading books, attending courses, dealing with parents – the list is virtually infinite.

The modern coach however is also a *smart* worker. If hard work is the brawn, the modern coach adds the brain and 'smart' to the equation. Brian Clough, former European Cup winning coach with Nottingham Forest, once deplored the use of note taking by managers during the first half of games so they can relay relevant information to their players at half time. But unless Clough was superhuman (which I am pretty sure he thought he was!), the human capacity to remember on command the full detail of 45 minutes of soccer is not possible! Considering the detail involved in the modern game, it may be the minute detail, that a coach notes, that will be the difference between being successful or not.

Modern coaching is about being analytical and understanding that the little details add up to make a big difference. I once heard a story that Paul Ince had a falling out with former coach Gérard Houllier and was aghast when the coach informed him that his 5-a-side team had lost more training games than any other over the period of several months! Pep Guardiola is documented as being a workaholic that locks himself in his office and watches opposition videos until he finds the nugget of information that will help his team to victory.

…is a Teacher AND Learner, is a Mentor AND is Mentored

A coach teaches the game to young players (something we will explore in more detail in Chapter 3), but the modern coach is also a learner, or what is commonly termed a *Student of the Game*. He will crave ways to develop his knowledge to maximize the ability of his players. This learning may be attending a coach education course, or it may be that document you found on Twitter that details how to teach ball manipulation to 9 year olds. It may be buying a sports psychology DVD.

The game of soccer is moving so quickly that the evolution of the coach through learning is imperative, and is what Jamie Houchen, Head of FA Learning, describes as "self-responsibility". The modern coach recognizes that he is not, and cannot be, the font of *all* knowledge. He will be an expert in some areas, have real strength in others, but recognize that there are gaps in his knowledge base that require filling. Roy Hodgson, the much travelled English coach, epitomizes this notion: "Every training session that you do can be a learning curve for you [the coach] because you are learning from the players, you are learning from mistakes, you are learning from what you see on the field. Sometimes players can do things that you have not thought about, so I think every training session is a learning session for you."

The one failing of many soccer coaches is doing it all alone. They form a cocoon around their work and their team and can be extremely territorial. Seeking assistance from others is extremely important. Having a mentor to help guide and advise is invaluable. This is not something that ought to embarrass or question your authority. It is something that will take your coaching to a higher level. The most impressive coach I have ever had the privilege of watching and training under was Dick Bate. He could captivate a room with his lectures and astound players on the practice pitch. Into his sixties, Dick has kept firmly up to date with the game by constantly learning and insisting on feedback from others. It is my understanding that he will pay someone to observe his work and provide him with feedback on his performance. Likewise, in an interview about Sir Bobby Robson, former Manchester United manager Sir Alex Ferguson freely admitted: "I was never too big or too proud to ask him for advice which he gave freely and unconditionally."

If someone of the calibre of Dick Bate and Sir Alex Ferguson can freely use a mentor, and is open to ongoing feedback, then all soccer coaches can.

...is Positive

Arguably the key ingredient in pulling all this together is positivity. We have all been in dressing rooms that are overtly negative[6]. We have all been in environments where problems and mistakes are dissected, rather than solutions sought. We constantly hear negative feedback rather than positive. This kind of atmosphere can be energy-sapping, however well-intentioned people may be. Living or working with an individual who is constantly negative is draining, and that is the same with coaching. *Do not let negative people near your players!*

The modern youth development coach accentuates the positives. This does not mean that problems or issues are overlooked, or that coaches make excuses for players. It means that the coach is able to step back, analyse what is happening and move the team or player forward knowing that there is light at the end of the tunnel, even if things seem particularly bleak.

Being positive with players allows you to get some positivity and energy back from them. John Robertson, Former European Cup Winner under Brian Clough (and long-term assistant to coach Martin O'Neill), said of his manager in his playing days: "When Brian Clough came to Nottingham Forest, everyone at that time picked on all the things I couldn't do... I couldn't tackle, I couldn't head, I wasn't the quickest person – but it didn't seem to worry him at all and he concentrated on things that I was good at."

Conclusion

We always give players advice to help maximize their performance. "You would be a better player if you did x, y and z." Coaches however must strive to maximize their potential too, many of

---

[6] As a teenager I once played in an adult amateur game that happened to be near the grounds of a psychiatric hospital. At half-time I was told my performance was like one of the hospital's residents!

which are detailed above and throughout this book. That is what great teachers do – they use their ability to innately inspire their subjects to greatness. In Chapter 3, we will look at the role of the coach as teacher and players as learners.

Summary

The modern coach…

- Has some of the traits of the traditional coach, but adds more and evolves as necessary.

- Is open-minded to new ideas, but recognizes ones that do not fit.

- Is emotionally controlled and does not behave like a soccer supporter.

- Is player-centred rather than coach-centred so he can help the autonomy and decision-making of his players.

- Uses a range of styles from *The Coaching Continuum* from autocratic to democratic.

- Believes in himself and his ideas and can sell these ideas to players, rather than expect them to blindly follow them.

- Works hard *and* smart, in an analytical way, displaying the attention to detail that players require.

- Recognizes that to be an effective teacher, he must be an effective *Student of the Game*.

- Acknowledges the gaps in his knowledge and seeks help when appropriate.

- Uses a positive outlook with players to maximize their development and coach effectiveness.

Real Coach Experience

A Coach, Not a Fan!

(Steve Round, former assistant manager, Middlesbrough, Everton and Manchester United)

As much as possible, I have tried to steer clear of using high profile coaches in this section. This story from Steve Round however is an exception. Steve relayed this story to a room full of youth coaches in 2007 in which I was present, and such was its impact that it caused me to re-evaluate my coaching and behavior around players.

Steve was a young youth coach working with one of the Derby County FC Academy teams. His enthusiasm for the job was without question and he displayed many of the traits that we have dealt with in this chapter.

Prior to a fixture, Round asked a colleague to video the game so he could use it to complete some performance analysis, to which his colleague obliged. The players got on with playing, the coach got on with coaching and managing the game, and the game was recorded from start to finish.

When Round sat down with the video however, he was horrified. Rather than record the ebb and flow of the soccer game in action, the camera was fixed sorely on the touchline – onto the coach. It captured fully the behavior of Round throughout the game. He went on to describe how misguided his manner was – screaming and shouting at players and at officials; gesticulating and bounding around on the touchline. He was behaving like an erratic supporter in the stands. He was full of emotion, misplaced enthusiasm and rose-tinted bias, rather than conducting himself like the educated, knowledgeable, diligent, professional coach he was.

The thought that other coaches, colleagues, players and opposition had witnessed him do this caused him great embarrassment and to seriously reflect on his coaching approach. His story embarrassed me also, and most of the other coaches in the room. There was a slight shuffle of shameful feet amongst the laughter in the audience. We had all been guilty of this at some point. You would not expect a youth tennis or swimming coach to behave in that manner, so use Round's embarrassment to expect better from yourself.

3

Understanding Teaching and Learning in Soccer

"You train dogs... I like to educate players." (Brendan Rodgers)

I have always felt there are two professions that everyone thinks they can do better than the expert – a teacher and a soccer coach. I have trained as both and it is amazing how many times someone, with no experience of either field, will offer convincing and bold observations about how it should be done correctly. I guess it comes from years of being on the other side of the fence – sitting in a classroom or running around a soccer pitch.

To successfully do both jobs, however, needs a serious amount of study, hard work, qualifications, experience and understanding. The further along the path as a schoolteacher and as a soccer coach I travelled, the more closely both disciplines began to align. I realised that many, if not all, of the same principles of a classroom-learning environment could and should be implemented on a soccer pitch. After all, countless club and national association documents use the words that are commonly found in mainstream education – *development, learning, understanding*, soccer *school, academy, school* of excellence and so on. Indeed the word *academy* is considered a place of 'study or training'.

Being a 'soccer teacher' may sound very tricky to some, maybe even undesirable. However, the wonderful advantage that soccer coaches have over mainstream teachers is the motivation of the learners at hand. The motivation of millions of youth players the world over surpasses that of those millions trudging to mid-morning maths, science or history lessons.

Make no mistake about it though, the coach is a teacher, a soccer teacher, and his players are learners, possibly the most attentive, stimulated learners that exist.

Creating a Positive Learning Environment

At the end of Chapter 2 we noted that a positive approach to coaching is integral to the success of the modern youth development coach, and it is an excellent place to start here. If we consider many of the other traits discussed in the previous chapter, and embed them in our coaching, the learning environment we create for players *will be inherently positive*.

Constructing a positive learning environment is again a common theme within well-established youth development programs. For example, The Derby County FC Academy 'Mission' is "To identify, develop and support talented young players in order for them to achieve their maximum potential in a positive, supportive and professional *learning environment*." (my italics). The Manchester United Soccer Schools echo the need for a player-centred approach to coaching, within a positive learning environment (see the *MUSS's Player Development Model* below).

In an article for *Insight* magazine, Dick Bate detailed several factors that may help to create this type of environment, which I have added to:

- How the practice is designed (realistic, challenging, involves all players, involves a ball![1])

- How players are grouped (consider differentiation, avoiding cliques, etc.)

- How recognition is given (with praise and enthusiasm)

- How performance is evaluated (development outcomes, rather than the result alone)

- Congratulating ability or effort[2] (the more you give, the more you get back)

- How a coach reacts to a defeat (focus on positives, using negatives as learning outcomes)

- Establishing realistic expectations (as detailed by Beswick in Chapter 2)

- How players are taught and encouraged ("Kids don't learn from people they don't like" – Rita Pierson, Talks Education)

The Coach as a Teacher

It is key to teach your players the game and accept the label of 'teacher'. You are, after all, influencing and shaping players through a period in their lives where the capacity to learn and develop is strongest.

The England Under-17 Head Coach, John Peacock, openly discusses his role as a teacher while preparing the best players in the country for competition, and is a fantastic example of the many details we are discussing here. Peacock explained: "Going into the classrooms we work off the board tactically, showing them what they did last time; the positives and the areas where we need to improve on - we do visually. We then get them to come up with some of the answers, which really helps with their learning. So our training is two-fold really: practical work with some theoretical work alongside it."

---

[1] Involving a ball in all sessions and practices is almost non-negotiable, even in warm-ups and fitness-based sessions. There are very few non-ball-based practices that cannot be adapted to include a ball. On a weekly basis, I witness countless sessions where up to half the practice time is spent with young players running around pitches and performing needless shuttle runs. Players hate this and it has very little value for their development.

[2] Studies have found that praising hard work and effort encourages further work-rate and aligns improvement with working hard. Those praised for their talent *alone* may lose motivation to work, as their talent is deemed to have come easy and is the result of natural ability, rather than work. Matthew Whitehouse presents this theory in a soccer context in an online blog entitled *A Lesson About Mindset from Cristiano Ronaldo*.

Although classroom-based learning for players has its place, most coaches' 'classrooms' are the grass pitches and artificial surfaces the world over. For coaches that are operating soccer *schools* and *educating* players, helping players to *learn* and *develop*, there is a catalogue of transferable knowledge that can be used from the world of mainstream education.

Below, I have included what I consider to be two of the most essential educational theories that can be applied to our soccer environments. Both theories have been studied intensely and a huge amount of literature exists on both, although predictably, mainly in relation to mainstream education rather than sport. It is my aim to take the best messages from them, and apply them to our soccer teaching to help players learn the game.

Maslow's Hierarchy of Needs

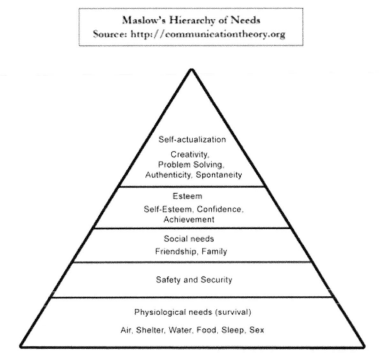

Let me paint a picture…

You are lying in bed one night and your partner is telling you all about their day. You are listening attentively until you hear an innocuous noise downstairs. You are not quite sure what it is, or whether it is just something that goes bump in the night. As human beings we are programmed to sense danger and threats to our well-being. When we perceive a threat to our person, it is all we can focus on. We shut down everything that is going on around us, which are no longer relevant to our human need, to remain safe. In this case, you listen closer for another noise, look for an exit, or decide whether it is something that you will need to challenge, call for help, or run away from. Meanwhile your partner's conversation, the one that you were so attentively listening to, is drowned out and becomes little more than background noise. You simply cannot listen to it or digest it with a threat to your person.

This is the premise for Maslow's work – you cannot learn effectively if there is a threat to yourself or, as you will see if the diagram above, not sufficient care is being taken towards your innate human and physiological needs.

This may seem a like an over-the-top place to start, but it is a vital one. Consider the impact of your coaching (teaching) if there is fear amongst your players. This may be as innocent as a coach's distant style, or as sinister as bullying. It may be pressure from a parent, or a strained relationship with a teammate or opponent that is blocking your player from learning effectively. Furthermore, when you take into account the wide-reaching life that players have away from soccer training (school, social life, social networking, other sports, family, etc.) they may take baggage with them that results in them being afraid when they attend your coaching session. If they are afraid, they will not learn.

The aim of coaches is to ensure that the base of the pyramid is catered for, before expecting a player to reach the top and fully realize their potential. The coach can directly affect this by ensuring that the environment he creates is free of fear and intimidation, that it is a positive and engaging place to come to, full of enthusiasm and well-intentioned people. For example, we can coach in line with the players' physiological needs by ensuring that they are well hydrated and given regular fluid breaks.[3] Complicated learning should not be attempted when players are fatigued. This is a mistake that coaches often make, notably by giving players long post-game debriefs, analysis and feedback. It is possibly better practice to allow players some recovery time before trying to impart specific or long-winded details on them.

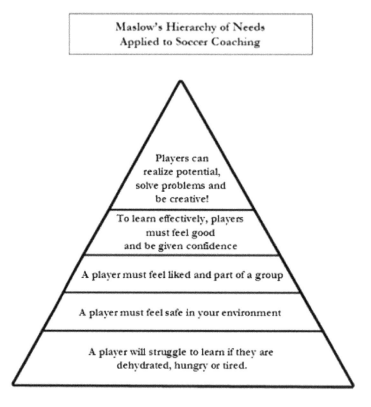

Bloom's Taxonomy of Learning Domains

The central thesis to Bloom's Taxonomy is that *you need to build learning in a naturally progressive manner.* For example, a mathematics teacher has to teach basic arithmetic, progressing the subject stage by stage before moving on to more complex equations.

I once watched a rugby coach work with players that were maybe seven or eight years old. He lined four players up and attempted to coach them an attacking pattern of play that involved all four players weaving in and out of each other, revolving around a central player who would receive the ball most often. The four players and the coach practiced this over and over again. They must have had twenty separate attempts at this ten-second pattern of play, *all* of which were unsuccessful, usually after just two or three passes. The core reason for this was that these young players did not yet have the ability to simply throw and catch consistently. Attempting even a slightly complicated tactical routine was scuppered by the fact that the players were essentially being asked, to use our maths lesson analogy, to attempt complicated mathematical equations before they were even able to count.

---

[3] I worked with a coach who once refused his players water at half-time as he considered their performance too poor and they were not deserving of it!

The central message in terms of soccer coaching is to ensure that players are challenged in the correct way, without being faced with tasks that are beyond their understanding and capability. For example, as coaches we cannot expect young players to perform technically, tactically or physically demanding exercises that are beyond their means. I have myself been guilty of this. Having heard about Manchester United's "six pass" rule[4], I decided to implement it with my Football League Youth Team. It failed. The intent was correct, the information I provided was correct, but that level was beyond the players' capacity at that time. I was trying to teach them to play like Manchester United, before any of them even reached adulthood!

Just like in school, soccer's learning process takes place over time. The best results are achieved when a curriculum is in place, and we recognize that this process has stages and requires age-specific considerations. A mathematics teacher would not set eight-year-olds calculus problems. He would make sure the student could do the basics first – count, add, divide, etc. This requires patience and it is often the case that the coach neglects this process, aiming instead to achieve instant results and replicate what they see in the adult game.

While ensuring our practices and expectations are not too far beyond the capabilities of our players, we *must* still ensure that appropriate challenges exist for them. Yes, they need some form of success in their development, but they also need a certain amount of stress[5] that puts them right on the edge of their comfort zone.

For example, during shooting practices, we often overload the numbers involved in the practice in favour of the strikers (e.g. two strikers versus one defender). Coaches do this so the striker can achieve success. This is a legitimate starting point, but once this success has been achieved, players need to be stressed. In the 'real' game defenders typically overload strikers. To develop, young strikers need to learn how to deal with this stress and overload. They must be involved in practices where they solve the problem of being outnumbered. Players need to be challenged with exercises that stretch them just beyond their current level, but not *too far* beyond it. Vygotsky (1996) usefully labelled this as the *Zone of Proximal Development* (ZPD).

Inherent in this process will be making mistakes, something the coach needs to manage. Encourage players to accept mistakes, as denying these mistakes will not be conducive to learning.

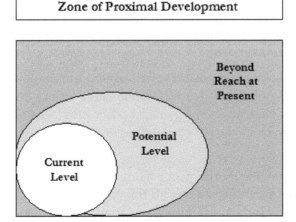

<hr />

[4] When preparing for a local derby against Manchester City, Sir Alex Ferguson and his coaches challenged the players to keep the ball for six consecutive passes on 12 occasions in each half. The intent was to take the sting out of a heated encounter. Once his team were able to keep the ball for six passes, they were able to control the tempo of the game.

[5] By "stress" we mean developmental stress. The stress that absorbs you and challenges you, as opposed to psychological stress and pressure.

Chapter 3

Let the Game Be 'A' Teacher

Most coaches will be familiar with the term *let the game be the teacher*. It is quoted around coaching environments time and time again. The term suggests that less time ought to be given to drills and exercises, and more time is provided for players to be involved in uninterrupted play – a genuine tool for teaching and learning. Unfortunately the underpinning message of this phrase has been misunderstood in many quarters. *Involving young players in uninterrupted play alone is not enough to teach them the game holistically.* The term ought to be *let the game be 'a' teacher*, i.e. let uninterrupted play be *one* of several teaching strings to a coach's bow.

By adopting this adapted approach, a coach is not dissolved from his core duties of teaching the game. Letting the game be *a* teacher cannot be considered a license to be a lazy coach, taking a night off, or neglecting to impart the knowledge that is required for players to improve.

England National Development Coach, John Allpress, uses the phrase of taking the "light footprint approach" to youth player development. In other words, letting the game be a teacher allows players to learn without overbearing input and instruction from the coach. Through using this technique, a modern coach will still use his observational and analytical skills to judge where improvements needs to be made, and what individuals need what help. He may observe the mentality of players. He may even use this less formal player-led environment to develop rapport with players. He will use this play session as a way of teaching players something relevant, just in a different way.

All coaches lament the changing world that our young players live in. After all, 'when we were young' soccer was all we had and it was all we cared about. We played soccer before school, at break times, and in the street after school. We didn't need a referee or a coach. We would pick two teams, use whatever area we could find and place jumpers for goal posts. It could be 1v1 or 16v17. If the teams didn't provide an even match-up, we changed them. If more players came, we absorbed them into the game. I regularly played against boys that were bigger, stronger and older, in limited space, which pushed me into my zone of proximal development. We had no bibs and only one ball. During holidays we played from sunrise to sundown. Rarely was anyone injured enough to require them to leave the game, and I don't remember anyone diving.

As a result of this 'street soccer' we received a huge amount of uninterrupted play. We could experiment; we could learn and would make mistakes all day long. This was the best *grounding* in the game we could have had.[6]

Due to cultural changes however, street soccer is a rarity, certainly in economically developed countries. Young players have other interests like the Internet, games consoles, and mobile phones. Streets are considered unsafe.

As coaches, however, we must understand that bemoaning the extinction of street soccer will not resurrect it. The days of young players that have a ball and a wall as their only interest and entertainment are gone. As students of the game, coaches now need to find a way of filling the void in a player's development that is left by the disappearance of this wonderful, informal learning environment.

Happily, coaches *can* recreate this learning environment by offering players the opportunity to participate in uninterrupted play. We can absorb this into our coaching plan and use it as one method of educating players. In fact, I know of one English Championship Academy that had a weekly evening session where the players would arrive, the coach would provide some balls, and the kids would just play. They would make up their own rules, teams and areas, and let the game be *a* teacher.

---

[6] Please note the use of the word *grounding* in this instance. This initial uninterrupted play is useful, but eventually players will need advice and guidance.

Teaching Games for Understanding (TGfU)

When can we have a game? Do we get to play a game tonight? How long do we get to play a game?

As coaches, we deal with these questions constantly. We sometimes even take it personally and feel insulted that the fantastic practices that we adapted from the Barcelona or Juventus Academy are not treated with the respect we feel they are due. The truth is that *game time is what players love.* They crave it. Game time is what intrinsically motivates them more than anything else a coach will ever do, regardless of what famous academy he got the practice from or what professional coach he saw deliver it. We normally trade off the question with a reply along the lines of: "We are going to warm-up first, then do some passing exercises, then we *will see what time is left for a game. If you do not do the first bit correctly, there will be no game.*"

By offering this answer we now change player motivation from intrinsic to extrinsic[7]. That wonderful practice that you have planned is, according to the players, something they 'must' do – a chore they need to complete before they get their wish of playing a game. It may even descend into a type of cold war where the players begrudge your practice, and the coach begrudges allowing them game time.

Imagine if you were our mathematics teacher again and a whole class-group arrived for your lesson desperate to skip some practice questions and jump straight into answering exam questions. What would you do? Insist they paid their dues with the time-consuming early questions or embrace their thirst for learning?

A *great* teacher would capture the enthusiasm and intrinsic motivation of the group and go with it. I would suggest that this teacher would let them loose on the exam questions and work backwards from any mistakes or stumbling blocks. He would praise any good practice or highlight the great strides and efforts of the students. It is only by challenging the students with exam-level problems that a true grasp of what those maths students are capable of is truly tested.

Sport's answer to this is the *Teaching Games for Understanding* method originally developed by Rod Thorpe and David Bunker. The basic premise of the method is hitting players immediately with game-like practices, and working backwards to solve any problems that may arise along the way. The players' motivation is very much intrinsic again but the coach is offering a legitimate learning tool to aid the players' soccer education.

Unlike the premise of 'just play', however, the coach sets out problem solving within these games. It is *implicit* learning[8] at its most powerful. It may be a tactical problem or one that asks players to make decisions that provide certain outcomes. It may be a game that has certain conditions or rules that players must abide by so that a certain topic can be the focus. The example below is taken from José Mourinho's *39 Preferred Practices* document. A game has been set up which involves six goals rather than two, a pitch that is wide and short, and an area for the full-backs to play unopposed. This game is designed to encourage switching the play, and in particular, the use of the full-backs.

---

[7] We will study intrinsic and extrinsic motivation in Chapter 4.

[8] Implicit learning is learning that takes place without the player consciously knowing he is taking on information (as opposed to explicit learning when players are consciously studying the game).

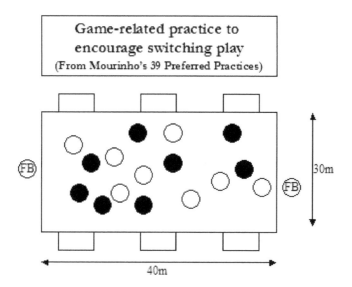

Technique is still practiced, but in a game-like situation. It mixes technical work and tactical relevancy all into one. Be very careful with pure technical practices that exist in isolation from the game and that offer little relevance to 'real' soccer. Players often are unable to reproduce these techniques unless they are constantly challenged to do them in real situations. Players will only improve when challenges exist that are just outside their current capacity, but not completely out of reach.

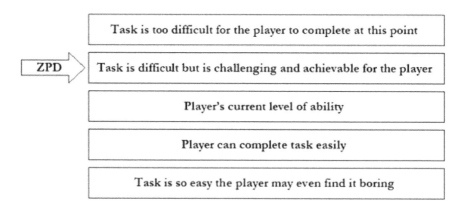

Remember however that *TGfU* is just one way of working. Again, it is another string to a coach's teaching bow. There is no need to throw your technical and skill practices out the window. These types of work are still of extreme importance and there are ways to test and stress players beyond their comfort zone. Indeed the use of *Whole-Part-Whole* type practices allows you pick a theme from a game-like situation, focus on it intently, then send the players back out into the real game. It shows players how the technical practices they are being asked to execute relate to the problems faced in the 'real' game.

In many ways *TGfU* challenges some traditional methods of coaching soccer where we use a 'practice ladder' to gradually move in a linear way from unopposed technical repetition through opposed practice and then finally testing players with a game-like situation. Both methods are valuable, and I am in no way advocating that coaches abandon the traditional session format, especially in the early days when players are learning a new skill. Using the Whole-Part-Whole method allows players to spend more time in 'real', game-related situations. More game-time increases motivation and joins the 'part' aspect of the session more closely with the 'whole' in the mind of the learner. The practice is no longer a 'chore' for the players or a grind they must get through before game-time.

Traditional 'Practice Ladder' Session Format	Whole-Part-Whole Format
ACTIVITY 1 – Warm-up	ACTIVITY 1 – Warm-up
ACTIVITY 2 – Unopposed Technique Practice	ACTIVITY 2 – WHOLE – Game-related Practice
ACTIVITY 3 – Opposed Skill Practice	ACTIVITY 3 – PART – Technical / Skill Practice
ACTIVITY 4 – Game-related Practice	ACTIVITY 4 – WHOLE – Game-related Practice

The Player as a Learner

Using the theory that soccer coaches are teachers, players are then, by consequence, learners. It is of great importance that coaches understand players in their role as soccer learners. All players are different, have different skills and learn in different ways. To truly fulfil our role as soccer teachers, and develop young players to reach their potential, we need to explore how they learn.

Learning Styles

Broadly speaking, all of us have an optimal way of absorbing and understanding information. Most of us have a favourite *learning style*.

In the 1980s, Neil Fleming popularized the VARK Learning Styles theory. He noted that people learn in different ways and education should tailor teaching approaches towards matching the following learning styles:

1. Visual Learners (those that learn best by seeing information through the use of graphics, diagrams, etc.)

2. Aural Learners (those that learn best by hearing information from someone speaking, lectures, etc.)

3. Reading and Writing Learners (those that learn best by seeing written, text-based information)[9]

4. Kinaesthetic Learners (those that learn best by physically doing something; learning in an active, hands-on manner)

As with any revolutionary theory, the VARK theory has been critiqued and analysed to ensure its validity and this particular theory can come with a warning sign. Many experts like Baroness Greenfield (Director of the Royal Institute and professor at Oxford University) and Professor Daniel Willingham disapprove of the theory. Just because someone may have an *optimal* learning style, *it does not mean that they do not need information presented to them in other ways also.* For example, if a player learns best through visual means, teaching him soccer through graphics alone will obviously not be sufficient. There will still need to be an aural explanation from the coach and for the player to practice it kinaesthetically. The trick is to *always offer the information you are conveying in a variety of different ways.*

Not many coaches have trouble telling their players what they require (maybe even too much!) and players ought to get plenty of time to physically attempt the exercise. What is vital however is to add more visuals and more reading / writing to practices. The best coaches that I have seen incorporate these styles will use a whiteboard or tactics board to:

• Write the session title and key points on the board to assist reading-based learners.

---

[9] Interestingly (as described by the European Club Association), at the Standard Liege Academy in Belgium, older players are regularly asked to take notes on their training sessions and are required to present these practices and the key information the next day. This is as part of their philosophy around "Brain-Centered Learning".

- Draw diagrams of the practice to aid their aural explanation of what is required.

- Refer back to diagrams during natural breaks in play and in debriefs to reemphasize key points, or to add progressions to the practice.

- Explain tactical points by moving markers around a tactics board.

The importance of visual material to modern youth players has not gone unnoticed by former German international and current US Soccer Head Coach, Jurgen Klinsmann. He points out "The young generation has a different curiosity that is more visual...We coaches have to learn how to deal with that: How do I get to each one best – with a talk, with video analysis? And what sort of tone? We need our own coaches for that. The sports psychologist coaches me too."

How Intelligent is David Beckham?

An 'intelligent' person is often measured in terms of their academic performance. Someone who is considered intelligent will have a Masters Degree of some sort, or is a maths whiz or physicist. Having 'brains' is being able to achieve a high score on an IQ test, retain lots of information or possess a large vocabulary.

Let's rebuke this common opinion here.

In 1983, Howard Gardner presented the theory of *Multiple Intelligences*. Gardner's central thesis was that everyone is intelligent, but in different ways. He outlined eight intelligences (a ninth, existentialist or 'religion smart', has been added since, although to much debate).

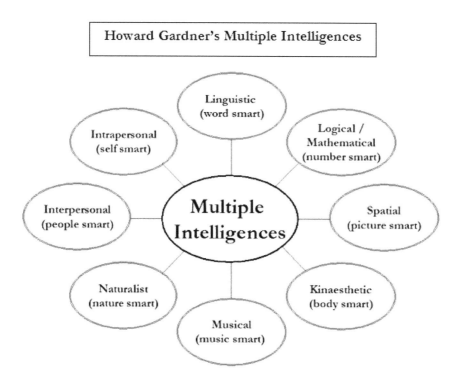

Soccer players are not normally considered to be 'intelligent' as defined by modern society. It is a bit of a running joke that they are notoriously under-educated. Let's take a step back, however, and study the intelligence of a soccer player in action.

David Beckham is famed for his ability to play accurate long-range passes to his teammates, but is also often the butt of jokes relating to his 'intelligence'. There is a wonderful clip on *YouTube* of an assist that Beckham gave Brazilian striker Ronaldo when playing for Real Madrid.[10] Feel free to take a minute to search for the clip and watch as you read!

As a technical piece of play it is outstanding. Consider the following calculations that Beckham would have computed after his first two touches:

- Is my teammate onside?

- How quickly is the closest opposition player pressing the ball? If at all?

- How tall is the left-sided central defender to ensure the ball goes over his head? What is his maximal standing jump?

- Can I get the required velocity on the ball to get it over this defender yet ensure it comes down to allow Ronaldo a goal scoring opportunity?

- Can I calculate the required curl needed to avoid all the defenders and place the pass into the path of Ronaldo?

- What pace will this pass need to ensure an element of surprise?

- Can I deliver this pass so it favours Ronaldo's 'safe-side' and is away from the second central defender?

- How physically strong is Ronaldo? Is he capable of holding off the second central defender?

- Is Ronaldo technically capable of finishing this assist? (Maybe the easiest of his calculations!). Is he prepared for what I am about to attempt?

- What is the goalkeeper's start position? Can I ensure the pass is out of his reach? Can I tempt him to come for the cross?

- Is there a wind factor that may affect the flight of the ball? If so, how strong is it?

- What is the state of the game at this moment? Do I need to take this risk?

- What are my other options? What are my teammates asking from me?

- If this pass does not succeed, what happens next?

- Where do I need to place my standing foot? What is the action of my left arm? What about the position of my head and hips?

A soccer player's intelligence then goes beyond what we conventionally mean by the term 'intelligent'. The Beckham example shows just how powerful a player's brain can be. The calculations involved in just *one pass* are considerable. I am not suggesting that Beckham could sit down with a scientist and describe any details about velocity, weight, wind speed considerations, the defender's height, his own arm position, etc. This intelligence comes from practice. It comes from repetition. It comes from muscle memory. It comes from an environment where Beckham was free to take such a risk. It comes from being spatially intelligent, intra-personally intelligent, and kinaesthetically intelligent. Maybe it even comes from being mathematically and inter-personally intelligent.

The most astonishing thing is that all of this will have been computed within a fraction of a second. As a coach, it is worth considering the varying forms of intelligence that may be before you.

---

[10] Search YouTube for: "David Beckham Crazy Pass (Cross)"

Differentiation

We have already noted in this section how different each player is. Each will learn differently, have a different type of intelligence and have personalities and characteristics that will determine different ways of learning and developing. Having redeveloped their youth development system after, by German soccer standards, a disastrous European Championship Finals in 2000, the central thesis of German Youth Development became that "every player needs individual attention" (*10 Years of German Academies*).

Having a focus on every player is very easy to state and acknowledge, but managing this differentiation is, arguably, the biggest challenge that a coach has to deal with.

Every group of players, like any group of classroom learners, can be broadly split into 3 groups[11].

1. Those that are striving ahead

2. Those that are coping with the challenge (the largest group)

3. Those that are struggling to keep up

We need to ensure that our practices cater for these 'copers', 'strivers' and 'strugglers'. On the back of this there are many misconceptions when differentiating soccer practices.

The tendency may be to pitch the level of the session towards the copers, which is often the most populated group. I suppose it is the natural thing to do. The challenge as a coach is to be more creative in the way we pitch sessions that ensure that they meet the development needs of all three groups and allow each group and each individual to enter their zone of proximal development.

Differentiating a group can often be misunderstood as a way to put more focus on your weaker players, the strugglers, in an attempt to lift them up to the standards of your more able players. While the thought is noble, and some would quote the phrase 'you are only as strong as your weakest link', you are actually positively discriminating against your strong strivers who also need your help to develop further. In times gone by, I found myself guilty of an over-focus on the weaker players, and putting more energy into them than the other two groups, thus neglecting my role to make over-achievers better as well. It was only when I took a step back that I realized I was putting probably ten times more time and energy into a player who was struggling than I was into a player who we believed (and still do!) will go on to be an England international.

On the other side of the coin, by focusing *only* on the strivers you may alienate the majority of the group, and potentially call your moral duty as a youth development coach into question.

How?

I suppose the remaining question is how? *How* do I differentiate accurately within a group environment? In *Youth Soccer: From Science to Performance*, Stratton, Reilly, Williams and Richardson outline two ways in which you can differentiate in sport:

> "Activities can be differentiated by 'task' or by 'outcome'. Differentiating by task requires the coach to set appropriate tasks for different individuals. In its simplest form, a coach may request some players to shoot with their preferred foot whilst the more able use their non-preferred foot. A coach differentiates by outcome by setting the same task for the group, but adapting it for individuals during the session. The task is made more difficult for the more able and easier for the less able."

Remember, however, that by applying restrictions and changing the normal rules of the game, you a tampering with the realism of soccer. If I 'have' to score with my non-preferred foot, I will

---

[11] There is a case to say that each individual in each group is progressing at an individual rate.

turn down a shot at goal with my preferred foot, which may have been the right thing to do. Ensure that you are happy with this 'trade-off'[12].

It is also worth noting that the dynamics of every group of players is different. I would suggest that no two groups are the same, even if they have age, level and experience in common. I have set up the same practices, for players within the same demographic who play at the same level, yet sometimes the practice works excellently with one group and not at all with the other. It is key for a coach to understand the individuals that make up a group, what motivates them, what characters dominate the group, and what types of practices get the optimal response from the group.

Conclusion

Youth soccer development is education. It is teaching. It is learning. This is something we cannot get away from, and there are certain theories from education that translate from classroom to soccer pitch. Use these to help your players achieve their peak performance.

Summary

- The top youth development programs across the world use educational terms and are set up as places of soccer *education*.

- It is important that a coach establishes a positive learning environment where players can learn and feel comfortable in making decisions and making mistakes.

- *Maslow's Hierarchy of Needs* identifies that players cannot learn unless their physiological and human survival needs are being met.

- *Bloom's Taxonomy* insists that coaches must build gradual learning into their program and not set challenges that are beyond a player's capability.

- The *Zone of Proximal Development* suggests that players must be pushed slightly beyond their current ability if they are to improve.

- *Let the Game be 'a' Teacher* has replaced street soccer – can the coach replicate this environment, leaving a "light footprint" on players?

- The *Teaching Games for Understanding* technique, and the use of Whole-Part-Whole Coaching can improve player learning but also satisfy their intrinsic motivational needs.

- Players will have different learning styles (visual, audio, reading and writing, and kinaesthetic). Coaches can use techniques that cater for all styles.

- Soccer 'intelligence' is different to conventional intelligence, but it is important to note that intelligence comes in many forms.

- All groups are different. All players are different. The needs of all players need to be met to ensure the development of all players.

---

[12] We will be discussing 'trade-offs' in your coaching sessions in more detail in Chapter 11.

Real Coach Experience

What if a Lionel Messi Arrived at Your Club?
(Observing a School Soccer Session - Anonymous)

What if a young Lionel Messi arrived at your soccer club? (I appreciate the obvious answer may be "great, my team will win more games!" but let's think deeper than that...)

How would you affect the development of this young soccer genius? I recently watched a junior school soccer session. There was one player who dominated the game. He scored goal after goal, and beat player after player. He showed an abundance of skill and seemed to cover every yard of the school playground. He was enthusiastic about the game and, like any young player, wanted to win.

The coach however, saw this as a problem and commenced 'differentiating' within the game, but did so through positive discrimination.

Firstly he instructed 'James' that he was no longer allowed to score. James reluctantly accepted the challenge and commenced continually beating players and setting his mates up for easy tap-ins, something as an onlooker I found endearing, cheeky, but James was merely solving a problem set out by the coach and was living within the boundaries of the outlined rules. Still dissatisfied, however, the coach conditioned James to a maximum of two touches, before making him go in goal and then confining him to his penalty box. All because he was *too good* for the session the coach had planned.

The coach differentiated but did so to meet his own needs. At times it had the feel of a battle of wits, with the player determined to show his worth despite being handicapped, and the coach wanting to restrict James' ability so the session would be more manageable. You got the feeling that he would prefer if James were not there at all.

If a Lionel Messi arrived at your club, would you tell him not to score goals? Not to dribble? Would you restrict him to two touches? Would you banish him and restrict him to a 10-metre square box? I wonder how many extraordinary young players have been made ordinary in this way.

4

Understanding Psychology in Soccer

"Forget all your phases of play and technical practices. You first need to light a fire under players." (Craig Short)

'Psychology' is an evocative word. To the layperson, it looks like something that is beyond their comprehension, something that is best left for academics and thesis writers, just like the rest of the '-ology' disciplines. We distrust ologies. We look at them with suspicion. We misunderstand them. Other terms are often used to take the sinister edge off the term such as 'mind coach', 'Peak Performance Coach' or a 'stretch' rather than a 'shrink' (Bill Beswick).

This fear and mistrust comes from a lack of knowledge around the subject and as a result, competent people even declare that they 'don't believe' in psychology in soccer. In a sense, that is like not believing in gravity. But although they cannot be seen, both psychology in sport and gravity are very much alive.

Summarising soccer psychology in one chapter is virtually impossible. I contribute to a sport psychology website called *The Sport in Mind*. When scrolling through the index there are well over 100 topics to select from. The wonderful book *Coaching the Mental Game* by H.A. Dorfman has an A-Z of topics for the coach – and another A-Z for athletes! Psychology is a minefield.

Therefore, instead of this chapter providing very little information about everything, I will endeavour to give you a 'one-stop' guide to psychology in soccer, based on the most useful, workable topics that I have encountered.

Two Exercises for the Non-Believers

I always find it a shame that when introducing the use of psychology in soccer, I feel the need to justify it, and then hope that people come on board. Indeed many of the other performance sciences, such as biomechanics, nutrition, etc. have been more readily accepted than psychology, when once upon a time they were also considered unimportant.

In an effort to substantiate embracing psychology in soccer I have outlined two exercises below. The first you can do in a matter of seconds, the second will require an assistant…

1. Even the Non-Believers Use Psychology!

I want you to think about the most old-school, narrow-minded coach that you know. The coach that is stuck in his ways and never embraces change. The one who talks, but doesn't listen. The one that would glare at you if you ever mentioned any word that ended in 'ology'.

Maybe a team-talk of his has gone something like this:

- Where was the effort today?
- You don't want it enough.
- You lost your discipline and that is why we lost.
- Some of you haven't got off the bus yet.

- We are losing because you don't care.

- You are not switched on.

- You lost concentration on the second goal.

- You are embarrassing yourselves.

- This game is all about who wants it more.

Whether you are a psychologist or not, you will notice that all the above statements refer to psychology and the mental approach to the game. Is this proof enough of the need to embrace it? Or maybe you need physical proof...

2. The Physical Power of the Mind

This is an extraordinary exercise to show fellow coaches and even your players the power of mindset and positive thinking. I won't claim it as my own, but will thank Susan Jeffers, the author of *Feel the Fear and Do It Anyway*.

Have a member of your team stand in front of the group. For effect, choose the biggest, most boisterous player.

Ask them to raise their arm so it is at 90 degrees to the body. Tell him you are going to push his arm back down by his side and to resist you.

Before pushing, however, tell him that he is "weak and unworthy". He is a feather in the wind. Get him to repeat that he is weak and unworthy. You will effortlessly push his arm down.

The second part of the exercise turns this on its head. Tell him he is "strong and worthy". Tell him he is a rock and an immovable mountain. Get him to repeat: "I am strong and worthy" four or five times. He must fiercely repeat it and really get into the emotions of it.

Try pushing his arm down – you won't be able to! He will have the physical power to resist your efforts.

All that has changed is your player's mindset. A mere 30 seconds worth of suggestion and feedback from the coach, and some positive self-talk, results in the physical performance of your player being changing completely – purely as a result of his mindset!

Confidence

There is a brilliant, if not rather bizarre, story told by England and Chelsea midfielder Frank Lampard about an incident with his coach José Mourinho[1]:

> "He knew how to get into people's heads. He got into mine the moment he came. He has that air of arrogance, that confidence, and it rubs off.

> I have never had a manager who, while I'm standing in the shower cleaning my balls, tells me I'm the best player in the world. He did that. I'll never forget it. So casual. "You're the best player in the world, but you need to win titles".

> 'From that moment the extra confidence was in me. Not that I thought I was the best player in the world, but the manager who had just won the Champions League thought it. *So I went out a different player.*" (my italics).

---

[1] Quotes courtesy of Martin Samuel article Lampard *Scrubbed up Nicely for Chelsea after José Showered Him With Praise.*

During the upcoming paragraphs we will speak in detail about how mentality affects performance. All of the factors below however, as understood by coaches like Mourinho, tend to come back to one thing – confidence. Being confident is one of the major tools a soccer player can have in his armoury. A lack of confidence affects creativity, risk-taking, decision-making, and will hinder a player's ability, desire and motivation.

Dan Abrahams, author of *Soccer Brain* and *Soccer Tough,* points out in *Mental Toughness for Soccer* (available for free e-book download at the time of writing[2]) the following as "enemies of confidence":

- Worry

- Uncertainty

- Fear

- Doubt

- Anxiety

- Nerves

These factors, according to Abrahams, "…strike at the heart of consistency. They slow you down both physically and mentally. They ruin your decision-making and coordination. They prevent you from being the best individual soccer player you can be…"

I cannot overstate how crucial the coach is to being a young player's source of confidence. You hold the key in helping them overcome these "enemies". After all, the coach holds a colossal amount of power in terms of feedback; his opinion is highly sought after and valued, and the coach is the one to impress.

As a coach, and consequently a role-model and power holder, it is vastly insufficient, but all too common, to simply order players to 'be confident' – the mind does not work like that, yet it is a phrase I have seen over-used time and time again. Confidence cannot be instructed like you would instruct a player to shoot, pass or tackle. It needs to be *fostered* from within your players. They need you to "light a fire under them", as creatively outlined in this chapter's opening quote by ex-Premier League centre-back, Craig Short.

There are thankfully techniques that you can use to help light this confidence fire:

Technique	Detail
Praise	The use of praise is the easiest way to foster a player's confidence. Tell him that he has done well, point out occasions where he has been successful and celebrate this success. If you praise correctly, you can then build an environment where any criticism is more readily accepted. In a 2012 Harvard Business School address, Sir Alex Ferguson described the term "well done" as the "two best words ever invented in sports".

---

[2] Also available as a free e-book at the time of writing is Tony Reilly's *An Athlete's Guide to Sport Psychology.*

'Anchoring' / Using 'Triggers'	Refer players to past performances where they have been successful – for example, "Remember, when we last played this team, you made four great saves in the first half". This 'anchors' positive thoughts in their mind, building confidence to be able to achieve their peak performance.
Success	Confidence comes from achieving success. Set up exercises where your players can be successful. This success breeds further success and a belief that "I can do this". Remember, success needs to be challenging also, within the players Zone of Proximal Development[3]. Success that is achieved *too easily* sends a message that things should be easy to achieve and do not require hard work. In fact, praising success as a product of hard work is very powerful, encouraging players to incorporate a *growth mindset*. Praising talent alone encourages a *fixed mindset*, where instant gratification is prized more than long-term improvement[4].
Be Positive	Encourage an environment where mistakes are not overtly criticized. Being too critical of a player can reduce confidence further. Praise and reward good performance and effort. To encourage this, the *Positive Coaching Alliance* created the *Positive Coach Mental Model*.
Goal-Setting	Set your players attainable yet challenging goals. Not only does this focus the player, it also gives them a chance to celebrate their success once achieved.
Bigger Picture	We are all familiar with the term 'form is temporary; class is permanent', a very positive message. Remind players that a fleeting drop in form is just that – fleeting. Remind players of the bigger picture – that other parts of their development are progressing successfully and with hard work, their form will return.
Visualisation	Encourage positive visualization. Visualization is a technique that involves mental preparation and rehearsal, rather than physical work. Although often met with scepticism, the value of this technique in improving performance has a growing following. Wayne Rooney is an advocate of the technique – "I lie in bed the night before the game and visualize myself scoring goals or doing well. You're trying to put yourself in that moment and trying to prepare yourself, to have a 'memory' before the game… I've always done it, my whole life."

---

[3] Refer to previous chapter for details of the Zone of Proximal Development.
[4] Players with a *growth mindset* have a desire to learn. They understand that their skills and ability can be developed. Those with a *fixed mindset* do not reach their full potential as they want instant success and readily give up on challenges. For more on this topic, see the work of Carol Dweck.

Give your Players a Sandwich!

Providing players with confidence does not mean that players are immune from receiving *negative feedback*. You *can* give players a negative message, but in a way that is also highly positive. I once witnessed a fantastic half-time intervention from a youth coach working with under-18 players. He highlighted the negative aspects of a player's performance, but turned this negative feedback into a positive, motivational message. It went something along the lines of: "Your crossing today... (sighs) you are better than that. I know you are better than that. You know you are better than that. Show me, show your teammates and show yourself how good you are." The message was simple but powerful. The coach is letting him know that this aspect of his performance was not good enough compared to how good he can be, and that he believes the player can improve.

A tried and tested formula for providing negative feedback is by using the *Feedback Sandwich*. It is a way of delivering criticism but simultaneously softening the potentially harmful impact it may have on your player. The technique simply involves sandwiching your negative feedback within two pieces of positive feedback. An example would go like this:

Positive: "You did really well to open you body up to receive passes from the goalkeeper."

Negative: "To improve, however, you have got to scan and check your shoulders for what is around you."

Positive: The occasion when you did that started one of our best attacks of the game."

It is imperative that coaches outline aspects of good performance as well as bad ones. Indeed, while coaching is about improving players by identifying flaws in their game, it is also about maximising the abilities they have. Perhaps that is ever more important. A good, player-centreed coach, will actively seek out aspects of good performance, rather than constantly dwelling on the bad. Would you go to work every day where the only time your boss speaks to you is to criticize? The sandwich technique allows us to temper negative feedback, and in addition there is a growing school of thought that coaches need to offer *five* pieces of praise before the harmful impact of negative feedback is accepted.

The Four Mindsets

Confidence is one of four pre-performance mindsets that influence how players perform on the pitch. Bill Beswick wonderfully outlined these four during a coach education workshop in 2007, which I have displayed along a continuum below:

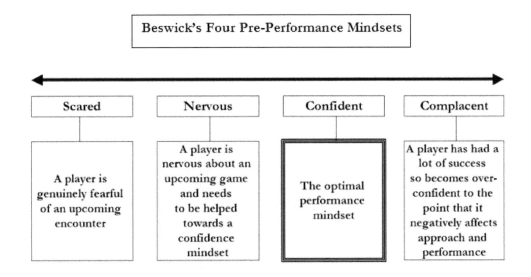

The optimal mindset to be in, pre-performance, is the *confident* mindset. If players find themselves at either end of the spectrum (scared or complacent), they will have major problems in achieving peak performance. A player who is nervous is nothing new, and a small amount of nerves is okay – after all, being nervous means that something is important. If nervousness is the dominant mindset of the player, however, he will also need your help.

Each mindset, away from confidence, is difficult to manage and players will need some help in getting back into a positive, confident frame of mind. There are ways that a coach can alter a player's mindset, guiding and motivating them safely towards the confidence zone. Let's explore ways that we can do this.

Scared

Players may be scared prior to performance for a multitude of reason. It may be external factors like the strength of the opposition, or internal ones like a run of especially poor form. Maybe the upcoming opponents have beaten the player's team heavily in the past. *This is where your players need you most.* They will need your support and they need your constant reassurance. Remember, you are their leader, role model and biggest critic! If they enter the field of play genuinely fearful of their performance they will be highly unlikely to perform to their best. If they start the game beaten mentally, they will be beaten on the field of play. Roy Keane, the great ex-captain of Manchester United famously pointed out that on many occasions he knew from the opponents' body language that they would lose the game – and that was before a ball was kicked!

Players who are scared need all the positivity you can give them. Give them lots of praise in the warm-up, even if you have to slightly exaggerate it. Set up a warm-up that is nice and simple – which will give them *success*. How you, as a coach, perform and what you ask of your players in the warm-up is critical. For example, you may normally finish the warm-up by playing 5v5 in a tight area because you know how good the opposition are at keeping possession. This is well thought out and justified *tactically*, but as *psychological* preparation, it may be very damaging. Players may give the ball away more often, they may misplace passes, and if one of them is stressed enough, he may even take it out on someone in an overly tough tackle. Emotions may run high as they are already in a stressful, negative mind-set. And that negative mind-set may be reinforced in such a warm-up. Change the warm-up by doing something fun and light-hearted where you can get your players into a more positive frame of mind.

In the changing room what you say is vital. Try understating the meaning and significance of the game. How many times have you heard a professional soccer coach in a press conference declare, "All the pressure is on the opposition"? That statement is not just a cliché, it is a very subtle way of de-stressing players and putting all the pressure onto the other team. If you tell a team that is fearful how important the game is, and how good the opposition are, that will only work to increase any fear.

Nervous

As we mentioned above, being nervous is okay, once those nerves come in small portions. As a race, human beings get nervous about something if it is important to them. That is something that can be harnessed and valued by a coach – your players care about their team and their game!

Again, praise is important. Remind nervous players what they are good at – or better still, get them to remind each other. Get them in pairs around the changing room and give them two minutes to tell each other two or three good things about each other. If you think about it, if someone tells you positive things about you, it makes you feel ten feet tall. That becomes even more powerful when it comes from a peer, a team-mate, someone your own age and in your own circumstance.

The coach can also positively anchor players by recalling times the team has played well, a specific game, goal, passage of play, or giant-killing result that will cause the players to feel great things about that particular event, and desire to apply it to the circumstance they are in now. It increases motivation and allows them more positivity to break through into a confident mind-set.

You can use this even if it is only one individual who is particularly nervous – ask him: "Do you remember that match when you marked their star striker out of the game? Then scored a goal at the other end? That is what you are capable of. Remember that." You may even take that player aside subtly to work with him. After all, you do not want to point out his nerves and raw feelings in front of a group. The key message is about reassurance. *That is what they will want to hear.*

It is important to tune into the mind-set of your players. If you do they will dictate how you prepare for a game. If you find them to be nervous, or literally scared about the task at hand, then it is time to go to work. It is time to be positive, pick them up and praise them. They need you more than ever and will be craving any glimmer of hope and positivity you give them. Ensure they get it.

Complacent

Complacency is the result of success over a period of time, where players become overconfident and overestimate their performance capabilities. So while coaches want their players to reach peak performance by adopting a confident mindset, there is a problem when players become *too* confident.

In a way, the atmosphere of a complacent changing room is far more dangerous and far more negative than when players are scared. We have no sympathy when teams lose because of complacency. In fact, we in the sporting world quite enjoy it when it happens to others. When players are scared, the desire for your help and guidance is strong. Players want to hear your solutions. When players are complacent however, messages are harder to convey and instill in them. It is almost easier to manage a group through a crisis of losing than a crisis of winning! Whether we like to admit it or not, we all suffer from it at some point or other. We have all underestimated the opposition only to come back down to Earth rather sharply when the test is much more difficult than first perceived. It is extremely important that the coach, as leader and elder, distances himself from complacent thoughts, as they will rub off on players very quickly. They may feel like they do not have to try, work hard or display effort to overcome their opposition. If a fall comes from a great height, it can be extremely painful.

For players to reach their peak performance levels, it is essential that they try, work hard, and show plenty of effort. This is what will maximize their technical ability and talent. Complacency undermines this effort and hard work, and obstructs players from achieving their potential. Only then will their perceived superior qualities and talent come to the fore. As the old adage goes, "hard work beats talent when talent doesn't work hard".

Guiding players through complacency is a tough task, but it can be done. We must recognize, firstly, that *no player chooses to become complacent*. It is not a conscious choice but a plague that seeps into the brain. We must also recognize once again that it is not something that can be instructed ("do not be complacent"[5]).

When I detect complacency I ensure that the standards we have set are maintained and maybe even pushed higher. I will overestimate the ability of the opposition, and use goal-setting to set challenges for players to meet. This allows players to refocus their minds by concentrating on specific facets of their performances.

During the warm-up I expect and demand more from the players. There is less focus on success and more on setting challenges. I accept sloppiness, indiscretions and mistakes less readily than

---

[5] The brain is wired in a way where it struggles to process negative instruction ('negation'), and instead focuses on the main body of what it hears. The most common example to emphasize this is "don't think about a big pink elephant". Needless to say, we think of an elephant that is big and pink! This applies to other soccer instructions like "don't give the ball away". All the players' focus becomes about giving the ball away. Change the instruction to "keep the ball" to rule out the negative connotation.

normal. It is probably the most confrontational and command-like I ever am as a coach – when things are perceived to be going well!

The techniques above are all intended to increase confidence and prepare players well for performance. They are intended to be inspiring and motivational. Remember all groups, and indeed all individuals, are different so need motivating differently. A close friend of mine, and professional sports psychologist, Kevin Clancy, describes this as "one of the most important roles of a coach, from a psychological perspective."

Motivation

Motivating players is the Mecca of sport psychology for coaches. Being able to motivate and "light a fire" under players is a wonderful mission for coaches and produces a great feeling for a coach.

The Epic Team Talk

Coaches can often misinterpret how to motivate players. We tend to want to devise and replicate Al Pacino's hair-raising speech in the movie, *Any Given Sunday*. We measure the success of our motivation by the noise-levels of our players as they leave the changing room, or by the look of their 'game face'. In reality, however, these types of forced speeches never really live up to expectation because of one simple reason – they are forced.

Human nature dictates that when a person speaks passionately about a subject – any subject – people naturally gravitate towards them and listen more intently. Their body language will give a coach an indication of their response – they will lean in, make eye contact and hang on your every word. Alternatively, of course, if what is being said is void of that passion and natural intent, it can come across as being quite hollow or inappropriate. Therefore by over-preparing and over-scripting these speeches, we actually lose their key, passionate meanings.

With coaching moving from being coach-centred to player-centred, more coaches are abandoning these epic-type team-talks in favour of a more individual or smaller-group approach. Coaches will talk to the group about their tactical approach, but then only to individuals about their individual role and preparation. If you have a squad of 15 – 18 players, it is difficult to transmit the exact message that you intend to every player. It is also difficult to use the same message and hope that it resonates with *every player*. Often, during long, coach-centred, dialogue-only team-talks, players switch off. They may be bored, disengaged, or maybe the epic message you are intending to provide is not quite hitting the spot. By tailoring your messages to individual players, the meaning becomes more powerful as you are speaking directly to the player. It builds rapport with the player and increases the coach-player bond.

Intrinsic and Extrinsic Motivation

Broadly, how people are motivated can be grouped into two categories – intrinsic (internally motivated) and extrinsic (externally motivated).

Those who are motivated intrinsically are driven by enjoyment and the love of the game. These players tend to come across as more motivated, and are willing to improve their skills for their own gratification. Those who are motivated extrinsically do so for reward or often to avoid punishment. They can lose aspects of their stimulation as the task becomes more about the reward than their development. The most successful players will be motivated in both ways. I always find it quite strange when people accuse national players of not being motivated to play for their country, especially in England. This normally comes from supporters and the media following a defeat, below-par performance, or exit from a tournament. People suggest that they do not care and are more motivated extrinsically, by money, women, cars and the superstar lifestyle.

During the 1998 World Cup, David Beckham was sent off when playing for England following a petulant altercation with the Argentine player Diego Simeone. England ended up being defeated after a penalty shoot-out and knocked out of the competition at the Last-16 stage. Beckham became the fall guy and was blamed in many quarters for England's defeat and subsequent disqualification. On his return to England, images of burning Beckham effigies appeared, his Manchester United team bus was attacked, and fans across the country routinely insulted his wife and family. This reaction would be enough for most laypeople to quit, walk away and never represent people who criticized them so overtly again. Instead Beckham went on to score the winning goal to take England to the following World Cup with a superbly taken free-kick against Greece in 2001. I often wonder what his thoughts were, having scored a truly vital goal, as he ran towards the England supporters that day – his arms aloft to receive their adulation, this time as the hero of those who once treated him with such disdain. His motivation to carry on was simple, and intrinsic: "I love scoring goals for England and playing for England... I love playing for my country." This "love" saw Beckham go on to captain his country and achieve 115 caps.

That intrinsic love for the game should be present in every young player. Ensure this is fostered in the players that you coach. Be extremely careful when you change players' motivation from intrinsic to extrinsic. I have seen 10-year-olds being motivated by the promise of money for every goal they score. Will this child now prefer the money over the innocent self-gratification of scoring goals? As a result will his decision-making change by constantly going for goal rather than choosing the correct decision which may be to pass elsewhere?

There is a great story of changing motivation from intrinsic to extrinsic in young players...

A group of teenagers persisted in annoying an old man by playing soccer noisily outside his home. No matter how angry the old man got, or how much he pleaded for them to stop, the boys continued to play. One day he had an idea. Instead of pleading with them or becoming frustrated, he offered them $2 each to carry on playing, and would pay them the same every time they came back. Sure enough the boys returned the next day, the day after, and the following day, picking up their payment as promised. The money, not the game, became the motivation. After a number of days, when the boys came to collect their money, the old man told them he would no longer be paying them. The boys were outraged and they refused to play soccer outside the old man's house again. Once the old man removed the extrinsic motivation from the boys, they rejected doing what they once did and enjoyed for free – playing soccer.

Motivating Negatively

Coaches can use motivation in a positive or negative way to get an emotional response from players. Indeed, using negative motivation seems to be quite a common thing for coaches, and often something that is necessary at particular times, especially when coaches want to ensure that discipline meets the required standard. This type of extrinsic motivation, however, can be extremely short-term, and over the long-term can be quite damaging to a player's impetus and enthusiasm. Some examples of negative motivation are below, and what long-term message it actually sends to your players:

Examples of Negative Motivation Used by Coach	Actual Long-term Message Received by Players
Do this properly or we will put the balls away and you will run instead.	Physical training is a punishment, not a necessity of the game. It will now be much harder for the coach to get players to buy into fitness-based sessions.
You need to win this game or you will be brought in for extra training at 6am every day next week.	Soccer practice is a punishment, rather than something I enjoy and look forward to.
I did not come here to watch you perform like that. I could be at home now spending time with my family. (Motivating through guilt)	I am letting my coach down. He has much better things to do than to be here with us.
If you do not improve, I will substitute you and you will never play for this team again.	My coach believes that I will not recover and improve from this single poor performance. To ensure I am not punished, I will take no risks and play a safe game.

Some of the examples above are difficult enough for an adult player to accept, and are even harder for young players. These messages, sent on a consistent basis, will change the long-term mindset and motivation of players, and may result in a change in the way they perceive themselves.

Self-Talk

If you refer back to Susan Jeffers' exercise at the beginning of the chapter, we noted how mental self-talk affects physical performance. We found that sending messages of being strong allows us to perform strongly physically, and pessimistic messages of being weak cause us to feel weak.

This self-talk happens to people on a daily basis. We are constantly sending ourselves messages that control the way we perceive ourselves - producing consequences for our behaviour. These messages can be either positive or negative, and maybe elements of both.

Take a job interview as an everyday example. If your self-talk prior to the interview is *negative* (what if the company doesn't think I am good enough for the job; what if they ask awkward questions; I have nothing worthwhile to wear and look scruffy) your demeanour will be less than confident, the way you answer questions may be disjointed and any 'blip' in the process, however minor, could dramatically affect your ongoing performance in the interview. Your lack of confidence in yourself will manifest in a poor interview and you will not be offered the job. If your self-talk is *positive* (I have been granted an interview because they want to employ me; I am well prepared for any question; I look good, and portray a professional image) we approach the process more confidently, you can answer questions with certainty and you can handle any perceived blips without it destroying you.

In a soccer context, players use self-talk regularly before, during and after performances. We all have players that use it negatively and those who use it positively. Below are some examples that I have heard from players:

Examples of Negative Self-Talk
If I get forward I am scared that I will be caught out defensively (trialist fullback).
If you give me a penalty, I will miss it.
I always play badly on this pitch.
When I receive deep from the goalkeeper, I am frightened I will give the ball away.
My opponent is a better player than me so why try?

Examples of Positive Self-Talk
They beat us the last time, but I am keen to put this right.
I know I can commit when pressing the ball because I trust my team-mates to cover me.
I conceded a soft goal but that will never happen again.
I won most of my headers so *I can* compete with physically bigger players.
I scored 35 goals last year so *I know* I can handle missing some chances.

The examples above are only ones *I have heard* from youth players, but there will be countless examples of self-talk that we *do not hear*. Coaches have to interpret a player's self-talk by their body language, reactions to situations, and general demeanour. Most coaches know the inherent behaviour of their players so can spot any discrepancies in their conduct. It is important that coaches do not ignore any changes in behaviour and seek to understand the reason for their occurrence. As coaches, we can inform players and influence them to be positive, by using positive reinforcement and encouraging constructive, helpful self-talk. Using positive, rather than negative self-talk, inspires confidence in players, which in turn produces better performances.

We all have certain negative images of ourselves. For example, in an everyday context, this may be to do with our weight and we may use self-talk such as "I am fat. I am in bad shape. I eat too much and do not exercise enough. I look horrible." How hurt would you be if others told you the exact same thing? That you were fat and looked horrible? Why would you allow yourself to speak to yourself in a way that would hurt you immensely if somebody else said it? Encourage your players to use positive self-talk and ensure the messages you are sending them are affirmative also.

The Power of Belief

We may need to throw conventional logic out of the window to fully understand the power of belief in sport. Analysing the belief system is complex and intricate, but tackled wonderfully by Matthew Syed in *Bounce* and in the works of Dan Abrahams. I have plucked the workable knowledge from writers such as the aforementioned, and other psychological works, and married them to my own experiences to come up with a useful guide to understanding self-belief for soccer coaches.

The more I have studied football, the more I have studied successful managers, coaches and players, the more I have studied the behaviour of successful people, it seems their success all comes down to one thing. That thing is an unwavering belief in what they are capable of.

In fact, I am going to suggest that belief is the most important ingredient in becoming successful. If you do not believe in what you are attempting, if you do not believe you are good enough, you cannot possibly complete it successfully. Without belief, there is little confidence, a huge reduction in motivation, and a lack of belief sparks emotions that are closer to 'scared' rather than 'confident' on our pre-performance mindset continuum. A lack of belief will paralyse players with fear, thus inhibiting their ability to play to their maximum potential. As Syed unequivocally puts it, "...doubt, to a sportsman, is poison."

Belief is also what keeps you going when things are going wrong, when you are failing. It is that one shred of positivity that you can cling onto when everything else is disintegrating. The belief felt by sportsmen may not even be rational! Look at Steven Gerrard's reaction to his goal in the Champions League Final of 2005. From being 3-0 down at half-time, and utterly outplayed by AC Milan, getting one goal back was always possible, but nobody truly contemplated that Liverpool would recover completely to lift the trophy that night[6].

If a player can learn to believe rather than retreat (give up), even in the worst of circumstances, it is the only way to achieve any type of success from the situation. Having watched tens of thousands of soccer matches, I have yet to see a retreating mindset result in a team's victory. I have, however, on many, many occasions, seen unwavering, even irrational belief win games, launch great fight-backs, and cause David to beat Goliath. Certain occasions spring straight to my mind – Senegal beating France at the 2002 World Cup; Mali coming back from 4-0 down with 11 minutes remaining to draw 4-4 with Angola in the 2010 African Cup of Nations; Inter Milan beating Barcelona over two legs of the UEFA Champions League semi-final, although they had a man sent off in the first half hour of their away leg in Catalonia. As Arsène Wenger famously said – "To achieve great things you have first to believe it."

How often do you hear a player say "I can't do that", "I'm not good at that", etc? When you hear a player utter these words, this is your moment to intervene and help them. If they say, "I can't", then they won't.

People have an unquenchable desire to prove themselves right. How many times have people pre-empted their failure, then gloated that they correctly predicted their own downfall? Think of a player who steps up to take a shot at goal or a penalty for example. Even in an informal practice session. "I hate taking penalties. I am going to miss". He then wildly attempts to score and doesn't. His response, "I told you so!"

If you ever hear a player say that they can't do something, call it immediately. Ensure in no uncertain terms that players understand that there is far more value in attempting challenges, rather than disregarding their ability before they have even tried.

By consequence, it is essential that the coach shows players that he believes in them. If the coach's behaviour is void of emotional control, is panicked, is constantly critical – it will impact players' belief, and will thus impact confidence and the players' ability to perform to their maximum. We constantly hear elite coaches tell the media that they will 'focus on the positives'. Most viewers now look on this as a cliché. It is not. That line is a product of ensuring player belief stays intact.

Control

To achieve peak performance, players need to be in control, and they need to attempt to control the right things. If players lose this, their performance will be affected.

---

[6] Elite sportsmen often have the skills to 'doublethink'. They will believe without question that even the improbable can become possible, but all the while, have the ability to accept failure in a way that does not overtly hurt them. They will believe in themselves, but they also will not fear failure.

Control the Controllables

"Only control what you can control". The players I have worked with across different age groups will have witnessed me say this over and over again. This repetition is due to my unwavering opinion that it is crucial for their development. It is a key message we must send to players at the earliest opportunity.

The distractions around a soccer match are numerous, even a youth soccer match. The crowd, opposition, referee, weather, travel and many more all have the potential to divert the attention of players. The crucial message to offer players is that they must not worry about the things that are outside their control, and only 'control the controllables', i.e. put your energy into the things that you can affect directly, and put zero energy into distractions that will not assist your performance. Those things that are out of a player's control, if given undue attention and focus, can consume the thoughts of a young player.

Controllables	
Things Players Cannot Control	**Things Players Can Control**
The state of the pitch	The way they perform on the pitch
The weather	How they adapt to varying weather conditions
The referee and his decisions	How they deal with decisions, even if they deem them to be incorrect
The opposition's ability and performance	How they control the opposition performance through their own performance
Injured / missing team mate(s)	How the team can adapt and perform in their team mates absence
The fixture list	How they deal with fixture pile-up, time of kick-off, or playing tough opposition back-to-back
Spectators	Focus on the game and not the impact of spectators
Team bus stuck in traffic	Remain focused, stay calm and concentrate on the game, even if preparation time is reduced on arrival
The opposition are late	Remain patient, manage their time well and adjust to a later kick-off time

Emotional Control

Soccer can be an emotionally-charged game, even at a youth level. It is unfortunate that we routinely see images of highly emotional players on our TV screens, and a tradition seeing soccer as a 'war' or 'battle' gives the impression that soccer is an argumentative environment, where losing self-control is a sign of the passion or fight of the player.

When young players interpret this, however, they can often get it wrong. They lose control over an incorrect (or often a correct) refereeing decision, which may be merely over an inconsequential award of a throw-in. Their performance descends into arguments with the opposition, officials or even each other. Retaining self-control and making good decisions off the back of this control is vital.

Genuine adversity may hit a group of players. They may feel that a situation is unjust or unfair. They may be losing a game quite badly, resulting in embarrassment and a loss of self-belief and confidence. If this emotion is too much for a player, where the uncontrollables overawe his performance, his game will suffer. The coach needs to be there to assist them through this and sell the need for players to harness their emotions that are getting in the way of them playing their best game.

Conclusion

The breadth of psychology in soccer is huge, and far bigger than this single chapter. Abrahams uses the theory of "4 C's" (Creativity, Confidence, Commitment, Cohesion) in *Soccer Brain* while the English FA use the "5 C's" (Commitment, Communication, Concentration, Control and Confidence). I have only briefly mentioned the power of goal-setting, visualization, and mental strength, while I have not written about a player's ability to recover from setbacks.

I would encourage any coach that wants to further understand sport psychology to use the works of many of the writers included in this chapter. This particular '-ology' need not be feared any longer, as understandable, workable, practical information on the topic is now very much available.

I suppose the catalyst for all this work will be empathy - the power to share and understand the feelings and emotions of your players, and to tailor your coaching to get the best out of them.

Summary

- Embrace psychology in soccer coaching – everyone uses it!

- A player's mindset can manifest itself physically.

- Confidence is a major ingredient for players to reach peak performance.

- The four pre-game mindsets are: scared, nervous, confident and complacent.

- Players who are outside the confident zone need specific motivation.

- Beware of delivering your epic, hair-raising team talk!

- Motivation can be intrinsic or extrinsic – be careful when externalizing player motivation.

- Avoid using negativity when trying to motivate players.

- It is important that the language and messages players use when speaking to themselves (self-talk) is positive, rather than negative.

- The power of belief is summed up succinctly by Arsène Wenger – "To achieve great things you have first to believe it."

- Teach players to concern themselves only with the things that they can control, and to maintain self-control.

- Use empathy to understand your players and their mental needs.

Real Coach Experience

An Exercise in Building Confidence in Players

(Ray Power)

My favourite exercise that looks to build confidence in players is one I do with every group I work with. I tend to reserve it for an occasion when players need it most, maybe after a poor performance or when the group in general needs a mental lift and an increase in self-belief. There are three stages to the exercise.

1. Peer Assessment

I distribute a sheet of paper to all players. One column will contain the name of all the players. A second column will have a space to write a sentence or two. I ask them to simply write one strength of each of their teammates. When all members of the squad have completed the sheet, you will have a library of positive opinions, all transmitted by the players themselves, about the rest of the group. Each individual will hopefully have seven or eight (or more) positive traits. The fact that a teammate has contributed these strengths is powerful as young people highly value the opinion of their peer group, frequently more so than they do the opinion of adults.

2. Coach Input

Once the sheets are returned, I make a poster for each player, inserting his strengths. If one particular player's feedback is not substantial enough, I tend to add strengths from my point of view, ensuring the impact of the exercise is maximized. I will also often include a part of his game that may not be a strength, but something he is working on. This gives the player extra motivation to carry on improving.

3. Include an Area for Development

Once complete, with an abundance of strengths, there is enough positive information on the poster to include a weakness or area for development without it being deemed explicitly critical.

I then place the posters around the changing room prior to the players' arrival. The excitement of the players is noticeable and you end up with a highly motivated, positive environment. Players, who may have been suffering with self-belief issues, now have renewed focus, and it is a wonderful tool to gain further rapport with your group. This rapport allows you to take players on whatever journey you want to take them on. I know one particular ex-player who still has his poster, some five years on.

Squad Strength Table and Resulting Individual Poster	
Player	Write one strength of your team mates
Adam	*Great shot-stopping*
Stuart	*Very quick and direct runner*
Conor	*Excellent long passing with left foot*
Josh	*Leader and organizer*

David	*Brilliant first touch*
Tom	*Attacks the ball aggressively*
MacAuley	*Great pace on delivery from set-plays*
Matt	*Excellent movement off the ball to receive*
Robson	*Calm in possession, always finds his target with passes*
Jamie	*Very quick feet, tricky and goes past players*
Kyle	*Scores lots of goals from midfield*
Cornelius	*Works hard, never gives up*
Antonio	*Excellent when taking players on 1v1*

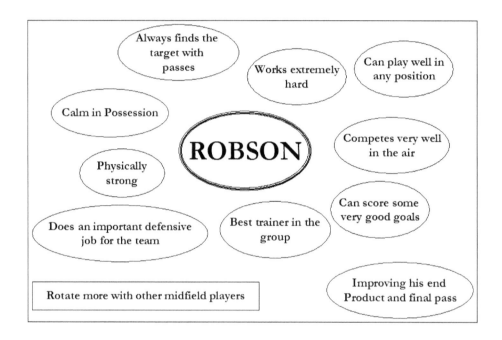

5

Understanding Communication in Soccer

"What does Martino transmit? Closeness. I like his way of talking, because he motivates you and explains things. He convinces you." (Barcelona midfielder Sergio Busquets on Head Coach, Gerardo Martino)

Communication is the most overused yet least understood word in soccer.

I gave the opening line of this chapter extra emphasis as it is something I truly believe. I am convinced of it. Communication is the most over-used yet least understood word in soccer.

I have witnessed this 'C' word in virtually every coaching session I have been party to. It is either a coach insisting communication needs to be better, that it is *the* key coaching point in a training practice, or that it is considered the main ingredient missing to make the practice successful.

Such is the emphasis that coaches put on 'communication', and the frequency in which the 'C' word is referenced that I have noticed players use it to answer virtually every question that is posed by a coach:

What could we do better? "Communicate."

What was missing from that exercise? "Communication."

What made that passage of play work? "Communication."

Such is the regularity of the use of the word, it is starting to lose all meaning and impact. Players know that if you ask virtually any type of open-ended question, they can respond with "communication" and have a pretty good chance of getting the answer right, even if it is not what the coach is looking for.

The Real Meaning of the 'C' Word

There is an assumption that communication in soccer means speaking. It is about what you say, being loud and talking a lot. Communication, real communication, however, is much, much more than that. Verbal communication, or *what we say*, is a tiny fraction of everyday and soccer communication.

Your players will receive and interpret your message in three ways:

- What you say

- How you say it

- Non-verbal communication (body language)

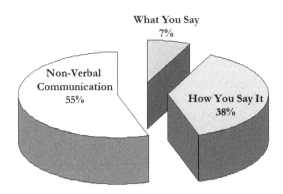

What You Say

Let's just put one thing straight first. Although *what you say* has a mere 7% of impact during communication, the information you provide still needs to be carefully considered. A great coach will use verbal communication to provide players with the detail and intricacies of the game. Then, the *way he says it* and his *body language* will reinforce or emphasize the message.

Do your players know what you are saying?

As you read this I assume you are in a quiet room or maybe alone in a busy area – on a train, in your work canteen or in a public park. If you are alone and reading this, with therefore no reason to be embarrassed, let me just ask you the following questions:

- When you speak, do your players really understand what you are saying?

- Do they truly understand the complicated technical information that you are transmitting?

- Is your focus more on displaying how intelligent a soccer brain you are, or how much you know, rather than actually looking to improve the player?

- Do you speak in riddles and use jargon constantly?

- Is the language you use too complex for the players to grasp?

- Do you talk so much that your players completely switch off and simply stand there waiting for you to finish?

- If there are players in the group that do not understand, is there a culture where they can ask and probe for further clarity?

- Do you pick up on a player's body language that suggests he is lost in all the information being hurled at him?

Carefully consider the above questions and, as an open-minded modern coach – investigate your habits. There can be a perception that the coach is expected to deliver these outlandishly long, complicated and information-packed team-talks. The reason may be as innocent as enthusiasm and an unbridled desire to improve players. It may also, however, be an attempt to make the coach himself feel über intelligent. Communicating with players does not have to be like this.

I worked with an academy coach a few years back – let's call him Rob. He was wonderful with the players. He showed empathy, had a great demeanour and made the players smile as soon as he walked in the room. He was enthusiastic and his vibrancy flooded through the players. He had a presence and infectious fervour that changed a passive group into one with real spirit who were fantastically engaged in learning about soccer. That was, occasionally, until he opened his mouth!

Team-talks pre-game, at half-time and post-match were often arduous. Debriefs after training sessions or between training exercises were gruelling. With all his enthusiasm came the obsession with blurting out every fathomable explanation for every conceivable occurrence – all at once, without a breath, with barely a question present for the players, or any use of visual materials to reinforce what he was saying. You got a sense that he wanted to throw lots and lots of information at players, expecting them to absorb all of it. If I am completely honest, there were frequent times where I stood to his side, and I could not follow what he was saying once he got going! If I couldn't understand it all, how were the players expected to?

What was brilliant about Rob, however, was his open-mindedness and his self-awareness. He knew that he was an excellent motivator and rapport builder, but he was also happy to take constructive criticism. His main goal was to improve himself to get the very best from the players. We had a working relationship where our ideals of soccer and methods of playing were so in-line that we could approach each other and have an honest discussion about our flaws (not a common trait of soccer coaches from my experience, who can be very defensive about their decisions and methods). That is why I know that he will read this and smile, rather than be insulted.

After a number of these team talks I approached him with my observations. He was dumbfounded. He did not even realize he was doing it! I pointed out that he had spent about ten minutes talking players through an exercise, with much of it being hypothetical occurrences about "if he does A, then B and C can happen. If he does something else then he can do this… then that. Or if he tried a third thing, then the team can do X, Y and Z".

After our conversation, Rob insisted that if he got into that over-talking mode again, to feel free to intervene and get us back on track.

Sir Alex Ferguson once stated that it was at half-time when a manager earned his money, so given its importance, and on the back of our discussion about Rob, let's have a look at our team-talks with players on game day.

Pre-Game

The closer you get to kick-off, players will be able to receive less and less detailed information. Use the pre-game period to reinforce work you have done with them and any goals that have been set. Any detailed tactical information ought to have been communicated with the group long before the kick-off time. Hitting them with lots of new ideas and detail will cause a rush, with little time for gauging player understanding. Last minute information often leads to the famous coach comment "I told him not to do that". Because he was "told" at an inappropriate time, the player is unable to fully process the information.

Detail should be transmitted to players in the days, rather than the minutes before the game. Pre-game, the coach can then briefly reinforce the key messages, along with individual comments and any motivational or inspiring techniques that are relevant. Remember you have a group of individuals in front of you, with many different needs. Some may be nervous, others confident, others scared or complacent. Pitch what you say to meet the needs of the group, and then deal with individuals as necessary.

Ensure that you are positive with players pre-game. Coaches can be nervous or anxious too, but remember you want to keep these emotions far away from your players. Never highlight the weaknesses of your team, or of individuals – only their strengths. That will be what your game plan is built around after all.

Half-Time Team-Talks

The half-time team-talk is an important chance to get messages across to players that the coach may not have been able to offer during an action-packed first half. Coaches can often obsess about pointing out failings and criticizing players based on one half of a soccer game. Please *do not* lose this brief yet golden opportunity to improve performance by obsessing with statements like "you should have…", "you didn't…" and "you were supposed to…" These comments can create such a negative vibe and ill feeling that players may not fully respond to your key messages.

If the first half has gone badly, this 10-15 minute period is a chance to reset and promote a way forward. If it has gone especially badly I see little relevance in lambasting players who probably already know their failings. The key is to find solutions to problems and focus on how you can affect the situation to achieve a more positive second half. Remind players what they are good at; encourage them to find improvement and offer detail and information that will promote this improvement.

In turn, remember that there are many, many reasons for poor performance. They can be technical, tactical, physical or indeed psychological issues. It may be down to the team's preparation.

One of the most overly cited reasons for poor performance is "you have not worked hard enough". The only direction players receive – after their failings have been publicly noted – is to "work harder". Players, to my knowledge, have never deliberately set out to perform poorly, so refrain from treating them in this way. Poor performance is not a criminal act, it is a consequence of something that the coach needs to identify and work through with players. If your boss at work baselessly pointed out all your faults and simply instructed you to work harder, I bet your productivity would wane rather than increase.

If the first half has gone well, reinforce the good things and tidy up any issues you deem necessary. If it is a very comfortable performance, guard against complacency by setting goals and resetting targets. For example if your team is winning 7-0, encourage a particular type of move, promote the idea of keeping possession, or challenge them to keep a clean sheet *if possible*.

Post-Game De-Brief

Contrary to popular belief, post-match de-briefs need to be quite brief. Most of your players will have played a full game and are physically not in a place to absorb huge amounts of information all at once. They probably need to eat and refuel. If we remember *Maslow's Hierarchy of Needs* from Chapter 3, we understand that players have several human needs that need to be met first before they are able to learn effectively.

Overly emotional de-briefs are to be avoided completely. Using anger, resentment or bitterness towards players is a little like throwing a grenade into a room. If you are feeling overly pessimistic, use some time to cool off after the game, while players rehydrate or cool down. *Remember, you want to show your players that you are an emotionally controlled, modern coach that uses detail in their coaching.* I got a great piece of advice from a colleague of mine a number of years ago – "The next time you meet your players, you will find them in the mood you left them in," he told me. Find a positive message to leave them with, regardless of how desperate the situation is. There is always another game that needs to be played.

Judging the mood of the group is imperative. If a player is angry, disappointed or otherwise emotional, it is probably best to analyse the key points in relation to his performance at a later point, when he is calmer and more receptive to accepting information. You will notice that players in this frame of mind often do not make eye contact, they provide short answers, and basically do not want to engage in the particular conversation. It is far more beneficial and effective to use the next opportunity you meet this player to analyse his shortcomings.

Using Buzzwords

The use of jargon in soccer is frequently criticized, and often rightly so. Indeed, a few paragraphs above, we referred to the use of jargon as being something very negative.

A coach *can* use jargon and soccer language, but the key thing is to ensure that the players are well versed in the language that is going to be used. There are often several different terms used by coaches that can mean the same thing, which can often lead to confusion amongst players, regardless of age. Indeed I have recently started to work with a coach whose soccer language and jargon is completely different to mine. It was therefore important that, as two unique coaches, we aligned out soccer vocabulary to meet the players' needs and allow us to be understood, and to understand each other.

Ensure that the players understand your jargon by turning them into *buzzwords*. Explain their meanings in situations where there is less time pressure and put these words into practice during your coaching sessions.

For example, I often use the exercise below with young defenders to introduce them to certain defensive buzzwords. The idea for his session stemmed from a lecture from well-known youth coach and former Everton FC Academy Coach, Tosh Farrell.

The setup is very simple. Ask the players to move together as a unit, by responding to the well-known terms – jog forwards, jog backwards, jog on the spot, side-step left, side-step right.

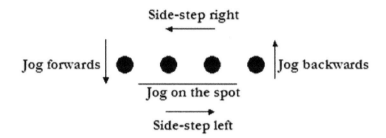

Once this is mastered, and players can perform these moves in sync, you can replace the phrases with the buzzwords you wish to use:

Common Language...	Replace with Buzzword...
Jog forwards	"Squeeze"
Jog Backwards	"Drop"
Jog on the spot	"Hold"
Side-step right	"Shift right"
Side-step left	"Shift left"

Asking Questions

One of the main coaching styles utilised by coaches is *Question and Answer*, as we explored in chapter 2. Asking questions allows coaches to identify whether learning has taken place, and engages players in the game/session. Probing answers from players through questioning is much more valuable to learning than simply providing players with all the answers.

How we ask these questions then is of vital importance as there are differing types of questions. We can ask questions that are *open-ended* or those that are *closed-ended*. *Closed* questions will have a specific answer, often a simple "yes" or "no", whereas *open* questions will give players the capacity to offer more information and will require a longer, more thoughtful answer. See some soccer examples below:

Closed-Ended Questions	Open-Ended Questions
Do you think we played well today?	In what ways did we play well today?
How many crosses did you catch today?	Outline some factors that determined whether you caught or punched the crosses today?
What were we working on in that practice exercise?	Can you tell me how this practice links into a game situation?

Using *open* questions with players challenges them to think deeper about the answers they provide. These questions offer a greater level of complexity and force the player(s) answering to use *higher order thinking*. This does not mean that closed-ended questions are not beneficial or should not be used. It is, however, more beneficial to long-term learning that they are used less frequently in favour of more open-ended questioning. Using an open question following a closed one can also be very beneficial. This probes further thinking from the players and allows them to evaluate, justify and expand their answers. The table, above, is also an example of asking a closed question, followed by a second, more probing open question.

Effective and engaged players will also ask questions to establish further clarity and understanding. Accepting these questions, and endeavouring to answer them satisfactorily, will help players to learn and will produce better soccer players. Questions should be encouraged and I would urge every coach to create an environment where players feel able to ask questions.

'Labelling'

The messages you send to your players are strong. After all, coaches are often judge, jury and executioner when it comes to assessing player progress and performance. With this considerable power, however, comes considerable responsibility.

People use *labelling* all the time when providing their opinions about others. We label others positively as smart, productive or hard working, or negatively as lazy, worthless or unreliable. We do this on a daily basis, and people do it when they are judging us.

I want you to think about that classmate of yours who was lazy in school - the one whose body language was languid and disinterested. Your teachers probably pointed out his laziness on a weekly, if not daily basis. Every report card he received would contain phrases like lazy, idle, and pinpoint a lack of effort and enthusiasm. When family and friends enquire about his future ambitions or exam prospects, even those close to him will dismiss his chances because "he is lazy". He himself will probably utter the words "I am lazy".

In the last chapter we noted the power of self-talk and the impact of feedback. Once someone utters the term "I am lazy", we find that a self-fulfilling prophecy will now go to work. *If a student or player is constantly labelled, he will become a product of that label.* Your responsibility then to produce and improve players will be completely undermined if your feedback is full of negative labels that stick. If you constantly point out players' deficiencies, especially mental ones, you are actually reinforcing these negative traits. If you are labelling your player as 'lazy' then, chances are, he is hearing this every day at school and at home also. To my knowledge, pointing out a player's laziness has never snapped him out of idle behaviour and made him work harder. Instead of using negative labels, invest some time to celebrate the occasions where he does work hard, point out their potential and the rewards that effort produces. Help players to replace their limiting, negative labels, with positive, empowering ones.

Labelling positively works. It may not happen immediately, but on a subconscious level, you will be causing a shift in behaviour that will help turn players around.

'Absolute' Statements

The detail a great coach provides to his players is important. Due to its importance, this information therefore needs to be actual, reliable and entrenched in fact. At times, coaches can be guilty of generalizing the information they provide to players when summing up individual and team performances.

Absolute statements are those definitive words like 'always' and 'never' (Karia, 2013). Avoiding *absolute statements* in coaching is a must. Such statements are inaccurate and are based on assumption and trend, rather than fact:

Absolute Statement	Fact
You *always* miss penalties.	You have missed two of your last four penalties.
You *never* pass the ball.	In the first half last week there were 4 times where you dribbled when the 'best' option was to pass.
You *always* win *all* of your headers.	You won 6 out of 7 aerial duels on Sunday.
You caught *every* cross you went for.	You caught eight of ten crosses.

How impressed would your players be if you used factual language and assessment, rather than incorrect guesswork? Would they buy into your methods and trust your opinion more? Would parents be more receptive to your feedback if it were factually solid? Of course the answers are 'yes'. By producing a factual judgement, players and parents will see you as a knowledgeable coach who is detailed and they will take negative feedback more readily.

The Other 93%...

The irony of this chapter is not lost on me. I began by pointing out that *what you say* has only a 7% impact on your audience, yet spent most of the chapter focusing on this verbal aspect. The other 93% however will support, back up and reinforce what you say. Getting the 93% right and what you say becomes even more powerful.

A few paragraphs ago, I introduced you to Rob, an ex-colleague who had an abundance of excellent coaching traits, but had a tendency to over-talk. For the period after our conversation that pointed out some of his communication shortcomings, rather than absorb himself in technical and tactical development, or study an endless amount of soccer 'drills', Rob studied his communication style. He consciously slowed down his speech (quick speech can often indicate that a coach is nervous or anxious – something you do not want to convey to players). He started to combine what he said with other forms of communication – using body language and visual aids to demonstrate, and changing his tone to highlight meaning and important statements. He started to focus more on *how he said it* to communicate better with players, something we will also do now.

How You Say It

"It is not what you say, it is how you say it". We all say or hear this on a regular basis – and often as a reprimand! In these circumstances we all know what the reprimand is getting at. We are pointing out that the words used are not aligned with the way they are being used. In a soccer environment our ability to communicate effectively will hinge on the way we use these words.

Flow Changers

When speaking to players, there are certain *key* parts to what you are saying that will need emphasizing. Speaking to players using the same tone, volume and at the same tempo can become quite boring - like a monotonous song that doesn't really 'go anywhere'. This one-paced approach makes it difficult to get our message across as clearly as we would like. There are a few techniques that can be used to make *what you say* become more engaging for those listening. I like to call these *flow changers*.

Tone

The tone we use when speaking to players is a giveaway for what we really mean. A coach's tone has the ability to compliment players highly, or cut them down mercilessly - even if he uses the exact same words. The sentence "you played really well today" is a compliment when said with a smile and with an authentic tone. When said in a sarcastic way, however, it's meaning changes completely. Be careful with your tone and use of sarcasm - it needs to reflect what you mean.

Players, especially younger ones, can take instructions very literally. If the tone of your instruction is not clear, it can result in players becoming confused. Recently I heard a coach of an under-12 team comment to his midfield player during a game: "That's it… You just keep passing the ball out wide. That will get us a goal!" I will let you decide whether this was a genuine instruction for the player to carry on passing the ball wide, or a cutting, sarcastic remark to stop him doing so. The one player who needed to know - the midfield player - stood confused.

Volume

Alternating volume is the ultimate flow changer. A sudden and unexpected increase in the volume of what you say can snap a group to attention and engage them with the key points that you are trying to convey. This change in volume may also re-engage those players who have switched off to what you are saying. Think of the way a boxing announcer uses the volume of his words to engage the audience, emphasizing and stretching the consonants to increase excitement and add emphasis. When you notice a group is not being as attentive as you like, hit them with a loud word or statement. Watch their eyes go from the floor to meet your eye contact. Suddenly they are no longer inactive in what you are saying, they are superbly engaged.

In his autobiography, former English Premier League manager, Alan Curbishley recounted his first meeting with Arsenal coach Arsène Wenger. He noted his surprise when describing that Wenger was quiet on the touch line, rarely shouting at his players, scarcely losing his temper, and refraining from bellowing instruction after instruction, as is commonplace in the soccer fraternity. When Curbishley probed this behaviour the explanation was simple - the less Wenger shouted and lost his temper, the more impact it had when he did. Cesc Fabregas, who in 2009 had been at Arsenal for six years, backed up this statement recalling how Wenger uncharacteristically lost his temper in a half-time team-talk during a fixture against Liverpool. The Spaniard told a post-match interviewer: "The boss screamed. I've never seen him like that before... In the second half, we turned it around." The impact of this clever approach is even felt at the top end of professional soccer.

The less Arsène Wenger shouts and gets angry, the more impact his message has when he does so. If you are constantly shouting and bellowing at players, they will soon become immune to it and simply switch off to what you are saying. It is akin to that teacher I think we all had in school who would shout and scream on a daily basis; once he started, the tendency was to think, "Here we go again..." and endure the verbal battering without giving it much credence.

In fact, speaking quietly can also be very advantageous. Done correctly, it can engage the audience further, stressing them slightly to hear what you are saying. Their increased efforts to hear every word you say will help you. Think of yourself straining to hear the TV or radio while someone else is in the room talking. You will not increase the volume, but strain yourself and concentrate more to hear what is happening. There are clear disadvantages to this also, but it might be a useful technique to use on occasion.

Tempo

Altering the tempo of what we say to reflect the intended instruction also aligns your verbal instruction with how you say it, making your directives more powerful. If you want your players to be calm and focused, you need to speak in a calm and concise manner. If you are promoting calm with your words, but are speaking fast and frantically, this will send mixed messages to players. If you want calm, speak calmly. If you want more energy, speak to them more energetically and quickly, although also ensuring you do not reflect anxiousness or panic.

By using these *flow changers* we add some flavour and engagement to that monotonous song that we so quickly forget.

Painting Pictures with Words

A colleague of mine, and fellow coach educator, is the master of using visual words to help with players understanding. The more we work together, the more examples he provides to literally 'illustrate' what he wants. We often associate shapes and other visuals to outline team tactics and formations such as the *Christmas Tree* formation, the *midfield diamond* and the infamous *'WM' system* from the middle of the 20th Century. Commentators and pundits also use visuals to aid the viewer's understanding of what has happened – his shot at goal travelled like an *Exocet*; the defender *swept up* the danger, etc.

My colleague however broke this use of visual aids down to individual technical work. He would explain to young goalkeepers that their hand position needed to be like they were *wearing handcuffs*. While dribbling around objects, he would tell younger players that the cones were *landmines*[1]. He would tell the holding, defensive midfield player that he was a *human shield*. By painting these pictures with words he made the technique and instruction more memorable, and added visual aids to the equation.

Having An Accent

I know first-hand what it is like to have a different accent compared to the groups of players you are working with. It can sometimes be the source of humour, which I am afraid needs to be taken on the chin![2] Just like the occasion when we speak quietly to grab attention, an accent can be similar. Players can lean in and strain themselves to pick up exactly what you are trying to convey. It is, however, of utmost importance that you learn to annunciate, and figure out what terms you may use that players may not be familiar with. Use this unfamiliar accent to your advantage, but ensure that everyone understands. If there is any confusion, use demonstrations and other forms of non-verbal communication to make certain your players comprehend.

Non-Verbal Communication (Body Language)

Body language experts will readily tell us how we are constantly communicating by the way we use our body and that we are *never not communicating*. Some non-verbal messages are quite obvious and we all pick up on them – for example, someone who is disappointed will slouch their shoulders, have their head down and look at the floor. There are other, subtler, signals that experts can more readily identify – like subconsciously pressing our tongue under our upper lip when we want to 'push someone away' when they say something we do not like.

---

[1] Although this land mine analogy is most effective with younger players, it can still be used with older ones, just sold to them differently. We again use our words to help us – "If I were coaching *younger* players, I would tell them that the obstacles were land mines. You are too old and mature for that now, but the importance of avoiding them is the same."

[2] It may even help you to develop rapport with players by laughing it off!

Coaches do not need to be body language experts, but they do need to seriously consider what their body is doing when we are coaching or interacting with players. Ian Holloway, current manager of Millwall and former manager of Leicester City, Blackpool and Crystal Palace, told a fantastic story a number of years ago at a coaching convention. During games, if he is happy with the performance of the team, he will stay seated. If something needs to be changed, monitored or improved in the game, he will leave his seat and stand in the technical area – a simple yet effective way of sending messages to players.

It is evident that Holloway considers the messages his non-verbal communication is sending players. Consider what messages *your* body language is sending players. Here are a few examples:

Coach Body Language	Inherent Message to Players
Flailing arms on the sidelines when players make a mistake	The coach is emotional so the player cannot take any risks for fear of making a mistake and upsetting the coach
Jumping around when his team have goal-scoring chances	This reflects the coach's anxiety and nervousness – something that is easily transmitted to players
Displaying dejection when a player has missed a chance	The player's confidence may drop due to this reaction as he has interpreted the body language as meaning that he has clearly made a very important error
Over-celebrating a goal scored	This can lead to an over-reaction from players as they may think the game is now over and gives them license to also over-celebrate and possibly lose concentration

Even though we see professional coaches display these mannerisms on a weekly basis, we need to again remind ourselves that youth players are not mini-adults. Professional players are thought to be able to deal with setbacks and refocus. Young players are far less able to deal with these emotional responses. Remember, players will reflect your behaviour, so if you are flailing your arms at your striker for missing chances, his team-mates will feel that they are free to do this also.

In the same way that coaches need to match *what they say* to *how they say it*, it is as important that they use non-verbal body language to add emphasis to the message.

We all have a mental vision of coaches on television frantically making hand gestures to position players differently, call them back into a defensive line, or ask them to execute a certain move. As confusing as this may sometimes appear through our TV screens, these gestures will be something that *these players are well versed in*. If you have a penchant for these gestures, your players need to be primed to ensure they understand their meaning. Otherwise, these may again cause confusion and misunderstanding. More broadly, use hand gestures and other bodily cues to emphasize key points and engage the listener. It is far more powerful as a means of communication than standing rigidly.

Listening

Communication, by definition, is a two-way process, involving a giver and a receiver. Listening is therefore a fundamental way of interacting with players. Players have a huge amount to offer that will help the coach and the team to function better. Listening is not a sign of weakness and it is nothing to be embarrassed about – it is a sign of self-confidence and understanding.

In the previous chapter's *Real Coach Experience* section I detailed a technique for boosting player confidence where the team outline each other's key strengths. I cannot tell you how many times I have used this exercise, but every time I do, I learn something from what the players say. On a couple of occasions players point out strengths of a team-mate that I have never noticed! This does not embarrasses me, and ultimately I now have more information to think about the players I work with, and am equipped to do a better job.

How to Listen

Do you remember being in school and, as the teacher was speaking or reading a passage from a book, your mind and attention wandered? I think all of us did at some point. While you are in your daydream, the teacher noticed your lack of attention and asked you to repeat what she just said… Somehow, you *were able* repeat what she just said, even though you treated it as little more than background noise. You getting the answer right somewhat upset the teacher, no doubt, who then hit you with the phrase: "You may have heard what I said, but you were not listening to it", before carrying on. You are not really sure what she meant, but you are just glad to get yourself out of a tricky situation! Let me explain how this works now you are not on the spot…

Listening is not the same as simply hearing – it is more than simply hearing. It is more than just being quiet and waiting for someone to finish their sentence so you can add your information. Being an effective listener involves putting everything aside and concentrating on what you are being told. It involves displaying open body language, making eye contact with the speaker, and showing you are attentive by nodding along in agreement, and maybe even asking a question from time to time to show that you want to get the full message.

How annoying is it when you are talking to someone and they do not even make eye contact with you? They appear rude and it is something that frustrates me a lot. Now, if I am speaking and the listener is distracted and not making eye contact with me, even in social settings, I will wait until the person I am speaking to does. I do not expect that from people when I am talking, so I am not going to be rude enough to my players or fellow coaches by doing the same!

But **They** Don't Listen!

Just like in a social setting, speaking to players who will not listen attentively is a cause of frustration. The coach will have a huge amount of knowledge to share and it is a cause of player irritation when players are not receptive to this knowledge.

What if the players are not the cause of this? *What if it was actually the coach who needs to change and adapt to the group?* If players cannot concentrate on long speeches, like in the case with Rob above, surely it is easier and more appropriate for coaches to alter their delivery than expect 16 players to alter how they process information?

Consider the following points to increase the ability of your message being heard and absorbed by the group.

Quiet!	Ensure the players are completely quiet before you speak – make a point of creating an awkward silence if necessary. It will save you the battle of shushing and quietening the group, and the group will probably end up shushing each other.
Balls still	Players are happiest with a ball at their feet. To gain their full attention, keep the balls away from the situation or insist that they are still. If players must do this, then so must you. Speaking while rolling a ball under your foot, for example, takes the focus from your words to what your body is doing.
Consider the weather	If it is sunny, take the glare of the sun in *your* eyes; if it is raining or windy, take that in the face yourself. Players then have less to

	distract them.
How much you speak	Make your points clear and concise, and involve players more by using question and answer.
Vary delivery	Vary the method in which you deliver. Use visual aids, videos, and use *flow changers*.
Use famous people!	Start by saying "I once heard Pep Guardiola say…" This gives your message some fame and mystique. It is not just your opinion but also the opinion of one of the most respected and successful coaches in world soccer.
The stare!	This is a well-established technique from the classroom that is actually promoted within teaching degrees. If one or two players are engaged in conversation at an inappropriate time, use a rather blank stare to show your displeasure!
Share a joke	Smiling and getting on the players' level with an appropriate joke increases rapport and can get groups aligned to your thinking. It will get them into a situation where you are the focus, rather than whatever else is going on at the time.

Developing Rapport

Rapport

From Wikipedia, the free encyclopedia

For other uses, see Rapport (disambiguation).

Rapport occurs when two or more people feel that they are *in sync* or *on the same wavelength* because they feel similar or relate well to each other.[1]

When setting out to write this book, I made a deal with myself that I would not start any section with a dictionary definition, but I am going to bend this deal here. This is to firmly establish the role of rapport in communicating and getting the best from the coach, his sessions and the group of players concerned. Below is a screenshot of the first line of Wikipedia's definition of rapport:

In her absorbing and inspiring TED speech[3], Rita Pierson, the late American educator of forty years, made two statements about rapport that really stood out:

"Kids don't learn from people they don't like"

"No significant learning can occur without a significant relationship"

The best youth coaches I have seen across age groups are ones that become *in sync* with their players and get on their *wavelength*. They show a genuine interest in the players, in terms of not only their soccer, but also their wider life. They develop a *relationship* with their players that allow them to coach and teach in a wonderfully effective way.

Methods of how to develop rapport in a soccer-coaching context are presented in an excellent document by Newcastle United FC Academy Coach, and excellent Twitter contributor, Neil Winskill. He kindly allowed me to share this below.

---

[3] Find Rita Pierson's wonderful speech *"Every Kid Needs a Champion"* for TED on YouTube.

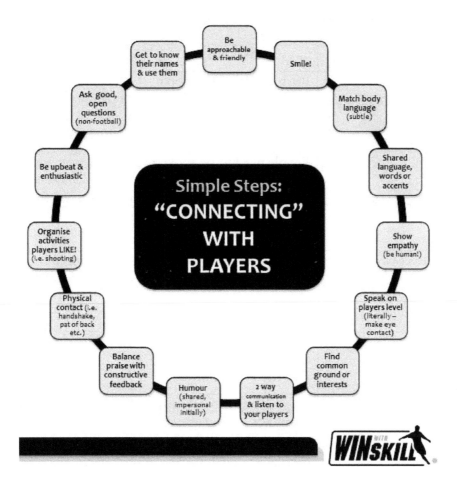

'Connect'

Personally, I make a conscious effort to speak on a one-to-one basis to every player, every week. This may be about their performance, their life outside soccer, their education, or whatever. I do this to show players I care and am 'in it' for them. This may be a conversation as they arrive to train, helping them to solve a problem outside soccer (for example, a phone call to a teacher in school), a text message praising their effort or performance, or simply listening as outlined above.

Kids, as per the quote from Rita Pierson, learn from people they like, and this personal time or *connection* facilitates rapport and helping players achieve peak performance. There is a fine line between achieving rapport and *befriending* players, which can undermine your role as leader and disciplinarian. Players need to know you are there for them, but accept that you will be required to discipline the very same players on occasions.

In his extremely useful book *How to Get Instant Trust, Belief, Influence and Rapport!*, Tom Schreiter takes the reader on a very concise yet comprehensive journey through 13 simple techniques people can use to develop rapport. Although he does not specify sport in particular, the lessons learned can be adapted for use in our soccer coaching. I have outlined his suggestions below, and also added a soccer context (the example below is a potential conversation with a midfield player who needs to alter his game).

Technique	Meaning	Soccer Example
Tell the player something that you will both agree on	People agree with people who they are similar to, and who share similar beliefs	"We both know the type of player you want to be – a quarter-back-type midfield player"
"Pacing"	People need to be spoken to in a way they understand and at a speed that reflects the way they think and operate	"A quarter-back midfielder is one who takes the ball from the defenders and tries to start attacks"
Tell the player two things that you will both agree on	This reinforces that you have similarities in thought	"Your current position does not get the best out of you. We both want you in the team every week.
Smile!	Human instinct tells us to trust people who smile as they offer us no threat	Smile!
"Most people…"	Another aspect of human instinct is to be part of a group – it is a method of survival. These phrases help align people to your way of thinking	"Most people understand that this position requires discipline and bravery on the ball"
"Everybody knows…"		"Everybody knows that this type of player is coveted by top level teams"
"Everybody says…"		"Everybody says that you have the attributes to play in this position successfully"
"Well, you know how…"	Using these phrases makes us think "if I already know this, or there is an old saying about it, then it must be true"	"*Well, you know how* we have been working towards perfecting you in this position"
"There is an old saying…"		"*There is an old saying* that the deepest midfield player is the most important in the team"
"What would you like to know first?"	This is a way of allowing the player to control the conversation, and allow him to focus on himself.	"So we want to get you training for this position. What would you like to know first?"

Technique	Meaning	Soccer Example
Pay them a compliment, and then ask them a question.	Paying someone a sincere compliment, rather than an overly obvious one, shows that you are looking deeper at them. Follow it with a question to take any embarrassment away.	"You have an excellent way of receiving the ball across your body to allow you to play forward" "Where did you learn that?"
Get your player to do the talking	Getting the player to do the talking is an effective way of getting them to share their ideas and feel comfortable with you	"So tell me about your background and the positions you have previously played"
Avoid a question beginning with 'why' that your player has to defend	Choose how to use 'why' questions carefully. This type of question, asked negatively, puts the prospect on the defensive and forces them to justify their decisions	"Why did you turn into the opposition striker when there were better options?"

On-Field Player Communication

Just like coaches, players will use all these forms of communication between each other while on the pitch. They will communicate verbally and non-verbally, and of course, there will be implications in terms of the way they say things.

As coaches we sometimes obsess about players' *lack* of verbal communication while playing. I personally believe that coaches over-focus on this and are needlessly over-critical of it. I have seen players, with an obvious introverted personality, lambasted for their lack of verbal communication.

During a recent FA coach education course, I asked the cohort of candidates how many of them felt that their young players communicated enough. An astonishing 11 of the 15 present felt that their players *were too quiet and did not 'talk' enough*, particularly during matches. I have found that this sort of statistic is replicated across youth soccer coaching.

When assessing these stats then, should we assume that 70%+ of young players do not communicate enough? Or should we see this as a trait of young players that needs honing and developing as they age? In the same way that their passing, heading, shooting and other technical qualities need improvement over time? I am convinced of the latter.

There are many reasons why young players may not verbally communicate enough:

- They do not understand the game well enough yet.

- Younger players especially are egocentric and will be focused on their performance only.

- Some people have an introverted personality.

- They do not know what to say!

Remember, however, a player's body will be communicating all the time. While you are watching your players during a game, consider what physical cues and signs they are using. Pointing, a hand in the air, waving and other hand gestures are common. Eye contact allows players to understand that, for example, a pass will be played between both players. Other body language in terms of their movement will influence each other - think of a striker shaping his body to make a run behind the defender, a midfielder opening his body when about to switch the play, a defender dropping off to receive the ball, or a goalkeeper shaping and reshaping his body to distribute. All these cues help players to understand each other. All these cues are methods of communicating.

Body language also allows players to evade opposition players through the use of *disguise* while dribbling, passing or shooting[4]. Our bodies are saying something all the time, even when our mouths and voice boxes are not.

I have no issue with coaches' desire to improve the communication skills of players. I often see coaches asking for soccer training exercises to use to promote the importance of communication. The normal response is to get players to play a game, but ban them from speaking – this reinforces the need to prize the moments where you can talk. My jury is still out as to how effective that strategy is *long-term*.

Your team will have players who are extraverted and those that are introverted. Some will be loud socially but maybe not understand soccer well enough to be loud on the pitch, and others may not speak much off the pitch, but talk constantly on it. This comes down to player personality, something that is inherent in someone. Are we, as coaches, insisting that players change their personality? It is well worth investing more of your coaching time to other, more pressing parts of the game.

Conclusion

Fortunately, knowing whether you are communicating correctly or not as a coach can be measured – by the actions and reactions of your players. Can you pick up on their verbal answers and non-verbal body language to see if they are engaged? After all, what is the point in speaking if people are not listening?

As a way of concluding this chapter I will share a story that happened to me recently in a coaching session while working with a group of under-19s. As we did not have a game the following day (as we normally would), the practice was essentially an extra training session. My prelude to the players was: "We do not have a game tomorrow so this is a bit of a free session. There is no pressure on us in terms of match preparation so we can enjoy ourselves and just play!"

In my head the message was clear, but the session that followed lacked everything we normally base our work on – willingness to learn, tempo of play, quality of play, decision-making, etc. My message, as heard by the group, was that the session was not that serious, so required minimal effort or interaction. It was *my message* that underpinned all that went poorly and I will never do it again. It is important that you ensure that the message you want to send is the one the receiver hears. The success of your communication is how others interpret it.

Remember, *you cannot not communicate*. Even silence is a form of communication. For those particularly interested in their communication habits, and further developing ways of gaining rapport with players, it is well worth looking into the use of *Neuro Linguistic Programming*. NLP; it is an area with a growing influence on sport.

---

[4] A study of the French Football Federation's work at the Centre Technique National du Football in Clairefontaine, noted the emphasis put on disguise when receiving the ball, and also when in composed possession.

Summary

- Communication is the most overused yet least understood word in soccer coaching.

- Communication is made up of 7% of what you say, 35% of how you say it, and 55% of the non-verbal body language you use to accompany it.

- Ask yourself if your players really know what you are saying when you speak.

- Provide players with reinforced detail rather than new information pre-game.

- Help them at half-time and seek ways of improving, rather than pinpointing mistakes and errors made in the first half.

- Keep post-match team-talks brief.

- Change your soccer jargon into usable buzzwords.

- Use more open-ended questions than closed-ended ones.

- Use tone, volume and tempo as flow changers.

- Can you paint pictures with your words to aid understanding?

- Consider what messages your body language is sending your players.

- Learn to listen to players – you will learn something.

- "Kids don't learn from people they don't like" – develop good rapport.

- Players communicate on the pitch all the time. Be careful when you are critical of this.

- The success of your communication is how others interpret it.

Real Coach Experience

Communication Skills Stretched to the Limit

(Tony Mee, Academy Manager, York City FC; FA Coach Educator)

It's easy to take communication for granted. This was brought home to me when working as a tutor for the Football Association, delivering a Level 2 coaching course at Doncaster Deaf College. I had delivered courses there before to a 'hearing' audience, so when I discovered the candidates were exclusively deaf, it was a bit of a shock!

On the first day we turned up to deliver and were introduced to the students and the two people who, over the next few weeks, were to prove invaluable - the translators. Their job was to take our 'soccer speak' and transfer it into appropriate sign language to those members of the course who were totally, as opposed to partially, deaf. The interpreters, however, were not 'soccer' people, so this prompted us to have to think very carefully about our choice of language, and also use our body language to 'paint pictures'.

An additional challenge for us in practical exercises was our coaching position. If we were physically in the middle of the practice, many of the players and interpreters were unable to see. This meant thinking carefully and strategically about the best position to coach from, and the most effective way to make interventions.

The fact that we had to wait for the interpreters to translate our words into sign meant that there was always a slight delay. This led to the sessions being much more deliberately paced. Since then, this is something that I have absorbed into my everyday coaching. I learned not to rush through things, but rather ensure that the messages I am conveying get across to players.

As a coach and tutor, I was already fairly animated in my delivery, but working with this group reinforced my belief that a coach's body language is very important when dealing with players. You can use it to reinforce points, explain yourself visually or you can use it to either increase the tempo of the action or calm things down.

The classroom sessions were another great learning experience as it was important to maintain eye contact with the person asking a question rather than just the interpreter and then deliver the information back to the questioner and trusting the interpreter to understand what you were saying.

Working with this group really pushed me out of my comfort zone and each day brought fresh challenges in terms of how best to present information. For me, as a tutor, the days were mentally and physically tiring, and although I could fall back on my experience, each day brought a new test.

I went into the experience expecting it to be a challenge (which it was!) but I came out of it better having learned how valuable communication in coaching really is.

6

Understanding Leadership and the Team

"Coaches have often been compared to conductors. Every musician plays his own role and instrument in an orchestra. It is not only the task of the conductor to ensure that every one of the individual musicians is able to contribute, he must also ensure that the result is harmonic." (Rinus Michels)

Ultimately, a soccer team, full of unique individuals, needs to be brought together. The team is the framework through which all these individuals must flourish. The analogy of the orchestra conductor, above, from legendary Dutch *Total Football* coach, Rinus Michels, outlines vividly the role of the coach in bringing a team together and the necessity for every member of a team to be in harmony. It is the youth coach's responsibility then, through his leadership, to bring developing individuals together within the structure of a team.

Leadership

Soccer players don't just need leadership – they want and crave it. In some shape or form, we all want to be led in certain situations. Not everyone can perform the task of a natural leader, but *everyone needs leadership*. Although it may seem unlikely at times, it is succinctly put by Dorfman in *Coaching the Mental Game*, "Young people want consistent parameters, direction, order, structure, organization and discipline. They need it, whether they know it or not. It gives them security, and that, in turn, helps them to be more confident". Ensure therefore that the leadership you provide is constructive and has a positive effect on people.

There is a magnificent story of leadership from Italian Fabio Capello during his spell as Head Coach of AC Milan in the 1990s. Having won the *Scudetto* (Italian League Championship), the vastly talented and experienced squad of players were celebrating on the pitch, taking the applause of their supporters and enjoying their achievement.

Amidst this joyful occasion, Capello waved one arm from the sideline, summoning the players off the pitch and into the changing rooms beneath the stadium. These were grown men, professional soccer superstars and champions. These were players who had spent almost two years unbeaten in Serie A, a succession of 58 games. Yet a single gesture from their coach saw them fall into line and follow his command without question or disapproval.

In many walks of life, people in positions of power can only dream of exerting that sort of influence over people.

Types of Power

The type of leadership displayed by Capello, above, can be interpreted as *Legitimate Power*, one of five varieties of power as identified by French and Raven way back in the late 1950s.

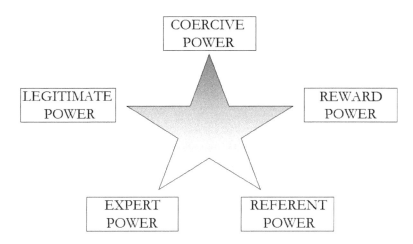

French & Raven Power Model

The Legitimate Leader

Legitimate Power involves using your natural position of authority to gain control or influence over a group. We have all witnessed or been part of a session where the Head Coach or 'boss' enters the pitch and the tempo and focus of the session increases immediately. I was once told by an ex-Nottingham Forest player of the immediate effect manager Brian Clough had on the approach and behaviour of the group. As soon as he appeared on the training ground - tempo, quality and professionalism increased dramatically.

Be warned, however, that *this type of leadership does not happen automatically.* Even if you hold a position of power, it takes more than barking instructions to make people truly follow your leadership. Players will not necessarily follow simply because of your position or your reputation. You must first prove yourself and that you are worthy of following. For example, a former international player will command instant short-term respect and authority, but longer-term, proving himself with leadership beyond legitimate power is essential for players to continue to admire and follow him.

The Expert Leader

Being considered an expert in soccer coaching is the ultimate praise in my opinion. *Expert power* is embedded in the fact that the coach is knowledgeable and has an expertise in the game. In the previous chapter we emphasized the need to avoid *absolute statements*, and to focus more on the detail and facts. If you can build this type of power, your position as coach and leader will take an upward curve in the eyes of players, parents and other coaches. This expertise in soccer may come from a distinguished playing career, experience, or from the study of the game and coaching qualifications. For youth coaches, however, it cannot always be about the results and the league titles that have been won. I have seen impersonal coaches who have won leagues and cups in abundance through the use of coercive power, and ruthless recruitment, rather than any form of expertise.

The Reward Leader

Reward power is the use of incentives to influence people. In a soccer context this may involve intrinsic rewards such as verbal praise. In youth coaching, this form of leadership is vital as it is the type of appreciation that kids feed off. It is no coincidence that when children are praised for their efforts, they are more willing to replicate behaviours again and again. The key here is using the power in an effective manner.

Former Tottenham Hotspur and West Ham United manager, and current manager of Queens Park Rangers, Harry Redknapp has based much of his work on this type of leadership. He frequently speaks about his team and players in press conferences and interviews as being "magnificent", fantastic", and "a different class". Former Tottenham midfielder (under Redknapp), Rafael van der Vaart, was drawn to comment that training sessions under the manager were not complicated in a newspaper interview. You got the feeling that Redknapp's intention was to ensure his players felt good to ensure they achieved their peak performance.

The use of praise and reward power can also have a shelf life. Ensure that you balance this praise and leadership style with constructive criticism and by using coercive power when necessary.

The Coercive Leader

Coercive power relies on the use of punishment to achieve the desired reaction from followers. This, in youth soccer, is often the threat of physical punishments like press-ups or running laps of the pitch for misbehaviour or poor performance. The long-term value of this type of leadership is minimal.

We discussed, in an earlier chapter, that using fitness exercises as punishment creates a player who will be demotivated when it comes to doing physical work that is part of the course. I do, however, accept that there are always negative consequences to negative actions. Sometimes players will need a stern conversation if their standards are not high enough. There have been countless times when I have had to release players for the benefit of the rest of the team and even for my own sanity!

As coaches, however, we cannot be *real leaders* if players are unwilling to follow us. If players are forced to follow, based on a more coercive type of power, they will not achieve peak performance. There will be a fear factor that affects performance. Motivation is extrinsic as the players are simply working to avoid punishment. As David Hunter points out in *Become a Leader – Understanding and Applying Life-Changing Leadership Skills*, "if you can encourage people instead of threatening them, they might become more productive".

The Referent Leader

Coaches that display *referent power* lead players through mutual respect, loyalty and admiration. Players will have a high regard for this coach through their compassion and people skills. This 'personal' power is developed through rapport building and trust, and players will follow you based on that conviction and respect. This type of leadership can be very effective with players who are difficult to manage or those that require more discipline than others. If this type of player knows you care about them and have their interests at heart, they will be far more likely to follow your lead. A local coach on a coach education program recently told me about one of his female players who was difficult to manage and was especially confrontational and moody. She was ecstatic to receive a text from him enquiring about a slight injury she had. It turned out that she had very little support or care at home. A simple, compassionate text message affected her so much that her work rate and attitude has improved immeasurably ever since.

My favourite leader used to lead in this way. Once a player entered the room, or arrived on the pitch, he would celebrate them and make them feel ten feet tall. I clearly remember him making such a fuss over a young pro who was training for the first time after a lengthy layoff. He called his name as if he was a fanatic supporter in the stands and praised his first few touches of the ball with an enthusiastic "welcome back son!"

A number of years back, David Bolchover wrote a fantastic piece in *The Sunday Times* newspaper about rugby coach Wayne Bennett called *Good Leaders Care for Their Staff*. Bennett, the much decorated Australian coach, was in no doubt about the value and importance of *referent power*. "When I had a manager that I cared about, and I knew he cared about me, that I was important to him, I would have done anything for him. I would have worked any hours, any time. I wouldn't have questioned anything. Then when you get another boss coming in who doesn't care about you or the rest of the people, you become demotivated.".

As we mentioned, in the previous chapter, there is a fine balance between developing this rapport and closeness with players, and simply befriending them. Befriending them clouds your judgment of their performances and distorts the disciplinary line that needs to exist.

Which Leadership Style Should a Soccer Coach Use?

Dr. Sue Bridgewater, Director of Sports Research at Liverpool University and deliverer of the *Certificate in Applied Management for Football* (Soccer) course details the issue of leadership in soccer coaching and management very well in her book *Football Management*. She points out a theory that there are external effects on leadership that are beyond the coach's immediate control. These factors include: the role and makeup of the followers (players), and how resources affect performance and leadership, especially at the top level.

Dr. Bridgewater's conclusion was that *no one type of leadership is effective in all situations*. Context, circumstance, the characteristics of your players and the extent of your resources will ultimately have an influence on how you approach your role as leader.

There will be times when it is important to lead through your expertise ("To get back into this game, we need to do A, B and C"), reward ("Your performance today in training will get you a starting spot in tomorrow's team), or indeed through coercive, referent or legitimate power. Hopefully you will possess a concoction of these styles in the way that you lead and work with players, as illustrated by the jigsaw of styles below that will create the final picture of your leadership.

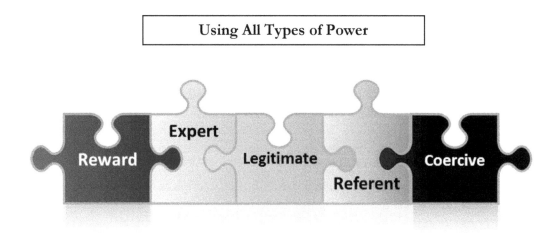

The Body Language of Leaders

In the last chapter we spoke a lot about communication skills, and had a look at the messages our body language, through our gestures, reactions and movements, send to players. In this section we will explore the body language used by leaders and how we can apply that to our soccer coaching.

In *The Body Language of Leaders*, Brian Night explains: "strong body language will give an impression of power and strength... One reason that many leaders have difficulty inspiring and motivating a group of people, is conflicting verbal communication and body language". Our non-verbal communication then, can have a real impact on how coaches lead and how they influence people.

Add Gestures to Your Words

Politicians are (or should be!) experts in leadership body language. They will emphasize a key point by matching what they say to a gesture or motion. They will use slower, defined movements, rather than fidgety and uncontrolled ones that reflect a stressful demeanour. Prior to attaining the Presidential Office, Barack Obama used lots of hand gestures to reflect his energy, his specificity, and positive nature.

Politicians will not hide their hands, as people do not trust those who look like they are being secretive. People that are anxious or unnerved will often resort to sticking their hands in their pockets or folding their arms in a subconscious effort to hide them from their audience.

As coaches we can also match key phrases to well-defined gestures, emphasizing the important parts and developing a relationship between the message and the gesture. If players need a quick reminder of a key message when playing in games, you can use the gesture without having to detail and explain the message. A colleague of mine who works as a coach educator uses this masterfully. On one occasion I observed him work from a distance and I could pick up virtually all his coaching points by simply watching his gestures and body language alone.

The 'Power' Posture

How you stand and present yourself to people matters. A coach I recently spoke to told me about taking over the running of a team that played at a regional standard. He was put in place to revamp and reinvigorate the operations of the squad. He described to me how the previous coach had been "chomping on a burger" during the pre-game team-talk for a National Cup semi-final! I will assume the coach was saying words that were trying to inspire or relay detail to his players, but his body language contradicted this by suggesting the occasion was unimportant and not worthy of his entire focus. This created a deflating, anti-climactic experience for the players.

With a powerful posture, there are several golden rules. You should have your feet spread apart at shoulder length. Ensure that your chest is visible and pushed slightly forward, and keep your head up. How much greater would your body language and power be if you did this rather than recklessly standing, leant against a wall, burger in hand, trying to inspire a group of young players at one of the most defining occasions of their young playing careers?

This 'power posture' may not sit comfortably with everyone, and indeed faking or overdoing these actions can result in you coming across as cocky, over-confident and dislikeable. But fear not, *The Body Language of Leaders* advocates that you start slow and "as you become accustomed and more seasoned to body language you will begin to notice that you are incorporating these signals naturally. This is when the body language and posture control becomes second nature and you really start to see results".

The Art of Persuasion

The art of persuasion has been much studied in recent times. Books like *Persuasion* by James Borg and *Yes!* by Goldstein, Martin and Cialdini go to great lengths in offering tips to those who are looking to lead people.

Persuasion is the manner in which we get what we want by selling something in a way that the recipient wants to buy. The art of persuasion is frequently used in advertising, sales, and politics, and there are some wonderful stories in both the aforementioned books about how wording, phrasing and actioning things in a certain way make them more appealing to followers.

When You Speak – Mean It!

We commented in the previous chapter about the famous speech in *Any Given Sunday* by Al Pacino, where his words mesmerized and motivated a vast room of professional American Footballers. We noted how any half-hearted or forced attempt at replicating this type of speech can be flawed. Put simply, to pull off this type of speech, or any type of speech in which you want to sell something, *you must believe what you are saying*. With this belief comes power, and an audience that listens.

It's You, Because…

There are several words in the English language that are considered particularly persuasive. Along with words like *free* and *instantly*, there are two far more simple ones that, used correctly, can help persuade and allow you to lead *your* way.

'You'

Our name is crucial to us as human beings. It is possibly one of the first words we learn to read, write, and say. It is used daily.

Put us in a building of one hundred or one thousand people, and we will automatically turn if we hear our name mentioned! There is actually evidence that certain reactions in our brain become stimulated when we simply hear our name. Such is the power of our name that research from *Yes!* suggests that people favour things that relate to, or even sound somewhat similar to, their own name! As a result of this, we love to see our name in lights and feel proud when we are celebrated.

When you are working with players, *use their names*, or at least the name they want you to use, possibly even a nickname. It sounds too easy but I cannot tell you how simple yet effective this is to get people on-board with what you are doing. There are countless occasions where coaches refer to players, even in their presence, as "my goalkeeper", "the striker", "my number 4", etc. Worse still is forgetting names or getting them wrong!

In the *Real Coach Experience* section of Chapter 4, I shared with you the 'strengths' exercise that I get my players to complete when they are in a bad place and need a mental lift. When I used this exercise a few years ago, I collated all the information as normal, turned them into colourful posters, and placed them on the wall of the changing room prior to the players' arrival. As they arrived one by one, there was a real buzz around the group. I smiled as I watched them dissect the information and walked into my office satisfied that I had achieved the desired outcome. That was until my captain came to my office to tell me that there was no poster for our left-winger! His name was not up in lights like the others! I quickly printed off his copy (but this time in black and white) and waded through the crowd to place it on the wall. The impact for that one player was considerably diminished.

'Because'

If we are given an order, suggestion or question, our desire to comply is much stronger when we hear it followed by one simple word – *because*. This word, added to a phrase, helps to reason and justify what it is that you want. In general, people like to have a reason behind why they are instructed to do something, and this is the same with players. The better the reason you can provide, the better the chance that your players will accept it, and as a result you will get the most out of them in terms of effort and application. For example, how much more appealing do the following sound when backed up with 'because':

Without Reason	With Reason
To a right- back: "You are going to play left-back today"	*John*, you are going to play at left-back today. This is *because* you can use both feet really well and I believe you are the best man for the job"
To the team: "We are going to work on our fitness today"	"We are going to work on our fitness today *because* we do not have a game tomorrow and I want us to be physically prepared for the next three games"

With a legitimate leadership style, we can sometimes slip into a culture where "do it because I told you to" becomes habitual. I remember those words from adults as a kid and I hated them. Being told what to do whether positive, negative or just somewhere in-between was so much easier to take when it was supported by a reason, *because* people respond to it better.

Being the 'Boss'

With leadership comes responsibility. Leaders are expected to make good decisions *most* of the time. No leader I have ever known, in soccer, sport, politics or society has ever made good decisions *all* of the time. As human beings, we may demand high standards from our leaders, but we all know that judgments and actions will never be 100% perfect all of the time.

The Disease of 'Captainitis'

If you are the most qualified or experienced coach in the room, or had a distinguished playing career in professional soccer, be aware of a problem known as *captainitis*.

Captainitis is when the person who knows best makes poor decisions, but subordinates blindly follow them regardless. The masses bow to an order due to the leader's qualification, experience, or career. The term originated from a decision made by an airline pilot who ignored warning signs from the on-board computer system that had detected a fault. Although his co-pilot was worried and passed these concerns onto his superior, the headstrong captain was intent on taking off even though that problem existed. The airline staff readily accepted the captain's decision as he was considered *the* expert. The flight went down killing all on-board.

If you are a Head Coach, remember that - even given your status - you may well get things wrong, and the opinions of the staff under you, and also your players may well help you make better decisions. If you are an Assistant Coach, learn to question (in the right way of course) the merits of the decisions that are be being made.

Acknowledging Mistakes

A true acknowledgement that a coach is comfortable with himself is his ability to be comfortable when admitting his mistakes. Players will respect you more for getting it wrong than they would if you tried to bluff and sell a *captainitis*-type idea that is flawed. What would further emphasize a coach's expertise would be to go away, study the problem, find its solution, and relay it back to players correctly. Better still, if you are not sure about a particular style of play, formation or problem, get the players involved in *Trial and Error*-type coaching to help players take ownership of the problem *and* the solution.

Selecting Your Assistant Coach or Support Staff

There is one golden rule when you are considering an assistant coach (or any other support staff around your group of players) – *Never let anyone negative anywhere near you or the players*. Constant negativity or nitpicking will not leave a lasting, positive impression on players. Rather than *always* focusing on weaknesses, a true leader will celebrate and accentuate strengths, which can help players to grow and improve. He will also ensure that his or her support staff do the same.

Negative people and effective youth soccer do not mix. These *energy sappers* will take hold of your group and create an environment that is counter-productive and strained to work in. Do you, as a coach (or does your assistant) always moan at the quality of the players in the practice? Do they first point out a player's flaws rather than their strengths? Will they disrespect the player's ability before ever trying to coach them? Will they bemoan performance without ever helping players to overcome their limitations?

If there are people like this around the group that you are responsible for, it may be best to challenge them or move them on for the benefit of the group.

Selecting Your Team Captain

Choosing a player as captain is a decision made by every coach in world soccer.

The actual importance of a team captain, however, is rightly argued. Some coaches will be quite straightforward and say it does not matter. They will argue that regardless of who wears the armband or tosses a coin pre-kick-off, once the game is going, players will act and influence as they normally would. There is also evidence that the emphasis on the 'skipper' has cultural differences, where it is more of a focus and point of importance in Britain rather than in continental Europe, for example.

On the other hand others will highlight the captaincy as a vital role within the soccer hierarchy. These nominated leaders are the link between players and coach and will help to inspire, motivate and communicate messages on the pitch. A decision regarding the team's captain and vice-captain will be pored over and debated amongst coaches and club officials.

The Age Debate

Having an elected captain at younger age groups is not necessary. I would fully endorse the idea of rotating the player 'with the armband' on a game-by-game basis. The truth is, it doesn't matter what member of your under-8 team is captain. It will, in no way, impact performance individually or collectively.

However, the benefits of sharing and alternating the role are numerous. All players get a chance in the spotlight, feeling the pride and responsibility of the job. There comes a shared responsibility and group ownership of leadership and power. Along the way, the natural leaders in the group will come to the fore and it is possible that a natural leader may well develop through chance!

The dangers of appointing a single captain at the younger age groups is the presumption that they are the best player and will indulge themselves in insisting that everyone does what they say. Younger players are very egotistical so will use every opportunity to get carried away with their own self-importance. Remember, should you then take the captaincy away from a youngster, it is quite a fall from grace.

When you are dealing with youth players from 16 years and above, selecting a captain and leader on the pitch and in the changing room takes on greater importance. At this age players start to become more self-aware and really pin down their role in the social structure of the group. Some will be happy and proud to rise to the challenge of the role of team skipper, while others will rather play without additional pressure and increased responsibilities. They prefer to concern themselves with their own performance only; so clouding this focus with extra responsibilities is counter-productive.

Different coaches choose their captain for many different reasons. Some like a player to inspire, motivate and instruct (John Terry at Chelsea). Others like to use the best communicator to help relay messages to the team (Franco Baresi and Paolo Maldini for AC Milan). Some will choose the best player (Lionel Messi for Argentina; Luis Figo /Cristiano Ronaldo for Portugal) or the most dominant personality (Roy Keane for Manchester United and the Republic of Ireland). Many will prefer their captain to lead by example (David Beckham for England) or will elect a player that is entrenched in the fabric of the club (Carles Puyol at Barcelona; Steven Gerrard at Liverpool).

Using the Captaincy to Discipline

I have an interesting curveball to add to this captaincy debate. Rather than choosing a captain for *your* benefits, choose a player who *needs* that responsibility. Captaincy can be very beneficial if you have a problem player who is potentially influencing his team-mates negatively. This is a well-used and advocated technique in education where disruptive members of a class are given extra responsibility in an effort to focus their energy into something positive. *With this empowerment comes accountability and responsibility.* The player now has responsibility to the rest of the team, his peers, to behave and be a positive representation of them.

Sometimes players do not know how influential they are and can use this influence negatively. When working with an under-19 team a few years ago, I had a player of such influence. He had a powerful character and was respected largely because of his social status outside the soccer program. His team-mates, essentially young adults, were extraordinarily impressionable and lived under his 'spell'. If he messed around, behaved lazily or moodily, a huge chunk of the group would immediately replicate it.

Prior to a fixture one day, having warmed up, he made a seemingly insignificant comment about needing to tuck his shirt in, and remarkably, like a queue of lemmings, each teammate either tucked themselves in, or double checked that their attire was neat and acceptable. Because one powerful lad thought this was important, so did they.

On the back of this event, I used a free moment alone with him to address this. He had no idea how far his influence carried and was shocked when I told him the shirt story. I offered him a chance to lead positively – and he took it. We made a pact to work together and use his newfound influence to work constructively within the team. He began to echo my sentiments in team-talks and reprimanded anyone who was behaving inappropriately. It was like having a mini-me in the changing room - but with a lot more street cred! As a result his own performances improved, his work-rate increased, and he began to get the best out of himself.

Be very, very careful with decisions that offer problem players extra responsibility – *it does not always work in your favour.* You may be seen as rewarding poor behaviour, which affects the approach of the rest of the team. Think very carefully about the effects of your decisions on the group.

Getting the Best From the Team

A group of people is not a team. A team is something where all players work together for a common goal. This goal, or *vision*, once created, developed and maintained, may go on to create success for a group.

We use words like 'team' and 'team-building', plus phrases like "There is no 'I' in Team" and "Together Everyone Achieves More" a lot in our soccer environment. There is, however, much more to building team spirit and togetherness than simply asking a group to "be a team". *Telling a group of players to "play like a team" is not sufficient for creating genuine team cohesion.* It involves, on the one hand, allowing the team to grow naturally and accepting that all teams will go through phases in their development, but then also understanding when and how you, as a coach, can intervene.

Natural Team Development

In 1965, Bruce Tuckman coined the now famous *Stages of Team Development* model, which suggests that all groups go through four stages in their development before becoming a high performing team.

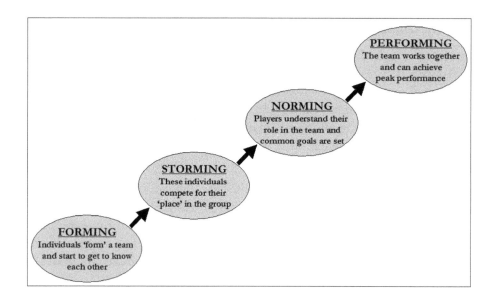

In his brilliant book *The Winner Within*, basketball coach Pat Riley gives us a wonderful account of his experience of working with a team in the early stages of its development. His team, the New York Knicks, had just recruited Xavier McDaniel, a dominant, physical character. Already on the Knick's roster was a similarly dominant figure in Anthony Mason. Within minutes of the first practice of Riley's first day of training camp, the two personalities clashed, ultimately leading to a violent, physical altercation. It was only through this 'storming' phase that both players began to realize that they had a lot in common, and working together would be very fruitful for them as individuals and ultimately as part of a team.

Hopefully, not all group forming will result in a physical brawl! It is worth understanding that a period of mistrust amongst a new group may ensue, will need to be worked through, but ultimately the team will become stronger.

Team Vision

In *Leadership*, Derek Stanza asserts that any "good leader will only be able to discern the right path (for his followers) if he or she has a clear vision of the destination" and the need to "start with a vision". Stanza goes on to categorically state that a team will enthusiastically follow you *once a clear vision is defined.*

Great leaders stand by their vision and use every opportunity to remind their followers of that vision - even to the point where it is repeated and over-repeated. If you watch Barack Obama's famous "Yes We Can!" speech, he uses the term over and over again. The audience loves the fact that they can see it coming and chant along to it.

During his 27 years at Manchester United, Sir Alex Ferguson constantly repeated that no player was bigger than the club and their duty was to win games rather than to accept even a well-earned draw. He coined a now famous phrase, "we didn't lose, we just ran out of time". Players and staff at the club, who wavered from this vision, were moved on, regardless of their ability. How many times did we hear Pep Guardiola tell his players, even through the media, that the players had a responsibility to the values and identity of Barcelona?

Louis van Gaal, a predecessor of Guardiola at the Catalan club set out the team's vision in a wonderful *Philosophy Vision* document, which is translated and available online. The three "fundamental principles" outlined by the Dutchman were:

1. Winning the largest possible number of titles

2. With attractive football (soccer)

3. And with the greatest possible number of players trained in the club

The document goes on to detail that the team is more important than any individual and that "the players have the obligation to meet and defend the idea of the club".

Guardiola built his Barcelona team around the same club identity as articulated by van Gaal, and took a personal stance in holding up the club's virtues through his team. This vision, when on the field of play, was about passing the ball, keeping possession and being patient. Below is a transcript of the team-talk used by 'Pep' before extra time of their 2009 Super Cup Final[1]. Note how many times he mentions possession of the ball and to do things "our way":

Pep Guardiola Team-Talk before Extra-Time of 2009 UEFA Super Cup

---

"Secure the pass. Don't take risks on the defence. Do it well. Don't make any passes to the middle.

As always, play to maintain the ball and go on. *Our way.* All of you before the ball.

They (Shakhtar Donetsk) are waiting for a counter attack and they won't change.

So *more than ever, our way: have the ball.* If *we have the ball we can do what we know.* In 30 minutes we can score.

Don't worry. Don't worry about anything. *Do what you know.* With patience. Don't go crazy because they will kill us. *Touch and touch.* Don't worry! Don't worry! *Patience.*

All 10 do the same operations like ever. Now, *more than ever. Move and move and create* a constant situation. *Open the field* and primarily seek the sides and the spaces in the middle will appear.

Ok gentlemen? *Like always!* Let's go!"

There are two distinct yet interlinked ways of looking at the functioning of a team. They are summarized nicely (above) in the case of Barcelona where van Gaal's vision was based largely on off-the-pitch detail, whereas Guardiola's team-talk brought that into existence on the pitch.

Teamwork

Teamwork off the Pitch	Teamwork on the Pitch
Group harmony	Formation, system, tactics
Vision, goals	Style of play
Aims, objectives	Training to replicate the game
Siege mentality	Attacking and defending
Team morale	'Job and a half'

---

[1] See this translation of Guardiola's lip reading on http://www.youtube.com/watch?v=iRhVGSKVYMU

Teamwork off the Pitch	Teamwork on the Pitch
Discipline	Positioning
Formation of cliques	Role of individuals within the team

Creating a Team Vision

A team vision is what brings all elements of the group together and gets them working towards a single purpose. Youth teams often do not have a club identity like Barcelona or Manchester United do. This identity needs to be created and maintained by the coach and the group of players.

Creating a team identity for you and your players to exist in can be immeasurably beneficial. Again, this goes beyond tactics or team formation. These are the core values by which your team lives. Hugo Langton, an English under-18 youth coach, provided a great example of this when he contributed *the Real Coach Experience* below:

"At home and at school, they have to abide by rules and people telling them off, and I hate to create that sort of setting within our soccer environment. Soccer is supposed to be fun, so I have just three rules that we all must live by, and that includes me:

1. Be on time

2. Tell the truth

3. Display excellence on and off the pitch

At the end of the current chapter, you will see how Langton's core rules or team vision led to great benefits when his team found itself in a difficult place.

A Team Vision in Action

Creating a team vision is also applied at the top levels of professional soccer. Prior to a Premier League fixture against Bolton Wanderers in September 2008, the staff and players of Arsenal FC gathered in their team hotel for a team meeting. In an extraordinary piece of opportunistic journalism, an A4 sheet detailing the focus of the team meeting was found soon afterwards and was published in the *Independent* newspaper[2]:

> ### The Arsenal Vision

> #### The Team
>
> • A team is as strong as the relationships within it. The driving force of a team is its member's ability to create and maintain excellent relationships within the team that can add an extra dimension and robustness to the team dynamic.
>
> • This attitude can be used by our team to focus on the gratitude and the vitally important benefits that the team brings to our own lives. It can be used to strengthen and deepen the relationships with it and maximise the opportunities that await a strong and united team.

---

[2] http://www.independent.co.uk/sport/football/premier-league/revealed-arsenals-win-that-was-all-in-the-mind-938723.html

---

Our team becomes stronger by:

• Display a positive attitude on and off the pitch

• Everyone making the right decisions for the team

• Have an unshakeable belief that we can achieve our target

• Believe in the strength of the team

• Always want more – always give more

• Focus on our communication

• Be demanding with yourself

• Be fresh and well prepared to win

• Focus on being mentally stronger and always keep going until the end

• When we play away from home, believe in our identity and play the football (soccer) we love to play at home

• Stick together

• Stay grounded and humble as a player and person

• Show the desire to win in all that you do

• Enjoy and contribute to all that is special about being in a team – don't take it for granted

---

The above example from Arsenal is what Rinus Michels calls the "Psychological Team Building Process". In the accompanying newspaper article, the consulting sport psychology expert, Martin Perry, described the document as having been evidence of "the team's core values, which they have clearly worked on and agreed as a group". By reminding the group of their values, the coaching staff at Arsenal were reaffirming their agreement and team spirit.

Making the Rules

The team's core values are the inherent rules that all players must live by. These values are at their most powerful when they are not just agreed by the players, but *when they are set by them too*. In basic terms, rather than the coach making all the rules – the players do. Like with our disruptive captain, responsibility brings accountability. If a player breaks these rules or is not compliant with the core values, the power is with his peers to bring him into line. In the Arsenal article, Perry again highlights the importance of this: "If some of the players don't buy into this process, it's up to the stronger-minded players to offer reminders about the team agreements".

In his autobiography, former Nottingham Forest and Derby County manager Brian Clough describes one of the methods that helped him empower, yet also discipline, his team. He allowed the players to choose what time they trained! Once they decided the time, it was up to them to be punctual. If they were late, they were breaking their own rules, and were fined.

A team's identity, vision, core values, and more, can be written down and agreed to. Sometimes, however, this is not required. At times, a group that shares existing ambition and goals will naturally come together as a team. For groups that do not, pre-season is the obvious time to sit down with players to devise the team's core values with them. Open the floor and let the players define, with your help of course, what constitutes success for the season, and what standards they need to uphold. This process of empowering players and letting them decide their vision gets an immediate buy-in from the team. Ensure these values are revisited regularly, like Wenger and his team did above.

Building a Team

We all want to recreate that moment from the movie *Remember the Titans* where a divided American Football team, while on an exceptionally early morning cross-country run, are led to a clearing. The area was an American Civil War battle site at Gettysburg, where an inspiring speech by Coach Boone caused a racially divided group to come together, with the strap-line "if we don't come together... right now on this hallowed ground…we too will be destroyed".

The process of team-building is a difficult one, and searching for that Coach Boone moment may prove elusive. We normally associate 'team building' with running around a forest completing tasks that involve people working together to find or make something. This is something I am personally not keen on. I am very much a team player but standing on a riverbank making a raft to get me and my team-mates across just does not resonate with me. Personally, I would much rather be on the soccer pitch with players.

When focusing on team-building I prefer to use videos and the game of soccer to bring people together. Players can learn how to work together by solving an on-field problem as well as building a raft to get across a river. I have a large number of videos that send very good messages to players and allow us to get away from the raft-building location onto the soccer pitch.

Useful Videos

The use of video and visuals with young players is very powerful. There are great messages about teamwork in videos like *The Battle of Krugar* and *Lessons From Geese*. Even more powerful is the use of an actual video from a world-renowned soccer team, and for this I will turn to Guardiola and Barcelona once again.

Prior to the Champions League Final in Rome in 2009, the Barcelona Head Coach consulted a local television company to put together a video montage of his players, depicting them as gladiators. Significantly, the footage contains every member of the team, giving them all equal time in the limelight. For example, superstar Lionel Messi receives the same attention as back-up goalkeeper José Manuel Pinto. All players are shown clips of their best bits, of them being successful but also clips of the team winning and celebrating together – all fantastic team messages prior to a significant occasion. The video is available to view on YouTube[3].

I also use videos about the unique on-pitch relationship between Brazilian Dani Alves and Argentine Lionel Messi, where they warm up together with a series of technically absorbing 40-metre length ball juggling exercises. Their relationship has seen the pair nicknamed 'Alavessi'. If we can build relationships like this all over the soccer pitch then our teams will be stronger.

Turning a Negative Situation Positive

It is always interesting to listen to the views of top coaches following a defeat. We usually have to wade through excuses about a refereeing decision, a missed penalty, or 'turning points' in games – those single moments that change the flow of the match. A number of years ago, following a rare defeat during his first spell as Chelsea manager, José Mourinho took a different standpoint. He claimed that the defeat was the wakeup call the players needed to work harder; needed to strive to reach higher levels of performance. He turned a defeat into a rallying cry for his players to kill any potential complacency and step up a gear.

During a recent pre-season, my own team had taken a step up and was preparing to play at the highest level of youth soccer; higher than any of them had ever played before. We had scheduled

---

[3] Search for 'FC Barcelona Gladiator Pep Guardiola's Motivational Video'

several friendly matches against opposition from the same level in an attempt to measure where we were at, where we needed to improve, and get a good feel about the standard we were going to face for the rest of the season.

All our early optimism was dashed after our first friendly game when we lost 5-1, and were given a pretty harsh lesson by an opposition that was also under-strength. Our confidence was shattered before we really got going. It affected me as well as the group and initially I thought our season was going to be a very long, very hard one, tested to the limit in every capacity.

We had four days before our next game. Although I should know better, it took me too long to snap out of the gloom and deal with the situation. It was my job as leader to turn this around. *Soccer coaches, as leaders, should be the first to recover from setbacks.* They are the inspiration for their players to get up and try again.

I decided the message needed to be 'to dust ourselves down', use the negative result and performance as a marker and learning curve, and move on. A colleague and I worked tirelessly over a few days and nights to get a video montage together of our best bits from the previous season in an attempt to emulate a low budget *Guardiola-Gladiator* style video. We clipped pieces from games and footage from training sessions. We then added photographs, motivational quotes, messages and an appropriate playlist of backing music. The video needed to be positive, energetic and give the players a sense of pride. It was all the things we were good at and what we needed to move forward. Thankfully, it hit the spot.

Having watched the 10-minute video, we agreed to draw a line under our poor game, and kick on with more focus and intent to improve and compete. We then went on to put together an incredible sequence of results and performances against very good opposition that turned our season around completely. Looking back, we needed that early hurt and negativity to refocus and move on positively.

The Individual within the Team

Throughout the youth development process, and thus far in this book, we have spoken primarily of the individual. We have looked at the need to consider individual differences when planning and conducting training sessions, when determining learning styles, intelligence, and differentiating. We, as coaches of young players, even put aside the result of the game and our league tables, to ensure the development and progress of the players as individuals.

Soccer, however, is a team game. On the pitch, the actions and reactions of the individual are constantly influenced by the performance, decisions, and acts of others. Soccer cannot be truly scripted beforehand, the individual is at the behest of the rest of his team and indeed the opposition.

I stand by the fact that youth development is about improving the individual. If you have an academy player, for example, he will be judged on his particular merits when the club decides whether to retain or release him. He is very much on his own. Some of his team-mates will be released from the club, others will be retained and continue their progression up the ladder at that particular organization.

Coaches often ask a player to sacrifice his strengths for the good of the team. This is a valuable lesson for players of course, as there will come a time where members of any team will have to compromise themselves and do 'a job' for the team. In a soccer context this may be playing a player in an unnatural position due to circumstance, asking an attacker with offensive instincts to operate defensively, or choosing one player over another as their strengths match the team's style or approach. Asking a player to constantly compromise his natural strengths for the benefit of the team can cause demotivation. To achieve peak performance, a player must be allowed the optimal amount of time to develop his strengths.

The key concept of a team is the old Aristotelian quote that *the whole is greater than the sum of its parts*. This can be difficult, especially in modern soccer. As Cary L. Cooper described in the

Independent newspaper article about the Arsenal team-building exercise above: "Football (soccer) teams used to be like close-knit families, this is what made them strong and effective" and "given the macho nature of football (soccer) players are more likely to take themselves elsewhere if asked to continually sacrifice themselves".

The real role of a soccer leader in team building is transforming individual merit into collective power. Or, as summed up by John Hindley, the Bolton Wanderers FC International Academy Manager in their *Philosophy to Youth Player Development* document: "Remember: We are looking at 'Long Term' development of individuals within a team structure."

The Maverick

Soccer is full of maverick-type players. The maverick is that player who is a little self-centred and far more concerned about himself than the rest of the team. They tend to be flair-type players who possess unique ability and believe that their single-handed ability to win games justifies a lack of effort around team-related goals and cooperation.

We often use the term that, as leaders, we will "treat everyone the same". This is inaccurate. You cannot treat everyone the same – different people need different management.

When Eric Cantona arrived at Manchester United in 1992, he already held this much-maligned tag of the selfish maverick. His time-keeping was poor, he ignored the dress code and upset the team ethic and 'all for one and one for all' notion. We noted earlier how Sir Alex Ferguson made many decisions in ridding his dressing room of players who thought they were bigger than the club. These players included superstars such as David Beckham, Jaap Stam and Roy Keane. With Cantona, however, he produced a wonderful piece of management to get the best out of a player who is considered a major catalyst for the team's success in the 1990s.

In the Frenchman, Ferguson saw a flawed genius. Rather than abandon his talent, he tolerated issues that he would discipline other players heavily for, much to the initial dismay of the rest of the team. Slowly though, by meeting the maverick halfway, Cantona began to turn up on time, in the correct club attire, and started to toe the line. Once a mutual understanding was found, Cantona's positive influence around the group began to show and he became a dominant figure in the success of the club, ultimately becoming the team's captain.

The maverick can be a difficult player to manage. He can undermine the coach's authority and push his patience to the limit. The tendency can be to 'label' him lazy[4], bemoan his lack of effort and poor body language, and ultimately discard the player. There is every chance, after all, that every other soccer coach, sport coach or teacher would discard him for the same reasons!

Before discarding, I would implore any coach to find a way for you and the maverick to meet halfway. Try to teach him the values of teamwork before thrusting him aside. Make it clear to the rest of the group that their journey to improve as a player may be a technical or tactical one, but the maverick's development journey is primarily a mental one, and like developing technique or tactical understanding, improving psychologically is a process that will take time. You may well end up with a player who is supremely gifted *and* absorbed in your team ethic. Alternatively, if there comes a stage where the behaviour of the maverick does not change, and it is pushing the rest of the team to breaking point, then you will have to do what is best for the team.

Conclusion

In an ironic way I am going to conclude this chapter on leadership and the team by introducing you to John Wooden, the famous and much admired former basketball coach. Wooden has become legendary for his leadership skills, which he grouped into his *Pyramid of Success*, that we have adapted below from his official website www.coachwooden.com.

---

[4] Refer back to Chapter 4 for the effects of 'labelling' players.

Wooden's Pyramid of Success

COMPETITIVE GREATNESS

Perform to your best at all times

FAITH

PATIENCE

POISE

Being in control. If you panic, everyone else will

CONFIDENCE

Knowing that your methods are correct and appropriate

CONDITION

Being physically, mentally and emotionally fit for purpose

SKILL

Being an expert at what you are doing and applying it consistently

TEAM SPIRIT

Using your strengths for the benefit of the team and encouraging the same from others

SELF-CONTROL

Being disciplined and emotionally controlled

ALERTNESS

Not being distracted by unnecessary things, or suffering from tunnel-vision

INITIATIVE

The importance of making decisions

INTENTNESS

Being determined and persistent

INDUSTRIOUSNESS

There is a difference between just turning up and actually working hard

FRIENDSHIP

This brand of "friendship" is based around respect and camaraderie

LOYALTY

Be loyal to your team and those you lead

COOPERATION

Work together to achieve common aims and goals

ENTHUSIASM

To reach your potential always love what you do. This rubs off on players

This pyramid is a very useful 'go-to' resource to identify what leadership strengths you possess, and where gaps in your team ethic can be identified.

Summary

- Although they may not know or admit it, young players need and desire leadership.

- There are five types of power – Legitimate, Expert, Reward, Coercive, and Referent. A coach cannot rely on one type only. He must use all five at different times.

- Great leaders use their body language to display power, influence people, and to add emphasis to key points.

- Be careful when leading that you do not consider yourself as being right all the time and suffer from *Captainitis*. Acknowledge mistakes and learn from them.

- Use players' names and provide reasons for instructions to help persuade players to comply and follow.

- *Never let anyone negative anywhere near you or the players that you are responsible for.*

- Having a set captain at younger age groups is not necessary. Share the job around.

- For older age groups, all coaches will prefer a different trait in their captain. The responsibility of the role can be a useful tool when disciplining or getting difficult players onside.

- A group of people is not a team.

- All teams will go through the stages of *forming, storming, norming and performing.*

- You need to perform as a team on the pitch *and* off it.

- All teams need a common vision or goal to work successfully.

- Focusing entirely on "the team", at the expense of the individual, is flawed.

- Give the maverick player a chance. If he can meet you halfway, you never know how good he can become. If he consistently affects the rest of the team, you may have to move him on.

- The team is greater than the sum of its individual parts.

- Use videos to inspire and show players examples of great team work.

- Don't despair about negative situations – find ways of turning them positive.

Real Coach Experience

Leadership in Action

(Hugo Langton, UEFA A Licence, Under-18 Coach)

I work with a group of 17/18 year olds, who are at that age when perhaps they feel they know it all. They think they are going to be professional soccer players and that the world also owes them something. So, when things don't go their way, they find it hard to deal with.

We have been through periods when we are not playing well, and poor results have affected the players. Whilst I place their development above results, they want to win, and I will never take that away from them. Instead, I prefer to take the pressure off and take any fear of making mistakes away, by telling them it is good to make mistakes – don't be afraid of making mistakes but ensure you learn from them. They are not yet in senior soccer, so results are unimportant.

I like to set my team three in-game targets, and if they achieve those targets then, as far as I am concerned, we are winning, regardless of the result. These targets will include things like attitude (don't give in… ever!), pressing (nearest player presses the ball), better passing, beating players 1v1, encouragement, etc. Use of strong words like 'destroy' and 'ruthlessness' I find help encourage players to go and give their all.

After one particular game, morale was low. Everything that could have gone wrong on the pitch had gone wrong, including players arguing amongst themselves and players giving up. We had been beaten 2 – 1, which was not an embarrassing scoreline, but the result was not the issue – it was everything else. We argued, blamed each other, and deflected responsibility and accountability elsewhere. We were in danger of completely falling apart. I asked them all to be in, the next morning, on time, and left it there.

The next morning we had a meeting. I made a decision to remain calm. I told them that we had come so far together but we needed to sort out our problems in an honest but non-confrontational way. I gave them a whiteboard and pens, asked them to write down their problems, no matter what they were, how we could solve them, and how we would avoid this in the future. I then left the room.

The players were alone in the room for an hour, while I waited outside. Not once did I hear raised voices, and they came together as a team, recognized the problems and came up with solutions, which I implemented. We have had our problems since, of course, but our team is a happier and one with greater synergy. When times are tough, it is now easier for us to stick together, and work together to improve.

7

Understanding Age-Specific Development Needs

"As in schools, there are teachers that, because of their personality, are more apt to teaching a particular grade. In soccer there are coaches that are suited to coach one particular age group." (Stefano Bellinzaghi, Inter Milan Youth Coach)

This chapter is a crucial one. It will underpin the content of the following chapters that specify tactics, physical and technical preparation, and exercises used with youth players.

At the time of writing it is probably fitting that we start with the visual below. In 2013, Bayern Munich swept all before them in Germany and in Europe, winning the Bundesliga and the Champions League, contesting the final with fellow German team, Borussia Dortmund. On their way to these victories was a dismantling of FC Barcelona, who up until then were considered by many as the greatest team of all time. A resounding 7-0 win over two legs was perceived by many as signalling a changing of the guard in terms of the domination of European football.

The youth development system put in place by the *Deutschland Fussball-Bund* (DFB) at the turn of the 21st Century has gained much acclaim for turning the fortunes of their under-performing national team and German football around.

I have taken (and adopted) the diagram below from the *DFB Youth Development Programme* document, which underpins their notion of development through the age groups. It shows a very definite age-related progression from players entering soccer to those entering the adult game.

7. Sustain Peak Performance	30 years+
6. Perfect Peak Performance	21 – 29 years
5. Prepare for Peak Performance	17 – 20 years
4. Affirmation of Learning	15 – 18 years
3. Learning the Game	11 – 14 years
2. Playing the Game	7 – 10 years
1. Learning to Move	3 – 6 years

Characteristics of Different Age Groups

Just like the progress of any skilled person, development takes time and involves a process. For example, young swimmers will start in a shallow play pool with armbands to keep them afloat. This is done to introduce them to the water. In time, they will move to the shallow end with floats and other apparatus, before ultimately completing multiple lengths of the full swimming pool. You would never stand a five year old at the deep end of an Olympic-size swimming pool and teach him to swim from that point! Learning to swim needs a process, and relevant stages, as the swimmer experiences the water, and grows and matures.

Effective youth development coaches *do not teach youth players an adult game* even though taking good practice from adult soccer and the professional game is obvious. It is tempting to replicate training exercises that their first team managers and coaches used with them during their playing career. We all tend to favour certain practices that we enjoyed as a player, or which were used with us as players. At other times we see a coach deliver a certain session that impresses us and we replicate it with our team, regardless of whether it is needed, or whether it is age-appropriate.

As we cannot leave an individual's development purely to chance and good fortune, we need to understand what players are capable of at specific ages and also what their limitations are. It is important that players move through certain stages of the development process, equipped for each subsequent stage by what has gone before.

Defining Age…

Age is measured in the number of years, months and days that a person has been alive. Much of our pre-adult life is dictated by this age – when you start school to the time you are legally able to drink alcohol. This is your *actual* or *chronological* age. Although this remains the means through which we band players together, development as a soccer player cannot simply or comfortably follow the same chronology.

Coaches can also use *'soccer age'* to measure the development stages of players. This soccer age (or sometimes known as 'training age') will reflect how advanced their game is technically, and in terms of tactical understanding, compared to others of the same chronological age. US Soccer determines this by three factors:

1. The rate of each individual's emotional and physical growth

2. The frequency that they are playing soccer

3. The soccer environment they are in

We refer to players' "emotional and physical growth" as their *'biological age'*. This reflects the way their bodies have developed physically and the psychological maturity they display.

As we re-consider what we understand by the term "age"[1], it is important that the coach recognizes the stage of his players and adapts his coaching accordingly. Ensure you do not wrestle against the natural age-related characteristics of your players. Becoming frustrated, for example, that your 10 year old does not concentrate, or that your 13 year old is struggling physically due to a growth spurt, or that your 18 year old is distracted by the temptations of early adulthood, is largely fruitless. Endeavour to work with these traits, rather than against them.

Long Term Player Development

The long-term development of your players is reliant on appropriate work being completed at certain times in the young soccer player's journey from age five through to adulthood. Clearly, in school, at home, or in any other environment, we do not expect the same from a five-year-old as you would from an 18-year-old, so why would we in our coaching program?

It is very difficult to group players, even players of the same age, into a rigid framework (or blocks). Indeed, a simple matter of a birth date within a particular age-group can throw up huge differences: physically, mentally and in other development areas.

---

[1] We will deal with relative age in Chapter 13.

What we can do, however, is group them according to 'normal' or dominant traits seen in players of a relevant age.

Note: It is easy, over the following pages, to play devil's advocate and come up with examples where players display traits outside of their age-related characteristics. For example I recently worked with a 16-year-old who displayed the same self-centredness of an eight-year-old. I have also worked with a pre-pubescent lad who had the maturity, game-sense and self-awareness you would want from a 17-year-old. As you read the following traits, remember *there will always be those who sit outside the presented framework*. Be adaptable and work with your individual players accordingly.

All national player development documents and club academies will differ slightly in where they precisely draw the line between ages. One of the most useful processes is the one outlined by the *Royal Dutch Football Association's (KNVB)* Albert Stuivenberg in *The Dutch Vision on Youth Development*. The diagram below, taken from this KNVB document, shows the youth development process as one that is fluid between the age groups:

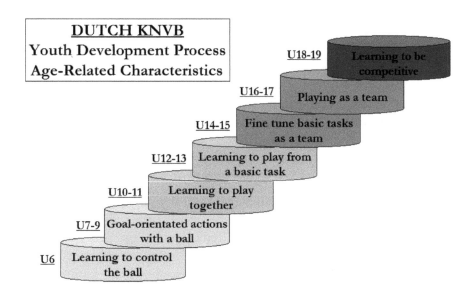

Allowing players to move effectively through the development process relies on certain work being completed before players can move on to the next stage of their development. All phases, as suggested by the KNVB above, are interconnected. For example, to effectively teach ball mastery skills to a 10-year-old, their physical motor skills need to be honed at the earlier age. By mastering the ball as an individual, and being able to control body movements, players can become technically stronger as they proceed through the age groups. Later in development, being 'technically able' makes carrying out tactics more effective. If players are not technically able to carry out certain game strategies, then any tactics will be flawed.

Long Term Player Development Model

Long Term Player Development (LTPD) Model Widely used across soccer and sport	
Technical Tactical	Psychological
Physical	Social

We often see the Long Term Player Development Model (above) expressed in boxes, with all categories given a distinctive place. This can suggest that a soccer player's development process can be neatly separated into categories. This is not the case. Each of the categories are interlinked and will overlap each other. For example, a player's physical make-up impacts their ability to perform technically, which in turns impacts on tactics. A player's psychological make-up impacts on his social and lifestyle decisions, which as a consequence affects his game.

The information below breaks the development process of young players down into age-related stages, with studies and examples of countless professional soccer clubs and national associations from around the globe. All these will vary to an extent, but the core processes in developing young players follows the same guidelines. In general the Long Term Player Development Model splits the development of players into six phases:

1. FUNdamental Stage
2. Learning to Train
3. Training to Train
4. Training to Compete
5. Training to Win
6. Retirement/Retainment

For the purposes of our focus on youth players, we will look in depth at the first five stages.

Stage 1 – The FUNdamental Phase

Ages 5 – 8 +/-

The clue is in the title when it comes to the *FUNdamental Phase*. Soccer training needs to be fun and with a focus on primary physical movements. Due to a young person's naturally low attention span and inability to stay on task for longer periods, a session that is a maximum of 45 minutes in length is enough.

Technically

Ages 5 – 8 +/-

Players at this age should be allowed plenty of time to explore the game and the focus should be on *playing the game*. Players need to become familiar with the ball – how it moves, spins and bounces so ball touches during a session need to be maximized.

Soccer sessions with this age group then need to focus on ball and game familiarization. Using 'drills'[2] where players are standing in lines, queuing and waiting their turn to pass, shoot or perform any other technique should be avoided wholesale.

Physically

Ages 5 – 8 +/-

As a priority, players need to learn the *fundamental movements and motor skills* required to be able to play soccer effectively as they get older. Coaches often bemoan the fact that modern children are less active in their general life. Competition from games consoles, digital television and the Internet means kids are no longer developing the basic physical attributes that come with climbing trees, falling over, playing hopscotch, etc.

Coaches therefore need to put on practices that help players develop Agility, Balance, Coordination and Speed (ABCs) to become *physically literate*. Mastering things like running, jumping, landing, falling down, rolling over and all such exercises help players become physically able to master soccer-specific technique later. *The better these motor skills are, the more capable players will become at absorbing ball mastery skills later.* Ensure that physical literacy work allows players to utilize multi-directional movements, and these are not just performed in straight lines. Do so in the context of fun play and using coordination games where ABCs are implicit.

It is also worth remembering that young children may run around with lots of energy, but may also fatigue quickly. Use plenty of breaks between exercises.

Tactically

Ages 5 – 8 +/-

Any 'tactical' work at this age group is about *learning the principles of the game*. 3v3 and 4v4 games are especially useful at this stage. I am a big advocate of 4v4 in particular as it is has the lowest number of players involved to replicate the 'real' game. Players get loads of touches of the ball, and the small-sided nature of these games allows them to learn the principles of both attacking and defending. Always include goals or a method of scoring as a way of stimulating players' interest.

Under no circumstances, even as a goalkeeper, should players be pigeon-holed into positions.

Socially

Ages 5 – 8 +/-

Players at this age are self-centred, which really lends itself to one-ball, one-player exercises. However, this egocentricity also means that the concept of team play is not even on their radar. A huge amount of team play and team ethic is too much to expect. The notion of the "team" can be introduced but is far from being the focus.

One of many young players' main motivations for playing soccer and sport at this age is to play and have fun with their friends. The environment helps them form relationships, so support from the coach and parents must ensure that they play in a fun, safe environment. As the young

---

[2] The use of the term 'drill' is a bugbear of mine. A drill suggests something that is military and robotic, something which soccer certainly is not.

players explore the game, work to foster their enthusiasm, and, as so prettily put by the English FA in *Their Game – Youth Football Development* "Help young people fall in love with the game"!

Psychologically

Ages 5 – 8 +/-

First of all, soccer sessions should be fun, engaging and lead to an understanding of invasion games.[3] Players should be involved all of the time, and not in queues, being asked to sit out, or having to wait their turn.

Kids love using their imagination and exploring new things – use imaginative games with names that capture their natural creativity. As players will struggle to focus on one thing for an extended period of time, keep altering and progressing the practices within the session. Do not get frustrated with their inattention, accept it as a normal character trait and work with it!

A five or six-year-old will not have the ability to understand the concept of cause and effect and their memory will be short-term. They will remember a practice or exercise because it was fun and engaging, not because of the technical detail taught. Using practices where *learning is implicit* is the coach's greatest teaching tool with this age group. Let them learn through experiences rather than theory.

Stage 2 – The Learning to Train Phase

Ages 8 – 11 +/-

At this stage, young players can begin to learn more about the game itself and start on their soccer-specific journey. Training sessions can now be longer but an optimal time would be around 60 – 75 minutes.

Technically

Ages 8 – 11 +/-

The main focus here should be on ball familiarization exercises such as those promoted by the Coerver® Coaching[4] brand and other such coaching philosophies. This is about having a ratio of one ball to one player to allow players to have the optimal number of contacts with the ball as possible. I have seen coaches use futsals at this point, and even tennis balls!

Controlling the ball in the air can also be introduced. In fact Cardiff City previously gave their young players a "Keep Ups" practice guide for homework[5] because "your first touch is the most important one in football!" It went on to insist that players "be creative [and] let your imagination run riot".

Being able to control the ball is the foundation for technical development. Without the ability to control the ball effectively, future development of other technical skills like passing, shooting, turning, etc. becomes harder to acquire.

As per Cardiff, encourage creativity, dribbling and staying in *individual possession of the ball*. Allow players to become comfortable and confident in 1v1 situations. Too often, when watching this age group play soccer, the majority of youngsters will use one touch to kick the ball as far as possible. In certain cultures this is even praised! Players should not be praised for aimlessly kicking the ball as hard or as far as they can. Conversely, encourage them to stay on the ball as long as they can.

---

[3] Invasion games are where teams (mainly) attack a space like a goal, end zone, basket, etc. and defend the same space. Other examples include hockey, American Football, rugby and basketball.
[4] Coerver is probably the leading 'brand' of technical development coaching, although it does receive criticism in some quarters for having queues of players and not taking technique into opposed practices enough.
[5] Or "post-training challenge" as we noted in Chapter 2!

These years are what the *Scottish FA Youth Football* advisory materials call the "skill hungry years". Players have an almost unbounded ability to develop their motor senses to acquire an abundance of new skills. Along with unopposed technical practices, use opposed practices and *Teaching Games for Understanding* to allow skill acquisition to flourish. Putting technique into game situations is vital for the development of 'skill'.

Resist putting limits on what players do with the ball or using absolute statements as rules. Unfortunately soccer has certain customs around "never pass the ball across the front of the goal" and to "only dribble in the attacking third of the pitch". I was once told by a ten-year-old that a classmate of his "had the skills, but could not pay the bills", a term clearly picked up from adults who prefer functional players rather than technically impressive ones.

Physically

Ages 8 – 11 +/-

Physically, I would like to hit you with an almost unbelievable fact – *children begin to lose their natural flexibility from the age of ten*! This may seem quite young, but as their capacity for learning physical literacy peaks, their flexibility begins to diminish also. Include and encourage static stretching in cool-downs to help with this. Likewise, the capacity of the pathways in the brain to support the development of new motor skills is strongest pre-11 years old, but begins to wane after 11 or 12 years old.

When warming up, ensure you include a ball and ABCs exercises. I rarely use absolute statements, but *never, ever have players warm-up by performing laps of the pitch*. If players arrive at your practice while you are setting up, do not use laps as a way of keeping them occupied – occupy them with a ball instead! Give them a ball each in a square to practice manipulating and further experiencing it. Even if the players only have 30 practices a season, replacing 5 minutes of running laps of the pitch with five minutes of having a ball at their feet means that they will spend *two-and-a-half hours extra* with a ball at their feet – that is maximising the time for players' long-term development!

It is very tempting to use physical size to win games at this age. Players who develop physically early will impact games greatly at this age due to strength, mass and running power. As discussed at the outset of this book, being motivated by short-term results will negatively impact the long-term development of *both* the bigger and smaller players.

Tactically

Ages 8 – 11 +/-

At this point, tactics still remain irrelevant. 'Individual tactics' can be promoted at this stage – in other words a player's decision-making on and, to some extent, around the ball. Again, use small-sided games and TGfU to allow players to experience game-like situations, rather than using 'drills'. Using too much "Stop! Standstill!" type interventions will disengage players, and will often contain information they will not understand. I recently witnessed a very well intentioned under-9's coach trying to stop a training game to make tactical points about space and off the ball runs, which the players simply could not understand. As they spent so much time standing around, players began having conversations, playing their own games on the side, and one even entangled himself in a dividing net! This upset the coach and caused a confrontation where there really did not need to be one. Remember, work with the traits of your players – let them play.

Players will still have a limited understanding of playing positions and the specialization of them positionally is discouraged. Using tactical terms that put limits on your players, such as "hold your position" are counter-productive. They discourage creativity, and the exploration of attack and defence, and do not resemble even the adult game – even a modern defender will join attacks when appropriate. Allow youngsters the time to practice this.

Socially

Ages 8 – 11 +/-

Players are still egocentric but start to engage in group-play and understand that cooperation and teamwork is important, although they may understand the concept more than how to put it into practice.

Players do not want to share, so expecting and insisting that they share the ball can be a tough sell. They want to be the centre of attention, scoring goals, creating chances, and their feedback will always be about *me*.

Players should be encouraged to participate in lots of different sports to allow them to learn lots of skills that are transferable to soccer.

At this age it is possible to introduce post-training tasks, like the ones produced by Cardiff City above.[6]

Psychologically

Ages 8 – 11 +/-

This age period is considered the "Golden Age of Learning". Players have a huge ability to learn and absorb a vast number of new skills. Use this time to teach players the fundamentals of the game, and the information you want them to carry through their later development years. Create a culture and environment where players are not afraid of mistakes and are free to take risks with the ball.

Young players will all harbour dreams about becoming the next Ronaldo, Messi or Landon Donovan, but cranking up any pressure about achieving this is fruitless. Believe it or not, one of the main reasons that young players stop playing sport is because there is too much pressure put on them!

If you step back and digest that last statement, it is quite disgraceful that adult expectations, whether from parents or coaches, actually drive eight or nine-year-old players out of the game. If the FUNdamental stage is about "falling in love with the game", this stage is about ensuring players "stay in love with the game".

Young players love to copy their heroes so encourage them to replicate the skills of their favourite players. Skills have a tendency to "catch on" – let them try and explore. Use videos and demonstrations that paint a picture to players of what you want; it is so much more powerful than simply saying or ordering it.

Stage 3 The Training to Train Phase

Ages 11 – 14 +/-

At this point, players are entering 11v11 soccer. This has consequences throughout the rest of their development technically, tactically, physically and mentally. Sessions are still very much about development, rather than winning, and can now last 70 to 90 minutes.

Technically

Ages 11 – 14 +/-

At this stage, players begin to learn about tactics but there is still a very strong emphasis on their technical development. During the previous stages, we spoke about the importance of players becoming familiar with the ball. To effectively make their technical journey through youth soccer, *players need to be able to master the ball before puberty*. At this stage efficient motor skills are needed.

---

[6] Incidentally this document, and others from the Academy, are available online.

Players in the 'Training to Train' phase are exiting the "golden age of learning". Their capacity to learn new ball manipulation skills is therefore on the wane. What they will start to do, however, is advance the skills that they have already mastered. *Applying these skills in competitive situations* is of paramount importance. I remember an under-13 running to a colleague of mine who was the technical development coach at the club and who specialized in teaching players individual moves and skills. The youngster excitedly relayed that both he and one of his mates had completed a particular move in that morning's game. The freedom to experiment with clever moves in games is of vital importance – allow players to do so, regardless of the risk of losing.

Therefore, applying technique in opposed situations is now a major consideration for players, whether during training practices or, of course, in games. The more game-like situations players are exposed to, the more practice they get at applying technique under pressure. Standing in lines, waiting their turn in unopposed practices, not only bores players, it is of little development value. Be innovative about your practices, knowing that - ultimately - players need to have their technique challenged.

Physically

Ages 11 – 14 +/-

The onset of puberty has a massive influence on players during this stage. Players' bodies are changing and growth spurts occur habitually. These changes affect agility, balance and coordination, as well as having psychological impacts. Players may temporarily lose control of their body movements (the brain is essentially trying to control and manoeuvre a new body), and begin to struggle to control and manipulate the ball like they used to. I have seen players simply fall over while moving for no reason. They are losing flexibility and agility but gaining size, strength and power at the same time – it is very easy to understand how this will impact their performance. It is essential to bear with players that may be affected at this point. You may find that an excelling player is suddenly not as effective short-term, but remember this is temporary and will settle down. Everyone involved should be patient and understanding.

In an interview with *Soccer Magazine*, Inter Milan youth coach Stefano Bellinzaghi made an interesting point about the impact of puberty on coaches' judgments of players: "If we have two players with the same technical ability, but one has gone through puberty, then maybe we have to look more at the other player, because he might improve more after he goes through puberty."

In this age group, size differences can become really obvious. You may have an early developing 13-year-old with the physique of a 16-year-old or a late developing one with the physique of a 10 or 11-year-old. Bigger players can control and win games making them effective match-winners at this age. However, ensure that they are not solely relying on physical power and strength and they are developing technically also. Do not throw away the smaller player as, once puberty and growth spurts are complete, they will have the technique *and* stature to deal with the game.

Tactically

Ages 11 – 14 +/-

Tactically, players will now start to learn how to work together and can be given unit and small group orientated goals and tasks. Their performance can be related to others on the pitch like never before and players will begin to understand the cause and effect of their actions. They will be able to relate their role to the role of one or two of their teammates and opponents. Beware though, that even the best players in your team will struggle relating the whole 11 v 11 picture to their performance.

Continue to play players in different positions, although some may start to show a tendency towards a particular position, and will certainly display a tendency towards attacking or defensive instincts. Goalkeepers can become more specialized and prominent.

The coach can start to teach players about different formations, which means being flexible by using different formations during games. Players can also develop *basic* roles and individual responsibilities at set-plays.

A team's organization helps you win games, but will not develop players longer-term. Players need to understand and experience the fluidity of the game of soccer. So although tactical work is gaining in importance, prioritizing skill development over organization is essential.

Socially

Ages 11 – 14 +/-

This can be a very difficult period socially for young players and their coaches. Players start to desire greater independence from adults and may become more confrontational as a result. They may push disciplinary boundaries further than they have done before. With an increased independence from adults can come a lot of newly formed opinions, which can lead to challenging behaviour.

With puberty comes the discovery of, and a greater interest in, other genders and their relationships with them. These relationships, and those with friends, may start to take priority over soccer development.

As a method of working with the traits of this age group, rather than against them, try giving players lots of opportunities to work together to solve problems. Encourage players to experiment with the game together, and try to mimic the good practice of others.

Players will start to recognize that their teammates can do things that they cannot, or that they are capable of things that their peers are not. Be careful therefore when making competitive comparisons between a player and a teammate.

Psychologically

Ages 11 – 14 +/-

Although the players' capacity to concentrate is getting higher, they still prefer and benefit more from *doing rather than listening*. Team-talks need to be concise, to the point, and allow players to experience the game and learn through it. Allow them to play, ideally give all players equal playing time and encourage making (but learning from) mistakes.

Because players are starting to become less dependent on adults, allow them to make their own decisions around soccer. By teaching them the game in your practices, and allowing them the appropriate amount of playing time, enable them, where possible, to make their own decisions, rather than make all their decisions for them (and thus creating robots). To help, set players individual goals to focus their decision-making around specific learning points.

The onset of puberty can also affect players mentally. The effects on their bodies can mean a loss of form, and a consequential loss of confidence. Stick with players at this age. Make them aware that change is happening and the mind *will* get used to a new body, ensuring parents understand this also. Persist with the player – they need your help and positivity to keep their confidence intact.

Stage 4 – The Training to Compete Stage

Ages 14 – 16 +/-

At this stage, players are starting to move towards adult-type soccer. The game begins to resemble that played by adults but, at the same time, players are also far from being fully developed. The coach at this age group should have a working understanding of the adult game they are working towards, and also a grasp of the game at a more junior level to understand where players are coming from.

Technically

Ages 14 – 16 +/-

Issues of the coach working with a team from a young age all the way through youth football can become really apparent during this phase. Coaches often come to me feeling that players have almost outgrown them. The practices that are put on may not be challenging enough and players can see them as being too easy and child-like. In the same way we do not teach adult soccer to younger players, we should not teach 'kids soccer' to older teenagers.

Players still need lots of technical work, but there is a notable shift towards tactical understanding and game sense. If they have come through the appropriate development at the previous stages, players should be competent technically and be able to apply technique to tactical situations, in a game that is now quicker and more physically intense.

Demand that players are more technically accurate and consistent, still understanding that mistakes will be made; learning from these mistakes still needs to be an important learning tool.

Physically

Ages 14 – 16 +/-

Although players have gone through puberty, they are of course still growing during this period. Hopefully those that are physically less developed have learned to use their size to affect games, but may still lose out in any battle based on strength, power or speed. A particular goalkeeper I know was released from several professional clubs during this period as, although he was considered "technically good", he was ultimately labelled "too small". By 17 he was six feet and physical tests predicted a peak height of 6 foot 4! Needless to say he has now re-ignited the interest of several academy clubs. Remember that players will go through a lot of physical transformation before adulthood.

The pace and intensity of the game increases notably here and 11 v 11 matches *start* to replicate the adult game more accurately. Regardless of the physical identity of individual players now, they must learn to find a way of coping with the game – and they will need your help in learning how to do so. Look at how the diminutive world-class players find space in-between opponents (often referred to as 'pockets of space'). They learn to release the ball quickly, play off fewer touches (or "half touches" as once famously quoted by Xavi Hernandez) or use a lower centre of gravity to evade defenders. There is a wonderful compilation video of Andreas Iniesta on YouTube that shows him quickly getting his body between the opponent and ball, allowing him to protect possession or develop a situation where the defender resorts to committing a foul.

Smaller players can still be strong physically, so encourage work around *core strength* so they can compete with more physically developed players. Core strength is almost the 'inner' physical strength of a player where muscles around his trunk are strong, meaning he can fend off opponents and retain balance even under physical duress.

Tactically

Ages 14 – 16 +/-

Tactically, players can now be stretched further than before. Players should start to 'link in' the roles of each of the team's units and begin to understand their role within the team. They may now start to link in players and movements "away" from the ball (third-man runs, movements to create space for others to exploit, etc.) Finding *ways* to win games (rather than necessarily winning them) is now significant, as that is what will be demanded of players when they enter adult soccer. They must also realize how their decisions affect the performance of the team. Players can further understand specific roles and responsibilities at set-plays and are comfortable working to a strategic game plan.

One particular academy I studied completely pigeon-holed players positionally at this stage. Players would spend 80% of the time working position-specifically. *Position-specific technical training* is introduced so that players practice skills that are relevant to them and their playing position. They are therefore not practicing skills they do not need (for example a centre-back will not spend time working on finishing or crossing). This has caused much debate and opposition among the game's thinkers, but, with the particular academy's excellent track record in producing professional soccer players, they have found a way of working that succeeds for them.

Phases of play and other tactic-based practices can be beneficial from this stage, once completed effectively. Coach interventions during these practices can often be about getting the players to stand still, whilst the coach points out what to do. This type of intervention can be very tricky as too much of it can result in a static practice, demotivated players, and although the coach may have a huge amount of information to impart, it can be lost as the players simply don't like it. Keep interventions brief, ask questions, and allow lots of free play in-between.

Other types of interventions and tactical challenges can be set. For instance, you can set up a small-sided game with a theme and team objectives (for example: "You are 2-0 up with 15 minutes left, can you find ways of holding onto the lead?") Alternatively you can set individual objectives – "Can you start in a wide position, but look to receive the ball infield in pockets of space?" or "Let's see how many overlapping runs you can make." These individual objectives can then link in as they would do when linking in the jobs of a winger and full-back, as above. Use breaks in the game or quick team-talks between practices to evaluate, reinforce, or set new tasks.

Socially

Ages 14 – 16 +/-

Players of this age will become more outgoing socially and may focus more on friendships and relationships. As a result players can have a lot going on in their lives away from school, family and soccer. Social networking becomes prominent and there can be social demands placed on players that they will be new to navigating. Due to the increasing importance of their social circle, players will often respect the opinions of their peers more than that of adults, and are less dependent on their parents.

Building rapport to get the best out of players is vital at this stage. A coach working with these players needs to recognize the huge social change that their players are going through and the impact this may have on their personality, attitude to soccer, and their performance.

Psychologically

Ages 14 – 16 +/-

Players' experience in the game thus far means that independent thought and problem-solving skills are starting to show. Allow them this independence. Players should not need the coach to solve all the problems they face. Challenge this ability further by creating situations and challenging thought processes.

Players can be encouraged to find ways to win games, without the result being the be-all-and-end-all. Players can also be introduced to mental skills such as recovering from setbacks, self-awareness, and being mentally tough.

Unlike younger players, cause and effect should now also become more prominent. As a result players should be encouraged to accept responsibility for their role and decisions, without it being used as a stick to beat them.

Players will also begin to start 'reading the game' more. This comes from their experiences and greater perception of tactics and principles of the game. They will be able to predict movements of team-mates and opposition quicker and with greater precision. This needs to be fostered and developed, as it is an essential tool for preparing them for older youth soccer and ultimately the adult game.

Stage 5 – The Training to Win Stage

Age 16 – 19 +/-

More stress is put on players who are entering this stage than during previous stages – the last phase of their youth development. Coaches working with these players are overseeing a transition from youth to adult soccer. Players will still need advice, guidance and a coach who can further develop the basic soccer traits they have learned until this point.

Technically

Age 16 – 19 +/-

At this age the outline of the players' technical ability will be set firmly in place. Of course, players can still improve, but their ability to learn new technical skills is diminished. It is vital from now that players look to refine and perfect their technique through practice; set standards that allow them to keep progressing. The coach can focus on developing more advanced skills (curling a ball, volleying, outside of the foot passing, etc.) Players can be challenged to complete technical work at increased speeds and consider the risk-reward trade-off in making technical decisions[7].

Their game understanding and physique should be improving and will, therefore, impact on their technique. For example, a better awareness tactically will help them play clever through passes, make better runs and understand what position to move into (to maximise technique). Physically, players' leg power will improve so longer passing, crossing, long-range shooting, volleying, etc. will become bigger weapons.

Physically

Age 16 – 19 +/-

Like technique, players are unlikely to develop new motor skills at this age. Their quest at this age is to maximize the physical characteristics they have. There is more emphasis at this point on soccer-specific fitness, endurance and speed. Core-stability training can become an ingrained part of their program. Many players will start to use gyms, where individual programs can be utilized to impact performance. Ensure that any strength work that is completed is relative to soccer. When young players first complete gym work they can focus on lifting the heaviest weights they can and muscle building can be cosmetic rather than soccer-specific. Remember, also, that lifting weights requires static power, whereas strength in soccer demands that players deal with moving objects (i.e. players).

Because the tempo and physical nature of the game is increasing, fatigue can often be a big factor in the latter periods of both halves. Much evidence from major international tournaments and national leagues show a larger percentage of goals are scored in the last 15 minutes of games than during any other period. This is often down to physical tiredness and a lack of mental concentration. Being physically able to affect games, even when fatigued, is imperative.

Tactically

Age 16 – 19 +/-

Players need to be challenged tactically at this point. We find that although their natural technique and basic motor skills will not improve dramatically, their tactical understanding will. They will begin to have a deeper understanding of their positional roles and the team's game plan. Most, although not all, will have a preferred position where they spend most of their time improving. Functional or position-specific training becomes more prominent and players should

---

[7] For example, should the player risk playing a probing pass to try to create a goal-scoring opportunity, or is it too risky and it will be intercepted?

spend a substantial amount of time completing technical, skill, and tactical work in their relevant positions.

In recent times I have explored and created technical and skill practices that are also position-specific and completed them on the relevant area of the pitch, as a reference for players. So a 7v7 small-sided game would not be played on a 7-a-side pitch with 7-a-side goals, it would be played from the goal line (with big goals, towards the halfway line. That way your goalkeeper and defenders are protecting a real goal in a relevant part of the pitch, and strikers are attacking the goal in and around the box.

Players will start to understand the game and notice patterns more, and will have a greater appreciation of the strengths and weaknesses of their opponents. With this, they need to develop their game understanding and be able to manage in-game situations. For example, if they are winning 1 – 0 with only a few minutes left, how do they approach the remaining minutes? If they are losing, what are the acceptable risks to take? Can they deal with a change in formation, focus, emphasis or personnel?[8]

Challenge players to think critically in small-sided games or other tactical exercises to make strategic decisions in real time.

Socially

Age 16 – 19 +/-

By this age a lot is going on socially. Players are drastically more independent from their parents and may not need or want adult guidance. Some show traits of young adults, whereas others are struggling to mature in a way to deal with their new-found freedom and level of expected responsibility. Players will be learning to drive, will be becoming eligible to vote, and will be making life-long decisions around work, university or, if they are lucky, their future in professional soccer!

Players may now even be living away from the family home, which brings about huge issues as to how they look after themselves in terms of diet, lifestyle, alcohol consumption, and other social temptations. You may even find that players in your teams are taking vacations together. Their topics of conversation also become more social and although the coach wants soccer to be the most important thing in their lives, this may be far from the truth.

Psychologically

Age 16 – 19 +/-

Players now need to be more accountable for developing their game and taking charge of their own potential. They should understand issues around lifestyle, practice, and off-the-field decisions, and take responsibility for them. Players should be fully involved and honest when reviewing and analysing their own performance. If you have an exceptional player, but he cannot get out of bed, or away from his girlfriend to train, then there are problems.

Fatigue not only affects the body, but can also affect concentration. Various studies across disciplines suggest that concentration levels last a mere 30 minutes, even if there is a concerted effort to focus, making the last 15 minutes of both halves particularly dangerous.

---

[8] In a recent tactical 11v11, I set some tactical problems for a new group of under-18s. We set up a hypothetical scenario where it was the last 15 minutes of a game. The reds were beating the blues 2 – 0. The reds were tasked with organizing themselves to hold onto the lead, and the blues had to set up to chase the game. Remarkably, both teams chose to play their biggest player (both normally center-backs) as their main striker – the reds to use him as a target man to launch counter-attacks, and the blues so they could play direct when trying to create goal-scoring opportunities! Both teams identified direct soccer as their best solution. This was doubtlessly based on their previous experiences and coach influences.

As the game is now physically quicker at 18, players are required to be mentally quicker to be able to handle the demands of the game. As wonderfully put by sport psychologist Dan Abrahams "In football (soccer) quick, nimble, athletic feet are a result of quick, nimble athletic minds". Essentially, performing at speed, means being able to think and make decisions at speed. By 19, players should have travelled through what FUNiño soccer call the *Four Stages of Problem-Solving*: Perception – Understanding and Interpreting – Decision Making – and finally Execution.

As players leave youth soccer, more decisions have to be made about their future in the game. Some players will begin to realize that their dream of being a professional soccer player is now over – something that needs a lot of support.

Conclusion

To conclude I am going to present some really useful visuals from the Belgian Football Association's *Philosophy of Youth Development*.

The adapted diagram below shows the relationship between the technical and tactical development of youth players and the shift from technique to tactics along the way.

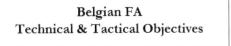

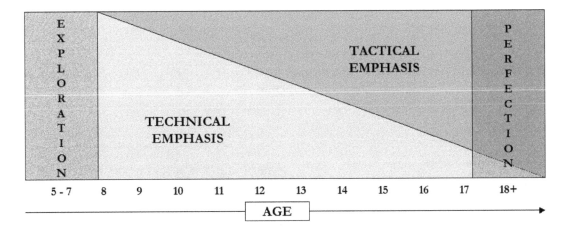

The diagram below shows the focus when moving from general capabilities of the body and coordination, towards endurance-based work later in youth, with work becoming more specific, the addition of flexibility work during the journey, and the importance of speed development throughout.

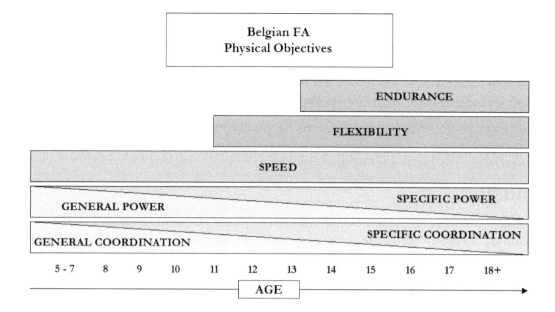

Psychological training can often be inherent in coaching. I recently heard it being labelled the "hidden curriculum". A coach will use mental techniques throughout his work, whether he knows it or not. For the more specific training of mental skills, the Belgian FA outlined the following:

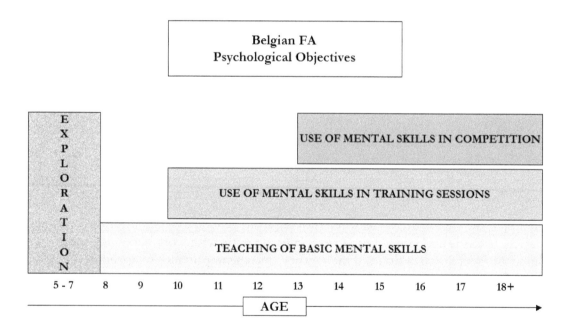

Summary

- Understanding different age-related characteristics is essential to develop youth players effectively.

- Chronological age is just one way of defining players. They will also have a soccer age and a biological age (and a relative age).

- Long Term Player Development (LTPD) involves the development of the following areas: Technical and Tactical, Physical, Psychological and Social.

- Although often presented as separate entities, the categories of LTPD are interconnected.

- The long-term development of youth players takes them through five stages prior to the Retirement/Retainment Stage: The FUNdamental Stage, Learning to Train, Training to Train, Training to Compete and ultimately Training to Win.

- The 5 to 8 (+/-) age bracket is all about exploring the game and the development of motor skills.

- From ages 8 to 11 (+/-) the focus becomes about mastering the ball. If this is not completed, more advanced techniques and tactics cannot be maximized.

- The onset of puberty greatly affects the performance of ages 11 to 14 (+/-).

- Tactical work becomes more prominent in ages 14 to 16 (+/-) as the game starts to reflect the adult game more and more.

- From 16 to 19 (+/-) players should be starting to take greater responsibility for their own development and perfecting techniques learned through their development.

Real Coach Experience

Observations of an Academy Coach

(English Academy Coach – Anonymous)

In a role at a previous club, I worked part-time with the under-15 and under-16 age groups. The academy was quite a modest one. Some teams had two coaches, as was regulated by the Football League who governed youth development, but, due to cost cutting, some teams only had one.

One coach in particular worked alone. Let's call him John. I have a feeling that he preferred it this way, and I've a suspicion that it was something he insisted upon with the management. He also insisted on working with the same group of players and was determined to follow them through the age groups. He considered the players to be "his" team, rather than part of the club, or individuals in their own right. During my three years at the club, John worked with the same players at under-9, under-10 and under-11 levels. I am sure he stayed with them for at least two years after I had left.

The older age groups trained after the younger ones so often I would arrive early, prepare my session, speak to colleagues and observe the sessions that were taking place. At the time the club did not work to a coaching curriculum so coaches essentially had full control over what work they carried out with the players.

Over three years, I consistently watched John deliver an identical session over and over again. The most worrying part was that at no point was there ever a ball manipulation exercise, something that is fundamental for young players. Lots of the practices were 'keep ball' 6 v 6 or 7 v 7 without targets, goals or a method of scoring. The work he was doing on a regular basis with these players was not only boring for the players, but also completely inappropriate for the age and level of the players.

The players achieved no real success from what I saw. His powerful character dominated them, and although he was young and enthusiastic, he coached a very out-of-date game. I despaired heavily when I once watched him sit all the players down and, while furiously waving a dominant finger at them, bellowed "if in doubt – put it out", which basically means that if you are unsure of what to do with the ball, then you should just kick it out of play. This flies in the face of the modern game that players need to be taught.

I am shocked that not only did John remain employed at the academy, but that he was allowed to teach the same thing to the same group of players for at least five years! As a result of this, I ensure that I work with the same players for a maximum of two, maybe three years depending on circumstance. I strive to be a specialist age-group coach, rather than a team coach, and I focus on the areas players of that particular age need.

8

Developing a Coaching Philosophy and Syllabus

"Long and medium term planning for your players will allow you to take into account their current abilities and outline what knowledge, skills and understanding you intend your players to acquire over a set time period."
(Mark McClements, FA Skills Coach Team Leader)

Like in school, a soccer syllabus is an outline of what you want the players to learn. The majority of the time it will be over the course of a season. It is developed prior to the season with the aims and objectives of the players at its core. It can, of course, then be updated as the players' soccer journeys progress. A syllabus will consider the age-related needs, ability and background of the group, and the individuals within it. The intent is to offer players a rounded, holistic soccer education.

Before going into huge detail on how to develop a syllabus, it is critical to point out that there is no 'perfect' coaching plan. There is also no one way of working that is the same (or will work) for all players. Many syllabi and session plans are contributed in the coming pages, all of which could be criticized in some capacity, even those from the greatest youth development programs in the world! The easiest thing to do as a coach is to stand back and critique the work and methods of another coach. We are constantly reminded that soccer is a game of opinions and, therefore, disagreement does not make something incorrect. It means that *you* may have an alternative way of working with your players. Different methods are not fully right or fully wrong. There is only good practice and poor practice.

Justifying Planning

Roy Keane once relayed that the team at Manchester United never had a wasted training session. There was a justifiable purpose to all the work they did[1]. Players at Chelsea also commented that all their sessions linked in with a task required to win the next game. When developing my own coaching philosophy, these stories inspired me greatly. I learned primarily that it is imperative to always have a rationale and justification for your methods, planning, and your coaching sessions.[2]

The sessions and syllabi outlined in the rest of this chapter are designed to be thought provoking and *offer* ways of working and coaching that are practiced at the top level of youth soccer coaching. Although I have taken inspiration from Roy Keane and José Mourinho, I am not interested in *their* coaching sessions. I am more interested in how the Italian's develop seven-year-olds, or how Atlético Mineiro work with their under-17s.

---

[1] Reportedly, during Manchester United's treble-winning season in 1998-1999, the players had a total of three days off, making Keane's comments about always having a justification for their training sessions even more impressive!
[2] I had a very surreal experience with a coach 'justifying' his methods. He set up a shooting practice for under-12s that contained a long queue of players, something in itself that is thoroughly frowned upon. When challenged, the coach insisted that his aim was to "identify technique in each individual player and work to rectify it". The first shot taken went high and wide and the coach told him to "go fetch his own s**t". That was not the technical detail I was expecting!

There may be some examples below that you do not like, whereas others will challenge the perception of how you coach. Use the examples to form your own experience, beliefs and way of working. Be adaptable, and *justify your methods*.

'Periodized' Coaching

Working towards a syllabus is also known as *periodized* coaching. A periodized coaching program is a planned, logical scheme of work, with the players at the center of your planning.

The traditional basis for our coaching tends to be *reactionary*. We spot that something from game day was not good enough, so we work on that during the next session. So if your team concedes lots of goals, the next session is spent on learning how to defend. This type of coaching is called *episodic* coaching. While this type of coaching is popular, its long-term benefits are minimal. When players reach the age of 16, there is scope for more episodic work, provided they previously have had a good grounding in the game.

Most of the time, *coaches only need to be reactive to performances once results start to have significance*. An adult professional team for example, if they are susceptible to conceding goals from set-plays (or 'restarts'), may spend more time focusing on defending corners. Often when a struggling team employs a new Head Coach, he may spend the immediate number of sessions working on the team's fitness and their defensive / offensive shape. We frequently hear these coaches talking about making a struggling team "organized and hard to beat".

As results are of utmost importance at this level, episodic coaching is a valuable method. To an extent, however, first team coaches will also work periodically to achieve medium and long-term objectives – we often hear of a coach having a "three" or "five-year plan". Unfortunately at the top level of the professional game, managers are given less and less time to work towards long or even medium-term goals[3]. It is understandable therefore that focusing on short-term objectives, supported by episodic-type coaching is quite forgivable.

In the world of youth soccer, however, the threat of being fired from your position due to league points is vastly reduced (although I am sure there are instances of this from poorly-informed decision-makers). Therefore, certainly up to the 16 to 19 age-group, a periodized approach to coaching is a necessity.

Periodized Coaching	Episodic Coaching
• Logical • Pre-planned • Comprehensive • Measurable • Ensures coaches don't just stick to comfortable sessions	• Illogical • Reactive • Immeasurable • Coaches tend to produce familiar sessions
Episodic has its place with 16+	

---

[3] As of December 2013, the average tenure of a manager in England's four professional divisions is less than two seasons (Source: League Managers Association)

How to Develop a Coaching Syllabus

One of the loneliest times as a soccer coach is sitting down with a blank piece of paper, staring at it, and wondering how (or where) to start devising a syllabus of work.

As you begin, you can wonder how on earth you can possibly fill a whole season with coaching topics. Then, of course, you will need to plan around missing weeks due to weather, popular holiday periods and countless other things that can interrupt the season. On the other hand you may struggle to fit in everything you want to work on.

The tendency may be to give up this planning altogether. Maybe you have looked at working towards a syllabus previously and, as it has not worked for whatever reason, you shy away from completing a new one at all. I myself have succumbed to this tendency. Looking back at a time when I was working without a syllabus, I do feel certain guilt towards the players I was developing. Admittedly, my sessions 'butterflied' between different topics, or similar topics were coached over and over again. My planning boiled down to *What Shall I Coach Tonight?*[4]

Having a plan in place negates all this. If you live in a part of the world where soccer coaching is halted due to snow for example, build in 'free' or 'catch-up' weeks where you can work somewhat episodically; or include a period where you will work indoors, utilizing *futsal* for example. *A syllabus must be a live or working document. It can be amended and altered as is necessary*, hopefully for the right reasons.

There is no correct way of developing or planning a scheme of work like this. The examples I have included below all differ. Some will insist on having a session around one theme, others will include aspects of certain work in every session. Other sessions I have seen happily jump around a number of topics in a 'carousel' fashion. *Your* syllabus needs to reflect how *you* as a coach operate and what you have identified as being considerate of your players.

Planning in Cycles

Normally, when we discuss planning in soccer coaching, we refer to the planning of our individual coaching sessions – the single hour or hour-and-a-half we spend on the field with the players. A good coach, we are told, will plan his practice prior to arriving at the coaching session. He will work towards this plan, and evaluate its effectiveness afterwards. A better coach will adapt this plan as the session progresses due to the individual needs of players, often using the STEP Principle[5].

An *excellent* coach, however, will go further than simply planning individual sessions. Planning an individual session should be the easy bit. If pre-planning is done correctly, you will already have an idea or topic set in stone, and session planning will merely require filling in the blanks on an individual session plan.

---

[4] *What Shall I Coach Tonight* is a coaching article written by Mark McClements, where this chapter's opening quote originates.

[5] The STEP principle is a term used for adapting your coaching session *during the session*. It generally means that some part of the set-up is not working correctly and requires an alteration to the *Space* being used, the *Task* itself or the *Time* involved, the *Equipment* we are using or the *People / Players* involved.

'Top to Bottom' Planning

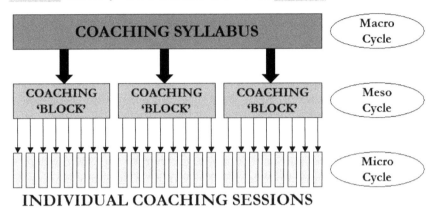

The diagram above illustrates the process involved in planning a syllabus or scheme of work. The process starts with a team's *philosophy*, then moves through *macro* (long-term), *meso* (medium-term) and eventually *micro* (short-term) pieces of work. Top of the pyramid is the coach or team's philosophy, which will include the culture of the club, what system or systems the coach wants to implement, a preferred coaching style(s) and the style of play.

'Philosophy'

The term 'philosophy' has been bandied around a lot recently. In England, the new *Elite Player Performance Plan* implemented by the *Premier League*, requires that each academy must have a playing philosophy that forms the basis for their youth player development. Some philosophies can be extremely well defined, whereas others can be general or even vague.

In 2012, the *European Club Association (ECA)* produced *the Report on Youth Academies in Europe*. This study detailed the major characteristics of 96 youth academies from 41 countries across the continent. This included very well established academies such as Bayern Munich, Inter Milan and Standard Liege, but also looked at the youth development set-ups at less renowned clubs such as Glentoran in Northern Ireland, Finland's FC Honka and Luxembourg's F91 Dudelange. Some of the key findings from the study relating to philosophies include:

- 91% of academies have a coaching philosophy, of which 65% are "clearly defined"; or have one in place "to some extent" (26%)

- More than 75% of academies work from a coaching syllabus and have a clearly defined vision for the club

- The majority of academies had a defined playing formation - 52% preferring 4-3-3 and 28% prioritizing 4-4-2.

Club Philosophy Case Study - Ajax Amsterdam

There are loads of great examples of the coaching philosophies used by major academies. For example, the cornerstone of Hoffenheim's *Philosophy of Youth Development* is to cultivate "independence, creativity and motivation". Each session at the Tottenham Hotspur Academy begins with the "10 minute rule", where each player spends time working on specific individual weaknesses. Therefore, Tottenham's older players, with six sessions over 43 weeks, will spend 43 hours a season working on specific aspects of their game that need developing.

However, when any discussion develops about a soccer academy having a well-defined philosophy, Ajax Amsterdam tends to be towards the forefront of discussions. Although the club's youth academy has been through some turbulent times over the last decade, the club has a proud and commendable record when it comes to developing world-class talent.[6]

The Ajax vision has been replicated and mimicked both in Holland and across the globe. The club has exported its 'brand' around the world, with partner clubs in Poland and South Africa amongst others, and its name and reputation frequently used across continents. Most notably, there is a significant Dutch and Ajax influence on the current academy philosophy of FC Barcelona, due to the link of famous coach Johan Cruyff between both clubs. On the back of this philosophy, Barcelona regularly has an abundance of academy players in their exceptionally successful first team.[7]

The *ECA* report is unequivocal in its stance that it is Ajax's "ideology" that has produced so many internationally renowned players. This ideology is based around a fluent, passing and attacking style of play. They want players to play with flair, improvisation, to press their opponents early and play the game in the opposition's half. Tactically the playing system is a mixture of 4-3-3, 3-4-3 or a mix of both.

The club looks to develop players that fit around four qualities known as the 'TIPS Model'. A visual of this model is below. This means that by the time the academy players are entering the first team, they are already fully versed in the way the senior players play, and have the individual qualities to do so.

Ajax Amsterdam Academy
TIPS Player Development Model

To be able to control the ball

TECHNIQUE

INSIGHT

Flair
Discipline
Team-Player

Football intelligence.
Decision maker

Mobility
Acceleration
Long distance

PERSONALITY   **SPEED**

According to Ajax, Personality and Speed are generally inherent assets possessed naturally by players. Technique and Insight however can be further developed through long-term player development. Each of the four TIPS are assessed against ten predetermined criteria. Due to the

---

[6] In recent years, Ajax as a club and an academy has gone through some changes. Johan Cruyff led somewhat of a rebellion against the running of the club, as there had been a notable drop off in the number of world-class youth players being produced. The hierarchy was instead focusing on buying talent from abroad rather than on producing it themselves, as per their tradition. In some quarters this change and reorganization has been labelled the "Second Football (Soccer) Revolution".

[7] Eight of the 14 Spanish players that played in the 2010 World Cup Final in South Africa were players from Barcelona. Seven of them (with the exception of David Villa) were schooled at the Catalan club.

focus on these areas, "Ajax youth are technically gifted, soccer wise, interesting personalities, with good basic speed." (*The Ajax Youth Development Scheme*, author unknown). Such is the popularity of the Ajax model, it is widely replicated across Dutch academies, such as at NEC Nijmegen. Dutch club Heerenveen use an adapted version of TIPS, known as STIM (using 'Mentality' rather than 'Personality').

The *Ajax Cape Town Youth Development Plan*, compiled by Marc Grüne, former Team Manager, Assistant Coach, Head of Youth, and Chief Scout at the club, sums up the philosophy of the club neatly: "The Ajax player has to have a very high level and broad base in all technical skills; he needs to be talented, skilful, tactically clever, fast, coachable and have a good personality. With[in] other words he needs to be at the highest level in all fields (also off the pitch). This means that the development must start at an early age and continue for many years to achieve these huge demands. The coaching for every age group becomes extremely important to lay a firm base (at youngest level) and continually expand, nurture and develop all necessary skills to the top level".

Having such a well-defined philosophy and playing style is celebrated at Ajax and by youth development enthusiasts across soccer. The club's official website boasts that the academy is "the breeding ground of Dutch football (soccer)"[8] and is known as De Toekomst (*The Future*). However, implementing and working around a single style of play has led to drawbacks when exporting players to other clubs, leagues and countries.

By the time Dennis Bergkamp joined Italian giants Inter Milan in 1993, the Dutch had successfully exported several plays into Serie A, including the trio of Marco van Basten, Ruud Gullit and Frank Rijkaard who formed the backbone of a tremendous AC Milan team in the early 1990s. Bergkamp, however, having been schooled in the 4-3-3 based attacking Ajax philosophy from his teens, could not (and possibly would not) adapt to a playing vision in Italy where defensive soccer was promoted, and forward players were left isolated. It was only when he transferred to attack-minded Arsenal, with a similar playing style to that of Ajax, that the world began to see the very best of Dennis Bergkamp.

Creating YOUR Soccer Coaching Philosophy

Not all of us coaches have a huge institution around us, like those working at Ajax. In fact, the overwhelming number of soccer coaches around the world work solo when coaching their teams. As a result, you will be in sole charge of developing *your* philosophy that *your* coaching will be based on. Indeed, the best youth soccer coaches I have met, whether working in a big academy or not, will unequivocally understand what their own coaching methods are based on.

Creating your own coaching philosophy takes much consideration. Once you understand the type of player you want to develop, this will go on to be the basis for the design of your syllabus and session planning. To illustrate, let's use two examples from Ajax. Because of their style and intention to dominate possession and outnumber their opponents, lots of work is done around overload possession games (i.e. 2v1, 4v2, etc). Dennis Bergkamp, now back at the club as a coach, bases his work and 'drills' around the concept of exploiting space, something he was renowned for as a player.[9]

It is important to remember that there is not just one philosophy that you *must* follow. It is easy to look at clubs like Ajax and Barcelona, with such celebrated playing visions, and replicate them because we are frequently told that their soccer is played "the right way". Not everyone agrees however. In February 2013, Italian soccer journalist, Michele Dalai, published a book called *Contro il Tiqui Taca* (Against Tiki-Taka), which lambasts the philosophy of the successful

---

[8] Seven of the 14 Dutch players that played in the 2010 World Cup Final in South Africa began their careers at Ajax.

[9] If you want a great resource for coaches or youth players from professional soccer, Dennis Bergkamp's *Stillness & Speed* is a must-read.

Barcelona-style that has been so honored in soccer circles over the last decade. Soccer, as we know, is a very debatable topic and is open to subjective thinking.[10]

Devising your coaching philosophy is therefore complicated and takes time. During my research for this book, I found an excellent, defined coach philosophy from a coach called Dan Wright. When I probed him further on how he devised it, his answer was long and detailed. I have summarized his answer below.

Dan Wright – Coaching Philosophy

"To me a coaching philosophy means how you view the game; your core values and beliefs.

I first started writing my philosophy in 2008 when I started my UEFA 'B' License. Until then I had an understanding of how I thought I wanted the game to be played but found it very difficult to articulate. My tutor said his outlook was as simple as "Player First, Player Centred, and Results Second." For me this was a great approach to coaching youth soccer but told you everything and nothing. It was a bit of a riddle. There was no talk of *how* and lacked personality.

It has to be *your* philosophy ... not Guardiola's, or Barca's, or Germany's or Cruyff's. It must be how *you* see the game, how *you* want your players to play, and how *you* are going to achieve it. This gives you and your players an identity.

I have recently re-written my philosophy and it's over 50 slides long! It discusses position-specific roles, player-coach relationships, creating the right environment, the demands of the game, my core values and everything that has shaped my outlook on the game. It is 50 slides before we discuss session plans. However, my overall aim is *to produce technically proficient players, who understand the game and make good decisions.*

I understand there are many different ways to play soccer – that is what makes it great. Whilst I have clear and defined opinions on the game, I *always* listen to others. Be prepared to have an opinion, to know why you think what you do, but know that the game is always changing and your philosophy may evolve with time and experience. As a coach you are never the finished article."

---

[10] Interestingly, I have never come across a written club philosophy that prizes defensive organization, direct soccer or physical dominance, although I am certain they exist, although somewhat in the shadows.

US Soccer offers an easy-to use document to assist coaches when trying to develop their own philosophy, basing this around four key areas – the coach's beliefs, motivation, experiences and methods. I have shared some of the questions they ask below.

US Youth Soccer – Philosophy Questionnaire

1. BELIEFS

    a) Why do you want to be a youth coach?

    b) Why do we have youth soccer?

    c) What are your responsibilities? To each player, to the team, to yourself and to the community?

    d) Define a successful season.

2. MOTIVATION

    a) I am interested in coaching because…

    b) What do you enjoy most about coaching?

    c) What do you like least about coaching?

3. EXPERIENCES

    a) PAST – what were your personal childhood experiences in soccer? Was it enriching or inhibiting?

    b) PRESENT – self-evaluation – what are you doing now?

    c) FUTURE – what experiences will I seek to improve my coaching?

4. METHODS

    a) What is my coaching style?

    b) At what point will I involve the players in the decision making process? Pre-, During, Post-Practice?

Macro, Meso, Micro

Once the overarching coaching philosophy is formed, the coach can then start to plan his team's long (macro), medium (meso) and short-term (micro) objectives.

Macro Objectives – The coaching syllabus, usually yearly (although possibly more if the club is well organized and connected), is devised based on the coach's philosophy.

Meso Cycle – The syllabus can then be broken down into a number of *blocks of work*, where for a certain period of time, players are taught around one or two particular topics. This period of time is usually from two to six weeks depending on the amount of contact time with the players.

Micro Cycle – Once the syllabus and blocks of work are in place, the individual coaching sessions are conceived.

The syllabus below brings the content of a previous diagram to life. This is taken from a "Women's Premier League Top Four Club" and is adapted from a presentation by Ben Bartlett, the founder of www.integritysoccer.co.uk. The full, detailed syllabus and presentation is available online.

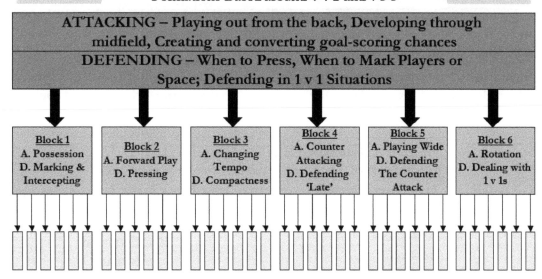

Stifling Creativity?

There is a school of thought that suggests devising a syllabus, and working rigidly towards it, actually stifles the creativity of both coaches and players. Although I understand these concerns, I do not necessarily agree fully with them. I believe an adaptable syllabus, which is used as a working document, rather than a restrictive document, is key. In that way you balance the logic of periodized coaching, while leaving room for episodic coaching and working towards the changing needs of your players.

Syllabi and Session Plans in Action

During the remainder of this chapter I will offer you various examples of syllabi and session plans and session plan templates from clubs, colleges, and professional academies all over the world. Like in the previous chapter, we will use the age-defined nature of the *Long Term Player Development Model*.

Stage 1 – The FUNdamental Phase

Ages 5 – 8 +/-

From the previous chapter, we noted that the focus of working with this age group is about exploring and discovering the game, developing movement skills, and helping young players fall in love with the game.

Sample Syllabus / Block of Work 5 – 8 Year Olds

Developing a syllabus for the five to eight-year-old age group is not an easy one. Considering the natural characteristics of these children, only a very basic coaching program can be designed and enforced. One of the most simplistic yet effective academy programs I have seen comes from a club playing in the English Championship. Although the club's first team is not in the Premier League, the academy has an excellent track record in producing players who have played at the highest level internationally, commanding transfer fees into the millions of pounds.

The syllabus runs over one season of *38 weeks*. During each week, there is a slightly different technical, tactical, physical and psychological focus. As these players are too young for tactics, this work simply involves "playing out from the back" and "through the thirds" which evolves from the club's possession-based philosophy. The psychological elements are simply based around confidence, commitment and emotional control.

The academy recognizes the importance, however, of concentrating more on the technical and physical development of the players. A breakdown of what type of work involved is below:

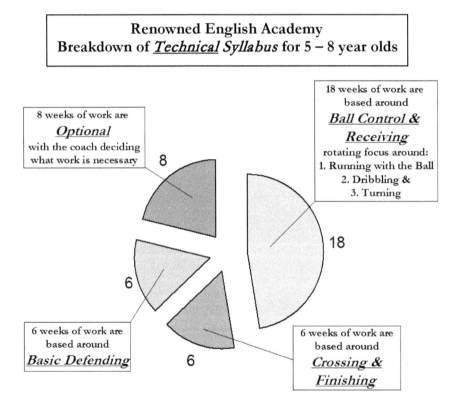

Renowned English Academy
Breakdown of *Technical Syllabus* for 5 – 8 year olds

8 weeks of work are
Optional
with the coach deciding
what work is necessary

18 weeks of work are
based around
Ball Control &
Receiving
rotating focus around:
1. Running with the Ball
2. Dribbling &
3. Turning

6 weeks of work are
based around
Basic Defending

6 weeks of work are
based around
Crossing &
Finishing

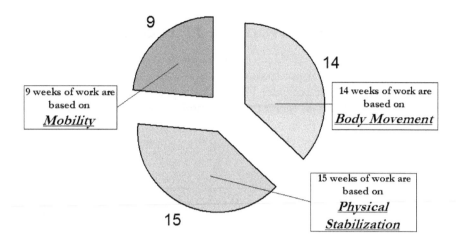

```
┌──────────────────────────────────────────────┐
│           Renowned English Academy             │
│  Breakdown of Physical Syllabus for 5 – 8 year olds │
└──────────────────────────────────────────────┘
```

9

14

9 weeks of work are based on *Mobility*

14 weeks of work are based on **Body Movement**

15 weeks of work are based on *Physical Stabilization*

15

Sample Session Plan 5 – 8 Year Olds

The session plan below is taken from the syllabus of an Italian Academy, adapted from the book *Youth Academy Training Program – New Methodology From Italian Serie 'A' Coaches*. Each session involves five activities over three phases.

Coaching Session Plan – Process From Italian Academy U5 – U8			
Timing	Phase	Content	Coaching Points
10 minutes	Initial Phase	**Warm-Up / Initial Game**	A team of 4 hold hands and try to tag dribbling players. Dribblers try to get to other side. Add cones for dribblers to collect en route
15 minutes		**Working Block – Technical & Individual Tactical**	Players dribble with a ball each. On coach's command they either stop or change direction using different parts of the foot. Add feints
10 minutes	Central Phase	**Technical Game – "The Canoe"**	Several 'rivers' are set out (as left). Players 'canoe' through the river & then shoot at goal. Shooting can be used to practice passing also
15 minutes		**Motor Game – "The Thief & the Guards"**	The 'thief' starts in the middle of two 'guards' & tries to 'escape' through either gate without being tagged. Start without then add a ball
10 minutes	Final Phase	**Final Game**	Players play a 2v2 free game

Stage 2 – The Learning to Train Phase

Ages 8 – 11 +/-

We remember, from the last chapter, that players at this age are living through their *Golden Age of Learning*. They have the ability to absorb lots of technical and physical improvement.

Sample Syllabus / Block of Work 8 – 11 Year Olds

The block of work below is a 12-week syllabus for players up to twelve years old and is taken from *The Football Coaches Library*. Although this is not from a famous academy, I like this example as, not only does each week have a specific focus, each week also links with the previous one, creating a solid, linked program of work. By linking topics with each other, it commits more to the players' long-term learning. So rather than jumping, for example, from defending to dribbling to possession, it works logically through topics, starting with basic understanding, then increasing the complexity.

Ball Control	Week 1 - Dribbling
	Week 2 - Running with the Ball
	Week 3 - Turning
Defending	Week 4 - Defending in Balance (1v1 / 2v2)
	Week 5 - Defending Out of Balance (1v2 & as a Team)
Passing	Week 6 - Possession
	Week 7 - Directional Passing
	Week 8 - Combination Play
Receiving	Week 9 - Receiving on the Floor
	Week 10 - Receiving in the Air
Goal Scoring	Week 11 - Finishing
	Week 12 - Shooting

Sample Session Plan 9 – 11 Year Olds

I must stress that the template below *only* is from Newcastle United. I contributed the session contained within. This template was shared on Twitter and I thought it was a simple yet thorough way to both plan soccer exercises, but also to consider communication, differentiation and a session evaluation is inbuilt.

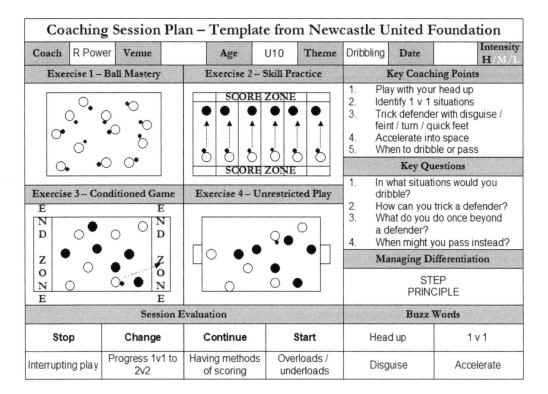

Coaching Session Plan – Template from Newcastle United Foundation										
Coach	R Power	Venue		Age	U10	Theme	Dribbling	Date		Intensity H/M/L

Exercise 1 – Ball Mastery	Exercise 2 – Skill Practice	Key Coaching Points
	SCORE ZONE ... SCORE ZONE	1. Play with your head up 2. Identify 1 v 1 situations 3. Trick defender with disguise / feint / turn / quick feet 4. Accelerate into space 5. When to dribble or pass

		Key Questions
Exercise 3 – Conditioned Game	Exercise 4 – Unrestricted Play	1. In what situations would you dribble? 2. How can you trick a defender? 3. What do you do once beyond a defender? 4. When might you pass instead?
E N D Z O N E ... E N D Z O N E		Managing Differentiation
		STEP PRINCIPLE

Session Evaluation				Buzz Words	
Stop	Change	Continue	Start	Head up	1 v 1
Interrupting play	Progress 1v1 to 2v2	Having methods of scoring	Overloads / underloads	Disguise	Accelerate

Stage 3 The Training to Train Phase

Ages 11 – 14 +/-

In the eleven to fourteen age groups, the focus is still heavily on technical work, although game understanding is of increasing importance. Coaches should be building on the ball manipulation and physical literacy work the players should have completed prior to eleven or twelve years old.

Sample Syllabus / Block of Work 11 – 14 Year Olds

The sample *technical syllabus* I have used here is actually the combination of two syllabi from two different English academies. The reason I chose two is simply because I do not feel that either are sufficient. The first syllabus is presented below in the titles. Each theme is used for six weeks. There is also a sixth block of work left blank for coaches to work on any aspect of the game they feel is required by their specific players. The second syllabus is presented below with bullet points, adding more detail to the type of work that ought to be covered.

1. Passing & Receiving	2. Running with the Ball & Dribbling	3. Shooting & Finishing
• Range / Variation of passing • To maintain possession • Passing under pressure • Off the front foot • With both feet • In attacking areas • To improve build up play • Passing combinations • Disguise of a pass • 1st touch – ground & aerial • Variation of control • Control under pressure • Weight of pass	• In attacking areas • Variation of running angles • Inside - shoot/outside - cross • To bring ball out of defense • Maintain control at pace • Opportunities to run with ball • Dribble in tight situations • Variation of turns & tricks • Feinting & Disguise • 1 v 1 work • Change of speed & direction • Skills & Tricks (creativity)	• Variation of technique: Inside / laces / volleys / heading • Variation of distances / angles / passes / crosses • Movement to create chances • Creative play to create shooting opportunities • Finishing in 1 v 1 situations • Finishing from through ball • Finishing under pressure • Timing of runs • Shot with back to goal • Finishing from crosses

4. Defending	5. Attacking
• Defend in 1v1 situations • Defending as unit • Defend crosses • Defensive heading • Dealing with overloads • Preventing shots / crosses / through balls • Pressing / Dropping • Delaying attacks • Dealing with pressure • Recovery runs • Challenging / Interceptions	• Creative play in the final 3rd • Attacking combinations • Importance of width & depth • Counter attacking • Switching Play • Build up play • Direct play • Maintaining possession • Movement in & out of possession • Committing defenders

Sample Session Plan 11 – 14 Year Olds

The session plan used for this age group is from Notts County, a Category 3 English Academy. Both coaches are former colleagues of mine and I consider them both to be students of the game. Both are currently taking their UEFA 'A' License. The template reflects the influence of the Premier League's *Elite Player Performance Plan*, with coaches challenged to consider the specific tactical, physical, mental, social and technical elements of player development. Each session is then evaluated with scores produced for the performance and application of each player.

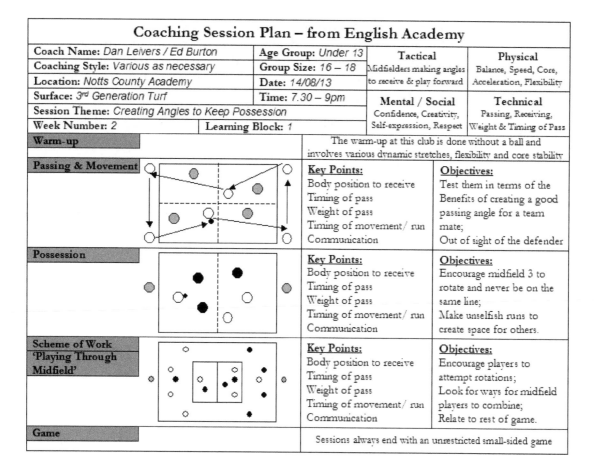

Coaching Session Plan – from English Academy				
Coach Name: *Dan Leivers / Ed Burton*	Age Group: *Under 13*	**Tactical** Midfielders making angles to receive & play forward	**Physical** Balance, Speed, Core, Acceleration, Flexibility	
Coaching Style: *Various as necessary*	Group Size: *16 – 18*			
Location: *Notts County Academy*	Date: *14/08/13*			
Surface: *3rd Generation Turf*	Time: *7.30 – 9pm*	**Mental / Social** Confidence, Creativity, Self-expression, Respect	**Technical** Passing, Receiving, Weight & Timing of Pass	
Session Theme: *Creating Angles to Keep Possession*				
Week Number: *2*	Learning Block: *1*			

Warm-up	The warm-up at this club is done without a ball and involves various dynamic stretches, flexibility and core stability		
Passing & Movement		**Key Points:** Body position to receive Timing of pass Weight of pass Timing of movement / run Communication	**Objectives:** Test them in terms of the Benefits of creating a good passing angle for a team mate; Out of sight of the defender
Possession		**Key Points:** Body position to receive Timing of pass Weight of pass Timing of movement / run Communication	**Objectives:** Encourage midfield 3 to rotate and never be on the same line; Make unselfish runs to create space for others.
Scheme of Work 'Playing Through Midfield'		**Key Points:** Body position to receive Timing of pass Weight of pass Timing of movement / run Communication	**Objectives:** Encourage players to attempt rotations; Look for ways for midfield players to combine; Relate to rest of game.
Game	Sessions always end with an unrestricted small-sided game		

Stage 4 – The Training to Compete Stage

Ages 14 – 16 +/-

We noted in the previous chapter that soccer starts to replicate the adult game at this age. The technical progression of players remains a central aspect of their development, but tactical issues and position-specificity take on a greater significance.

Sample Syllabus / Block of Work 14 – 16 Year Olds

One of the most interesting and thought-provoking schemes of work I have seen comes from the under-15 and 16 coaches at the Manchester United Academy. Former Manchester United Academy Coach, Mark Edwards, wonderfully presented the process. The syllabus has four main blocks of work that are taught in a logical order.

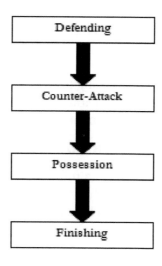

The logic behind the process was that, to play, you needed to be able to possess the ball and therefore, (1) methods of winning the ball back (defending) were prioritized. On the regaining of possession, the team then had to decide whether they could (2) counter-attack, or if not, how they could (3) keep possession. Eventually, either through a counter-attack or through sustained possession, the players needed to know how to (4) score goals (finish).

During his presentation, Edwards openly acknowledged that this process can be debated, and it was up to individual coaches to interpret and work to their own, justifiable methods.

Sample Session Plan 14 – 16 Year Olds

I observed the session plan below being delivered by an international youth coach working with an under-15 national team in Europe. It is a great example of using the whole-part-whole method that we discussed earlier in this book. The main theme of the session was to teach players how to defend deep (sometimes also known as defending 'later').

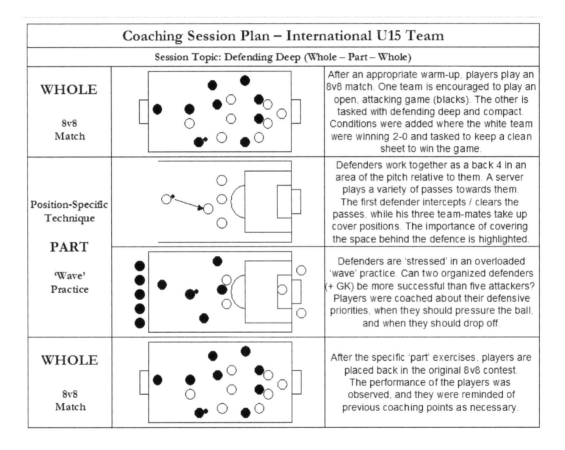

Stage 5 – The Training to Win Stage

Age 16 – 19 +/-

From ages 16 to 19, players need to start learning how to win games. For that reason, coaching can become a mixture of both a periodized syllabus and also episodic coaching. An increasing amount of time is spent on tactics and game understanding.

Sample Syllabus / Block of Work 16 – 19 Years Old

The six-week coaching segment below is from a full-time under-19 college soccer program. Like *The Football Coaches Library* example above, it shows that, not only are sessions linked, but are organized into technical and tactical chunks. There is also an allotted time for any necessary episodic coaching.

Sample Curriculum – U19 Soccer Academy					
Week	Topic	Monday Session	Tuesday Session	Thursday Session	Friday Session
1	Basic Possession	Technical	Tactical	Cool-down Analysis	Episodic Position-specific Physical
2	Playing Out From the Back	Technical	Tactical	Cool-down Analysis	Episodic Position-specific Physical
3	Defending Individual – small group	Technical	Tactical	Cool-down Analysis	Episodic Position-specific Physical
4	Pressing	Technical	Tactical	Cool-down Analysis	Episodic Position-specific Physical
5	Position-Specific DEFENDING	Technical	Tactical	Cool-down Analysis	Episodic Position-specific Physical
6	Mop-up week	Episodic	Episodic	Cool-down Analysis	Episodic Position-specific Physical

Sample Session Plan 16 – 19 Year Olds

The practice session below is taken from Brazilian club Atlético Mineiro, recorded by *World Class Coaching*. The specific age-group is the club's under-17 team. It shows an episodic approach to working with an older age group, and is the team's preparation session for a game the following day.

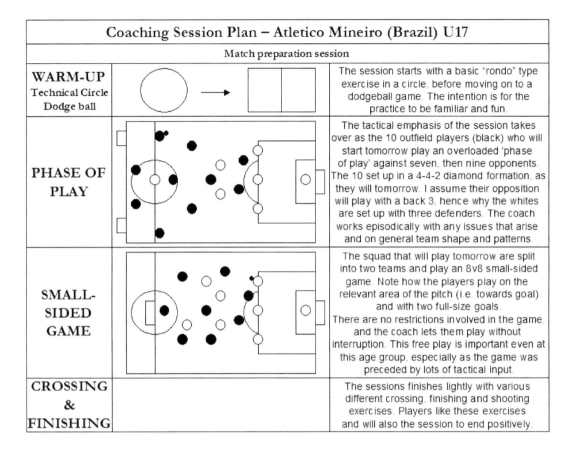

Coaching Session Plan – Atletico Mineiro (Brazil) U17		
Match preparation session		
WARM-UP Technical Circle Dodge ball		The session starts with a basic "rondo" type exercise in a circle, before moving on to a dodgeball game. The intention is for the practice to be familiar and fun.
PHASE OF PLAY		The tactical emphasis of the session takes over as the 10 outfield players (black) who will start tomorrow play an overloaded 'phase of play' against seven, then nine opponents. The 10 set up in a 4-4-2 diamond formation, as they will tomorrow. I assume their opposition will play with a back 3, hence why the whites are set up with three defenders. The coach works episodically with any issues that arise and on general team shape and patterns.
SMALL-SIDED GAME		The squad that will play tomorrow are split into two teams and play an 8v8 small-sided game. Note how the players play on the relevant area of the pitch (i.e. towards goal) and with two full-size goals. There are no restrictions involved in the game, and the coach lets them play without interruption. This free play is important even at this age group, especially as the game was preceded by lots of tactical input.
CROSSING & FINISHING		The sessions finishes lightly with various different crossing, finishing and shooting exercises. Players like these exercises and will also the session to end positively.

Conclusion

Regardless then of the varying methods of developing a philosophy, syllabus, or of individual session plans - having a clearly defined long / medium-term focus is imperative for all soccer coaches. Otherwise we will coach the same thing over and over again, or just butterfly around soccer topics, without considering long-term player development. Hopefully the examples above, bearing in mind that many, many more exist, will assist you in organizing your coaching to help your players reach peak performance.

Summary

- A soccer syllabus is an outline of what a coach wants players to learn, usually over the course of a season.

- There is no 'perfect' coaching syllabus. Even the coaching plans of top clubs will differ. Just because they differ, does not make them 'wrong'.

- Coaches should be able to justify their methods and the sessions they carry out with players.

- Traditional youth coaching sessions tend to be reactionary. However, 'periodized' coaching is best for young players. Episodic coaching becomes more justifiable once results become important.

- A syllabus should not be limiting. Use it as a working document that is open to change.

- The best coaches start from a coaching philosophy, and then plan their work in terms of short, medium and long-term objectives.

- 91% of the 96 European academies studied have a coaching philosophy. 75% work towards a coaching syllabus.

- Ajax of Amsterdam bases the development of their youth players around the *TIPS Model*.

- Creating your own coaching philosophy can be complicated, but is an evolutionary process.

Syllabi / Session Plan Summary

- 5 – 8 year olds – Renowned English Academy / Italian Academy

- 8 – 11 year olds – The Football Coaches Library / Newcastle United template

- 11 – 14 year olds – Combination of two English academies / Notts County FC Academy

- 14 – 16 year olds – Manchester United Academy / International Under-15 session

- 16 – 19 year olds – U19 College Academy / Atlético Mineiro Under 17 session

Real Coach Experience

Working Within a Syllabus

(Tom Johnson, U19 Academy Coach, Central College Nottingham; Performance Analyst, Derby County FC Academy)

In the past year I have been coaching a team where there has been a structured coaching syllabus in place to follow. I have found that this environment has helped me improve as a coach especially with the planning and delivery of my sessions. Preparing for my sessions has always been an aspect that I have seen as being very important. It underpins the success of the session you are delivering.

In the past I have been guilty of taking sessions where I have felt that I am under-prepared and this, I feel, has then shown during those sessions. Since I have been coaching with a structured coaching syllabus, it has allowed me to sit down with the other coaching staff and plan out what we are going to deliver in our sessions – sometimes even weeks in advance – rather than planning a session in the car en route to the club.

One of my roles with the team is to take them for an active recovery session the day after a game. This session can sometimes be a little 'lighter' than what may be expected at other times of the week, but this is an essential session in order to make sure that the players are recovering from games in the correct way so that they stay physically healthy throughout the season. It is in these sessions where I have been able to use the coaching syllabus and link it into an active recovery. If the topic during that particular week is switching play or creating space, I have been able to test my coaching skills by delivering a session that links directly to that week's topic.

Although there is a coaching syllabus in place, I still feel that is important to be able to implement my own coaching style on the sessions. As the players are training every day it is key that each coach adds their own style. I have found that this helps keep players enthusiastic and motivated. A new voice can be very refreshing for players.

Although the coaching syllabus is devised at the beginning of the season, there have been times when there has been a cause for change. In the days leading up to playing a team on a match day, I have been able to adapt the sessions to optimize the preparation for the game ahead. This has been the case a number of times this season. Therefore we have been able to focus our sessions around, for example, compactness of defence and counter-attacking. This has allowed us to swap and change certain topics of our coaching syllabus in accordance to our fixtures or the needs of the players.

9

Understanding Technical Development and Skill Acquisition

"Techniques learned by the player in isolation usually do not transfer to the game because the player has to essentially re-learn the skill within the ever changing context of the game. As a result it makes you wonder whether the skill would have been better taught within the game context in the first place." (Rick Fenoglio, Department of Exercise and Sport Science, Manchester Metropolitan University and co-founder of *Give Us Back Our Game*)

I am often asked the question "what is more important – technical or tactical training"? Although the question is quite simple, the answer is much more complex. Both are, in fact, interlinked. Technical ability forms the basis for everything a player wants to build on (assuming physical characteristics are in place and the player has the basic motor skills required to perform them). As wonderfully visualized by Rob Atkin in his blog article *Technique is Everything!?* "The wider the base, the taller the pyramid" – in other words, the more technically able the player (large base) the better the all-round player will be (the pyramid).

To answer the original question then, *the players' technical ability will determine their tactical performance.* For example, if you want to employ similar possession-based tactics used by the Spanish national team, the players firstly need to have the technical qualities to pass and receive. Add to that the ability to play quickly, play in tight areas, use different types of passes, pass 'safe-side'[1], use penetrative passes, etc. The receiver needs to have a good first touch, receive while on the move, while under pressure from defenders, and be able to see a 'picture' of what is around them. The other players then need to be able to support the ball, make off-the-ball runs, etc.

The same principle applies to teams that play a direct style of play. Although this style is considered less technically impressive, players still need to be able to: play longer passes, recognize areas to attack, have good aerial control (thigh, chest), hold off defenders, head, volley, make 'third-man' runs, utilise various crossing techniques, etc.

We therefore cannot simply talk about technical and tactical (or 'game sense') development in isolation from each other. They will link together more and more, especially as youth players grow older. Training practices therefore need to include elements of both, a principle we will talk a lot about over the rest of this chapter.

'Skill' Acquisition

To begin, a clear definition of 'technique' and 'skill' needs to be established, as both terms can be widely used in different ways across soccer. For example, a player like Ronaldo is considered 'technically excellent' based on his match performances. Freestyle soccer performers, such as Billy Wingrove, are considered to be 'skilful' as they can manipulate the ball with tricks and clever movements.

---

[1] 'Safe-side' is the term used when you want to pass the ball to the receiver on the opposite side of where the defender is. For example, if the defender is marking the player's right shoulder, the pass is played to the left. The defender therefore will find it more difficult to intercept.

Technique	Skill
Technique involves players and what they do with the ball (passing, shooting, defending, etc.). As a consequence, a 'technical practice' involves players practicing with the ball, but it is unopposed – i.e. the players complete the technique without any opposition.	A skill however is when a player can transfer technique into opposed situations. Therefore a 'skill practice' is one that involves opposition and is a more challenging situation.

> ## Sample 'Technical' Practice
> ## Real Madrid Academy 'Y' Practice

Iván Madrono Campos, an Academy coach at Real Madrid, contributed this technical practice to *Spanish Academy Soccer Coaching*.

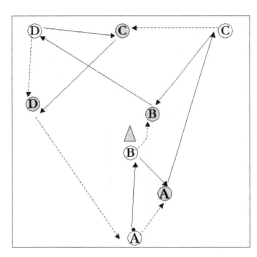

This technical practice is an unopposed, constant-type passing and receiving practice. Player A starts with the ball and passes to Player B. B then 'sets' the ball back for A to pass long to Player C. B, having spun off the mannequin, receives from C, and plays a first time pass to Player D. D plays a 'wall pass' with C and dribbles the ball back to the start. The practice begins again with the players having rotated positions.

**Sample 'Skill' Practice
The Spanish 'Rondo'**

The Rondo has recently been dubbed as the Spanish "secret weapon". Such is its influence, great Spanish international and Barcelona star Xavi Hernadez said of it: "Rondo, rondo, rondo. Every single day. It is the best exercise there is."

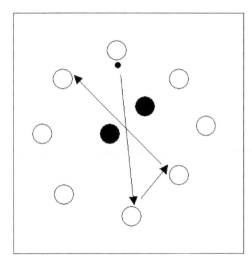

The basic premise of the rondo is that it involves a group of players looking to keep possession against outnumbered defenders. The players look to play a penetrative pass through the defenders if possible.

The example here shows an 8v2 situation, but any numbers and sized areas can theoretically work.

The exercise can even be adapted to involve tactical work, something we will look at in the next chapter.

During a recent conversation with Rahim Mohamed, recognized by *the National Soccer Coaches Association of America* as one of the "Top 30 Under 30" coaches in 2013/14 and founder of the free online coaching magazine *Coaching the Global Game*, he summed up the conflict quite nicely: "A technical player can perform an action on demand. A skilful player, however, can perform the technique under pressure." Mohamed went on to describe how he based lots of his early coaching on technical, unopposed practices, believing that they were the optimal way of improving players. On reflection, however, he found that the players, "were not always able to execute correct technique during the rigors of match play. The goal for me became about creating *skilful* players rather than *technical* players. In order to achieve this I had to modify my training sessions and the emphasis within sessions."

We have all heard players being accused of being unable to transfer their ability from training sessions into match situations, or transferring technique into *skill acquisition*. The concept of developing players' skill acquisition should be the primary role of the coach. Any talk of complicated tactics can only be fulfilled once players can transfer technique into skill acquisition and therefore affect live, random, chaotic soccer matches.

I would encourage any coach to read the short article *Practice, Instruction and Skill Acquisition in Soccer: Challenging Tradition* by Mark Williams and Nicola J Hodges.[2] The article criticizes traditional soccer coaching for an over-emphasis on technical rather than game-like, skilled practices and soccer research for the lack of study around skill acquisition in soccer compared to, say, physical development.

To fully understand the process of skill acquisition, we must examine what meaningful practice is, and the types of practices we are exposing our players to.

---

[2] This article was published in 2005 in *the Journal of Sport Sciences* and is available online.

Practice

We are all familiar with the old saying "practice makes perfect". In recent times this saying has evolved into "practice makes permanent". Practice, however, does not make 'perfect', nor does it make anything 'permanent'. What it does, though, is provide the vital ingredient in improving soccer performance – once practice is completed correctly.

Within certain circles, there is a war raging over the role of practice in the production of talented people – the *nature versus nurture* debate is alive and well. There have been some wonderful books released about the topic in recent years, most notably *The Talent Code* by Daniel Coyle, *Bounce* by Matthew Syed, *Outliers* by Malcolm Gladwell, and *The Complexity of Greatness* by Scott Barry Kaufman. When developing talent, lots of variables contribute to making an expert soccer player. Genetics, background, upbringing, influences, opportunity, love of the game, motivation, physical make-up, and many more are involved. Kaufman, quoting research from David Z. Hambrick and colleagues, notes however that practice contributes around 30% toward the success of a performer, by far the highest contributing factor. Vitally, it is practice that we, as coaches, can directly affect.

Guillem Balague, esteemed Spanish journalist and La Liga expert, has written several books, including one on the greatest soccer player of recent times – simply entitled *Messi*. In terms of any debate regarding practice versus natural talent, it is clear what side of the fence Balague sits, with the title of chapter six being "Leo is not a natural born genius. Nobody is". Stories from colleagues and coaches about Cristiano Ronaldo also highlight practice being the key ingredient to his success. In his article *Are Top Athletes Born or Made?* Mauro van de Looij reveals a tale from Dutch goalkeeper and former team mate of Ronaldo's at Manchester United, Edwin van der Sar. He quotes the goalkeeper as saying: "After training he was always practicing his free kick. If he needed a goalkeeper, to him I was the only option. If I asked him whether another goalkeeper could defend the goal during his free kick training he replied, 'I only want to train with the best so I can become the best'."

Top performers then, alongside motivation and many other factors, unsurprisingly put hour upon hour into practice. But how many hours are required for a youth soccer player to become expert? And how best can those hours be used?

10 Years; 10,000 Hours

One of the most interesting findings, discussed throughout the study of practice, and mentioned in various capacities in the works mentioned above, is the *10,000 Hour Rule*, often interpreted as the *10-Year Rule* (Simon and Chase, 1973). The theory is that any performer, whether in sport, music, science or any other field, needs 10,000 hours of practice to become an 'expert' in their field.

In *Team Sports and the Theory of Deliberate Practice*, Helsen, Starkes and Hodges presented their findings to support the notion that expert performers spend more time practicing. They scrutinized the practice history of Belgian professional, semi-professional and amateur players. At the point when players had been playing for 18 years, the professional players had accumulated 9,332 practice hours, semi-professionals 7,449, and the amateur players 5,079.

While there is significant evidence to back up the 10,000 Hour Rule, it *is not* and *cannot* be the only measure by which we develop youth soccer players. There are many examples of where, even after 10,000 hours of practice a soccer player or musician does not become an elite performer. There are also examples where an elite performer has not had 10,000 hours or 10 years of experience. As wonderfully summed up by Kaufman, "What has become clear is that the 10-year rule is not actually a rule, but an average with significant variation around the mean". In other words, using the measure of 10 years or 10,000 hours of practice is useful, but using it as a law or an exact science is dangerous, particularly if the practice involved in that time-period is flawed.

On Daniel Coyle's official website – www.thetalentcode.com – Coyle recalls a conversation with the head of a national soccer association regarding coaches' adoption of the 10,000 Hour Rule: "It's absolutely nuts. Coaches are tracking practice hours and the athletes are clocking in and out with time cards like they're working on an assembly line. There's no ownership, no creativity." Coaches, they found, were *measuring quantity rather than quality* by counting practice hours.

The greatest problem with this rule is that it has tried to quantify expertise. It has attempted to put a number on something that is a far more complicated process. On the back of its popularization, coaches began to count and work towards a 'magic number'. Coaching sessions became longer and more frequent without ever considering the *real quality* of the practice. When I started my current coaching job, coaching sessions lasted for two hours. However, after 80 minutes or so, we needed to finish. As the sessions were 30 or 40 minutes too long, the quality of teaching and learning involved diminished rather than increased. Incidentally, a typical session at the academy at Barcelona lasts around 70 minutes. Although this may seem short, the practice is a purposeful, high quality, high intensity *deliberate* 70 minutes.

'Deliberate' Practice

Deliberate practice, known as *purposeful practice* by Syed, was made popular by researcher Anders Eriksson in the 1990s. Eriksson and his fellow researchers found that the main difference between expert performers and the rest was *not the time they spent in practice hours*, but the amount of time they spent in *deliberate practice*. The cornerstone of the theory is that it moves away from the *quantity of practice* and shifts to the *quality of practice*. We all appreciate the concept of practice improving soccer players, but with deliberate practice, we are challenged to make the most of whatever contact time we have got with players.

Think of a young musician learning to play a song, let's say on a piano. They will attempt to play a new song and, inevitably, hit a snag. This may be a particular sequence of notes or chords that they cannot master immediately. They therefore isolate the particular section of music they are struggling with, and practice it intently and purposefully. Expert musicians will not just attempt it once and walk away. They will persevere, to the point where it is almost painful (and probably even more painful for those listening!) and frustrating. They may slow the sequence down in an attempt to master it before speeding it back up again. Once they 'get it', they will fit the piece back into the whole song and start again.

'Myelination'

Daniel Coyle first introduced me to *myelin* in his wonderful book *The Talent Code*. When humans learn, the brain creates new neural pathways that grow stronger with practice. As these pathways become stronger they are insulated in a white substance called myelin, which essentially protects the new learning. So, when a soccer player is learning a new skill, he starts to build a new neural pathway. When he practices it, this pathway strengthens and, with enough *deliberate practice*, the pathway is further wrapped in layer upon layer of myelin. A particularly successful friend and colleague of mine openly calls his coaching technique "myelination".

Players engaging in deliberate practice produce myelin more quickly, more strongly, and more effectively. The FA's *The Future Game* sums up its impact nicely: "Performers at the pinnacle of their sport have invested a significant amount of time in 'deliberate' practice over many years. 'Deliberate' practice requires focus and concentration and not just merely taking part."

With that sentence in mind, question whether your players are actively, purposefully involved in your training sessions, or whether they are simply "taking part". Is there a real focus on learning a skill under circumstances that will challenge and stress them? Or are they set up in neat lines and queues, kicking a ball, then falling back to the end of the line? To develop and improve, these players must be stressed and placed in 'hostile' environments. The foremost of these hostile environments is the game itself and, further down the line, the practices we use in our training sessions.

There must be a clear balance, however, in how players are stressed, without this tipping over into frustration, or even anger and resentment. If you find this occurring, the job of the coach is to change or modify the practice, offer words of encouragement and soften this frustration.

Types of Practices

If I am a high jumper, the variables of my sport are pretty much the same. They are the same whether I am competing at an Olympic Games, European Championships or whether I am practicing at the local athletics centre. It does not make a huge difference whether I am jumping in London, Paris, Sydney, Johannesburg or New York City. In my practices, I can set the bar to whatever height I want to replicate; exactly what I will face in a competition. I can measure the paces in my run up down to the very inch and I will use the same run up in a competitive situation. Aside from the extra pressure of performing in a contest, or extreme weather conditions, I can replicate competition accurately.

Soccer however is a chaotic game. It is a random game. Its variables, unlike the high jump, are endless. Replicating precisely an entire match, or even a moment of high action soccer is very difficult if not impossible.

Compromise and the 'Real Game'

Any practice that you put on for your players that is anything less than an unrestricted 11v11 game will contain elements of compromise with the 'real game'. That does not mean that it is simply enough to play 11v11 games within your practice sessions. In a top-level soccer match, each player will spend only about two minutes with the ball over a 90-minute game. Therefore to produce technically excellent or 'skilful' players, our practices need to involve players having many more frequent contacts with the ball. Your practice sessions therefore require two things – players regularly playing with a ball, in situations where these contacts are as game realistic as possible.

All the exercises you use in your soccer practices and training sessions *will contain a compromise with the real game*. The FA call this a 'trade-off' in their youth-specific training modules. To highlight, below I have I have included two very common practices, and detailed some of the compromise involved.

2v1 Attacking Exercise
Two attacking players try to score against one defender, plus goalkeeper

---

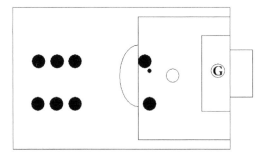

Compromise
The intent of this 2v1 exercise is to give attacking players lots of success. However, in the 'real game', attackers are more likely to be outnumbered, most of the time. Eventually these attackers will need to be able to be effective when *they* are outnumbered.

Zone Game
Players are placed in a small-sided game but are 'locked' into zones

---

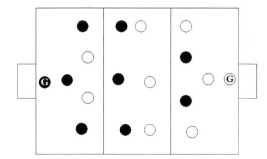

Compromise
Locking players into defined zones limits their movement. An integral part of soccer is that players have freedom of movement. A modern full-back, for example, needs to choose when he attacks, therefore restricting him to the defensive zone is counter-productive.

In the previous chapter we discussed the need for coaches to be able to *justify* the content of their practice sessions. In certain circumstances you could easily justify the use of any of the above, but *recognizing and being comfortable with the inherent compromise or trade-off is essential*. In both circumstances, to reduce the trade-off and give players a more game realistic challenge, the practices need to be progressed quickly. So, exercise one would involve more defenders than attackers, and exercise two would take limits off the where players are allowed to move.

Our practices can essentially be broken down into three categories – constant, variable and random ones. Within them there will always be an element of compromise – although some will contain a larger 'trade-off' than others.

'Constant' Practices

Constant-type practices are ones where players practice the *same technical movement repeatedly*. These moves will generally be practiced over the same distance and conditions, and the exercise will be unopposed. Because the emphasis is on the repetition of a specific technique, constant practices are best used to help players learn a new technique or develop a specific technique further. Often these practices are called 'blocked practices', or more disparagingly 'line drills' or 'cone-to-cone' practices given the static nature of their content.

Next, is a classic example of a constant practice, made famous at Ajax.

Sample 'Constant' Practice
The Ajax 'Square' (with progression)

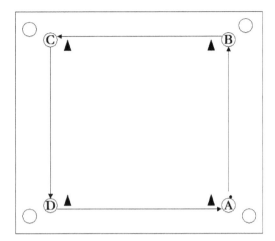 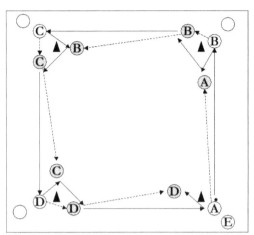

The practice starts with player A. As he is about to pass, player B makes a movement away from his cone in preparation to receive. A plays the ball, follows his pass and takes B's place. Players B and C replicate the exercise, and so on. The ball is rotated around the square until the coach either progresses the exercise or deems that the players have practiced enough.

The intent to pass the ball around the square remains. However, rather than simply passing and following the pass, the players start to combine with each other. So, A passes to B who, like previously, has made his movement to receive. B then makes a 'wall pass' off A before passing to C. This continues around the square as before. A second ball can be added when the exercise requires it.

In this exercise, the Ajax players pass and move in pre-determined ways. The passes are over the same distance and players make virtually the same runs. Repetition is the focus. If you were using this practice with younger players, you would be giving them lots of attempts to master the technique of passing – with older players, like the senior professionals at Ajax, the purpose of the exercise would be to refine their passing technique.

Again there is an evident compromise with the real game as, in the game, players do not wait beside cones and more often than not, do not simply 'follow their pass'.[3] Other techniques, even different forms of passing, are not evident.

'Variable' Practices

Unlike constant practices, variable ones start to introduce more decision-making and become more closely relevant to the game. There may be a focus on one particular technique, but other techniques will be required to solve the problems set by the coach. The moves are not as pre-defined as they are in constant practices.

---

[3] Players being constantly put into practices where they simply pass and follow their pass is a particular bugbear of mine. I would challenge anyone to watch any level of soccer match and find any evidence of players routinely following their pass.

Variable practices may contain interference or opposition. In the case of the exercise below from the Under-19 England squad, there is no opposition, yet there is interference, unlike in the case of the Ajax Square above.

Sample 'Variable' Practice
England Under 19 Passing Exercise

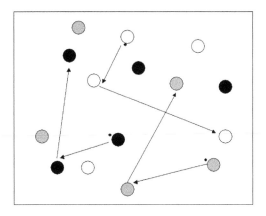

15 players are split into three colours. Each team has a ball and must pass randomly to teammates. The practice is progressed to where the passer must pass to a different colour, and further to pass to a different colour he received from.

Although there is no opposition in the above practice, it does contain interference. As the players can move randomly around the area, they 'interfere' with others simply by getting in the passer's way. This may cause the passing player to change his technique, or the height, speed and/or weight of the pass. The players decide how best to solve the problem posed by this interference. In certain circumstances, he may choose to delay the pass until a direct passing lane opens up, dribble to create an opening, or use a lofted pass. These are all problems that a passing player would face in a real game. The practice can be made even more variable by adding defenders and opposition.

So, although this practice is variable, and therefore links to the real game more efficiently, there is still a compromise involved. For example, there is no opposition so defending considerations are not involved, and other techniques, beyond passing and receiving, are not used with any frequency.

'Random' Practices

Random practices start to mimic the game a lot more closely than variable practices, and immeasurably more than constant ones. Random practices will generally be in the form of game-based exercises, and will involve players playing against opponents. The set-up and opposition add more interference and make the practices more game-realistic.

The learner resource book for the FA, *Module 2: Developing the Practice* course contains a wonderful quote to support the use of random practices: "Practice is a rehearsal and any rehearsal should be a 'word for word' run through of the event. Football practices should therefore replicate the things that are likely to happen in a match or the techniques / skills that are going to be needed."

The sample random practice, below, is taken from a document produced by the coaches at Chelsea Football Club's Development Centre.

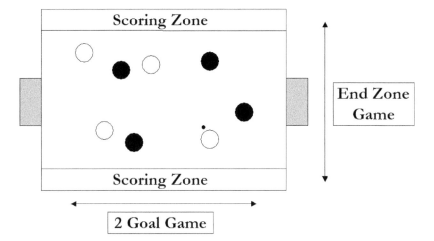

This random exercise is the blending of two games. Two teams play against each other in a 'normal' small-sided 2-goal game. On the coach's command, the game changes to the end zone game, where players must play a pass into the scoring zone for a team-mate to receive. Randomness is therefore evident, and through the coach changing the type of game intermittently, even more chaos is added.

Deciding What Type of Practice to Use

All three types of practices have their strengths and shortcomings, depending on the nature of the players in your session and what stage of their development they are at. The table below may help you in deciding what types of practices to employ.

	Strengths	Shortcomings
Constant	• Useful when learning new techniques	• Players required to make very few decisions
	• Useful when refining existing techniques	• Highly dependent on *explicit* learning
	• Lots of specific repetition	• Does not reflect the chaotic nature of the game
	• Lots of *short-term* success for players	• *Long-term* effectiveness is poor
	• Can be used to pinpoint specific technical issues	• Communication between players is seldom required
	• Controlled environment	• Overused with no technical detail present
	• Effective when dealing with lots of players at once	• Coaches use them simply because it makes them look organized

	Strengths	Shortcomings
Variable	• Useful for refining and improving technique • Adds elements of decision-making • Replicates the 'real' game more closely • Contains more variety than constant practices • Involves balance of *implicit* and *explicit* learning	• Ineffective if the player is unable to perform the required technique • Players achieve less short-term success than constant practices • Not as closely related to the game as random practices
Random	• Reflects the chaotic nature of soccer • Players need to make lots of decisions • Players have to utilize a vast array of skills • *Implicit* learning is inherent • Long-term learning is more effective • Problems faced are able to be transferred into the 'real' game • Aid players' muscle and 'game memory'	• Harder to pin-point specific technical detail • Players may not achieve success immediately • May look messy and disorganized

Making your Practices 'Deliberate'

For skill acquisition, we need to involve our players in practices that reflect the randomness of the game, by using far more game-like, variable or random practices. In these exercises, players have the opportunity to practice certain aspects of the game, but they are under more 'stress', and have to make more decisions. These practices involve opponents and more variables that players have to deal with to play soccer effectively. Suddenly our practices involve the game-specificity that aids players' muscle memory, goes further to strengthen neural pathways, and induces a greater production of myelin. Coaches will produce more technically able players, who can also deal with the randomness of soccer.

Herein lies the problem with an *over-emphasis on constant practices*. To make it abundantly clear, constant practices have their place. At times we need an exercise like the Ajax Square to pinpoint specific technical work or to introduce a concept to our players. Eventually however, coaches need to integrate this into purposeful, opposed, random activities.[4]

---

[4] How often have you heard players saying "Yeah…but can you do that in a match"? Unwittingly, they are pointing out that while it is one thing completing a skill in a stress-free, unopposed situation, it is quite another to be able to

To make your practices more deliberate, consider the following:

Choose Variable / Random over Constant Practices

In recent years there has been a *huge shift in the coaching community away from constant, static practices.* Although they allow for lots of repetition, their relevance to the chaotic nature of the game is limited. Players are required to make very few decisions, if any at all. The 'problem' they are required to solve is a very basic one and does not have the chaos present that the game of soccer inherently contains.

Coaches have the tendency to gravitate towards constant practices as they are easy to control and even look good, "preferring the security of grid and drill type practices to the instability presented by conditioned games and match-play." (Williams and Hodges, 2005). A coach once admitted to me that he would organize constant sessions so that observers would think he was organized and in control. By doing this consistently he was exposing his players to 'drills' that involved infrequent decision-making and problem-solving, thus reducing their ability to gain vital game understanding.

I once heard a story about Cesc Fabregas' first training session at Arsenal as a teenager. Whether the story is true or not I am not certain but the message is a valuable one for coaches nonetheless. During a constant passing practice, the Spaniard was asked to move away from the mannequin who was 'marking' him so he could receive the ball and play the next pass. Even after numerous attempts, he never made the exaggerated movement the coach desired! After several interventions the coach challenged Fabregas as to why he was not complying. His reply was something like: "The mannequin cannot tackle me, it cannot move, so I only need a small space to control the ball and pass it. I do not need to make a big movement to complete this exercise!"

While this answer might seem quite petulant and pedantic, it is very realistic. Players, and people in general, will always look to solve problems the easiest way. The problem presented to Fabregas on this occasion was to receive the ball from one player and pass it to another, under no opposed pressure, other than a static mannequin. His solution was the easiest one – make a small movement to receive, avoid the mannequin and play the pass.

Soccer is not the only sport wrestling with the questions regarding the benefits and consequences of using certain types of practices. *Volleyball Canada*, for example, is unequivocal in their support for practices that exist on the random end of the spectrum, even though volleyball contains far less variables than soccer. They acknowledge the fact that random practices can be more difficult for players in the short-term, but support the view that they assist with long-term development and learning of the game:

> "There is strong evidence that random practice, while sometimes associated with inferior performance in the short term, results in superior performance in the long term. In other words, when constant practice is used to learn a skill or task, the performance during the session is often better compared to random practice, but the latter promotes better skill retention and overall performance in the long run."

I recently spoke to Gerard Jones, an English academy coach and advocate of variable and random practices in his coaching. His passion was obvious when I asked him about the use of 'line drills' or 'cone to cone' practices, echoing the earlier sentiments of Cesc Fabregas:

> "A cone doesn't move, a cone doesn't teach a player to make decisions on time and space constraints, nor does a cone help a player think about compromise. For example, if I pass here what am I risking? Or when defending, if I close down here, what am I leaving behind me? Can I press or should I hold space? These, amongst many others, are the types of questions players are faced with and have to make very quickly, often subconsciously because of

---

do it within the madness of a free-flowing game. Coaches therefore need to place players in these hostile, random situations to test their technique when it really matters.

limitations in time. Yet we all, as coaches, at some point have been guilty of putting players in practices that don't allow them to make these decisions – i.e. constant line drills."

The evidence and opinion gathered then is quite unambiguous in relation to choosing practice-types that replicate the game, rather than those that take place in straight lines without any game-specificity.

Whole-Part-Whole

Whole-part-whole type coaching sessions are the soccer version of learning to play a song on an instrument using deliberate practice. The players attempt to play the whole tune (the 'whole' game), take specific parts out to improve (the 'part'), before attempting to play the 'whole' song again but with improvement.

Keeping Score

We noted earlier in this book that young players love competition – in fact all players love competition. I recently saw a picture of five members of the Liverpool first-team squad jumping with elation at winning a training-ground head-tennis competition! Using scoring methods in your sessions helps to focus and get the best out of players. It becomes more fun, engaging and increases the intensity and competitiveness of the session. As an example, I have included below a traditional 'keep ball' possession-type exercise, which can easily be adapted to involve keeping score, beyond the conventional method of counting the team's passes and equating them to a point.

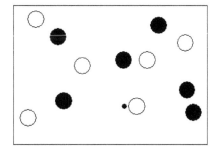

Traditional 'Keep Ball' Exercise

I do have certain issues with this traditional practice, although it is widely used across the amateur and professional game. For me, it is like asking basketball players to play a game, then taking the baskets away. Yes, the practice helps players to keep the ball, but compromises the real game as there is no way of scoring. At some point when keeping possession, there must be a decision as to whether there is an opportunity to score a goal. Also, without a goal or method of scoring, the only way the practice ends is with a player giving the ball away! So a team can hypothetically maintain a sequence of one-hundred passes, but it will only end with a negative - giving the ball away! If one team does really well and keeps possession for long periods, coaches direct irk at the team working to get it back. By adding a scoring method, players can achieve real success, and the inevitable giving the ball away is not emphasized so highly.

Alternatives to Include Scoring Methods

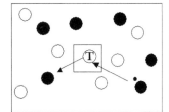 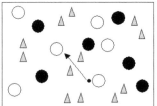 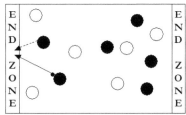

This game involves using a central target player to score. T could be a midfield player who has to receive and pass out to a teammate.

Using small gates as goals means there are constant decisions being made as to whether a player can pass to score, or pass to maintain possession.

This is particularly useful for penetrative passing work. Players have an end to attack and defend and can work on passing and also the timing of runs.

Poor Practice

At my current training centre we hire out our artificial surface to countless numbers of clubs to train under floodlights. I often stay on and watch. The session outlined in the first column below is one I have witnessed over and over again. Consider if the practice is purposeful and deliberate, or whether the players are simply "taking part".

Activity / Practice / Exercise	Time	Possible Justification?	Compromise or 'trade-off' with real game	'Deliberate' Alternatives
Warm-up with 2 or 3 laps of the training area	5 – 10 minutes	Players are adequately warmed-up	No ball involved No soccer player has ever run at the same speed over the same distance for several hundred meters	Use a warm-up game that *involves a ball*, changing direction, and which involves multidirectional movements that are sometimes slow, fast and medium
Static stretches with players in a circle	5 minutes	Players need to stretch before activity	Dynamic stretches[5] are required to replicate soccer movements	Within the warm-up game, disperse dynamic stretches throughout (and static stretches if required individually – some players feel they need certain static stretches to feel good).

---

[5] The use of 'dynamic' stretches will be explained in chapter 11

Activity / Practice / Exercise	Time	Possible Justification?	Compromise or 'trade-off' with real game	'Deliberate' Alternatives
A series of straight line sprints over anything from five to 30 meters	10 – 15 minutes	Sprints are an integral part of soccer It gets players 'fit'	Sprinting in soccer is not just done in straight lines. It involves changing direction and over varying distances. Sprinting is only a small percentage of the movements completed by players in games	The warm-up game can easily include some sharp, multidirectional sprints at the end
A constant 'line-drill' practice with players waiting their turn in queues	15 minutes	Players are organized and can learn, refine, or practice technique	Constant drills involve little decision-making, without the randomness involved in soccer	Use a variable or random exercise that involves decision-making, problem-solving and which is more game relevant
A shooting exercise involving a long line of players, taking their turn to shoot, then rejoining the back of the queue	10 minutes	Coach can pinpoint specific technical errors Players practice shooting Players love it!	Players shoot from the same angle, distance, and without pressure Distance is often too far for younger players Players in reality have very few attempts The coach has more touches than all the players combined!	A shooting game that involves opposition, an overload of defenders, shooting from various distances, angles and under differing pressures
A conditioned game, normally restricting players to 2 touches	What-ever time remains!	Two touches make players pass and move the ball quickly	Soccer involves using as many touches as are needed. It might to two, it might be one or multi-touch	Use an unrestricted game. Change the shape, size or emphasis of game if necessary

What a waste of an hour! When you consider the session outlined in the first column, there is virtually no evidence of the practice session being purposeful or deliberate. Players merely take part, have very little contact with the ball, and are stressed infrequently. The first three exercises are without a ball and involve very few movements that are even relevant to soccer. The players arguably spend more time forming, joining and rejoining queues than they do being involved with a ball!

On occasion any of the above could have *some* justification as part of the soccer session, but the popularity of this type of work suggests that it is seen as the 'norm' and thoroughly acceptable to do on a regular basis. It is not.

Other Methods of Technical Training

There are many 'other' methods of technical training and skill acquisition, some of which we will examine now.

Small-Sided Games

Small-sided games are a great way of immersing your players in game-related, skill-based training (once the numbers of those involved lends itself to players being in and around the ball consistently). These games allow players to acquire skill in situations that replicate the game. By 'conditioning' these games, you can help players practice one technique or aspect of the game more repetitively than others. A condition for example would be that players can only score using their non-preferred foot (weaker foot) or the opposition score is reset to zero if you score with a header. Particular players can be confined to particular areas of the pitch. You can use two goals, three goals, four goals or even six! You can outnumber one team or always restart games from a corner-kick. There are literally hundreds of ways to condition a game to tease out any particular outcome you may want – and conveniently, there are dozens of specific documents available for free online to help you come up with ideas!

There are, however, negative impacts when using conditioned games. There can be huge trade-offs or compromises with the real game. In real match play, for example, you take a shot with whatever foot is appropriate, scoring with a header gives you no extra advantages, and there are two goals in the middle of each end. All of which have implications for players' decision-making and actions. The *coach must carefully consider the use of conditioned games*, and what conditions are enforced. I have seen far too many teams and players conditioned to "two-touch" in every training session. Therefore if players need a third touch to complete a skill successfully it cannot happen, leaving little room for dribbling, and flair players become non-existent.

Up to 10 years of age[6] 4 v 4 games can be particularly beneficial. The *Cologne Study on Small-Sided Games*, researched through the Deutschland Fussball Bund and the University of Cologne, concluded that the use of this type of small-sided soccer is "a must for technical and basic tactical development", as did the independent *Small-Sided Games Study of Young Football (Soccer) Players in Scotland*, conducted by the University of Abertay, Dundee.

In the mid 2000s, Manchester Metropolitan University and Manchester United carried out a pilot study around the use of 4 v 4 in their games program. The club based all their under-9 and under-10 games on a four game format of 4 v 4. Their aim was "to optimize the 'window of opportunity' that exists for skill development". The 4 v 4 program, compared to the 8 v 8 equivalent produced the following results:

---

[6] 4 v 4 games can also be worthwhile for older players. Four players is the minimum amount you can use to reflect options in an 11 v 11 game, i.e. players have the ability to play backwards, sideways or forwards, something that 3 v 3 and below does not allow.

- 135% more passes

- 260% more scoring attempts

- 500% more goals scored

- 225% more 1 v 1 encounters

- 280% more dribbling skills (tricks)

Match day games for the younger age-groups were set up as follows:

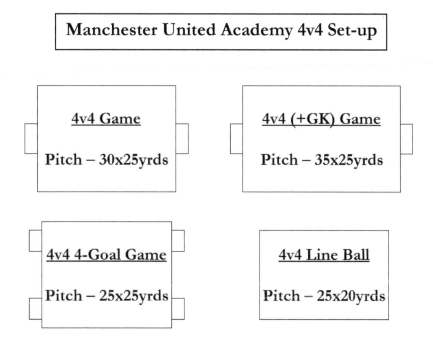

Manchester United Academy 4v4 Set-up

4v4 Game

Pitch – 30x25yrds

4v4 (+GK) Game

Pitch – 35x25yrds

4v4 4-Goal Game

Pitch – 25x25yrds

4v4 Line Ball

Pitch – 25x20yrds

Futsal

Futsal is a variant of a small-sided game that has its origins in South America, as do alternative versions of the game like 'futebol de salso'. Directly translated from Spanish, 'futsal' means 'room football (soccer)'. It is played indoors in a 5-a-side format. The pitch is a hard court with boundary lines, rather than rebound walls. The ball is smaller, heavier and has a reduced bounce.

A section of Coyle's *The Talent Code*, also quoted in Syed's *Bounce*, sums up futsal and its impact on youth player development wonderfully:

"One reason [for the success of futsal] lies in the math. Futsal players touch the ball far more often than soccer players – six times more often per minute... The smaller, heavier ball demands and rewards more precise handling – as coaches point out, you can't get out of a tight spot simply by booting the ball downfield.

Sharp passing is paramount: the game is all about looking for angles and spaces and working quick combinations with other players. Ball control and vision are crucial, so that when futsal players play the full-size game, they feel as if they have acres of space in which to operate... As Dr Miranda [professor of football at the University of São Paolo] summed up, 'No time plus no space equals betters skills. Futsal is our national laboratory of improvisation'."

Much of the justification of the use of futsal in the development of young players comes from the testimonies of notable players who have grown up with the game:

"In Futsal you have to think quickly and play fast. It's a great environment in which to learn." Zico, Brazilian legend

"Futsal is an extremely important way for kids to develop their skills and understanding of the game. My touch and my dribbling have come from playing Futsal." Ronaldinho

"I played [futsal] from the age of 9 until I was 16 when I had to stop to go on with my football career. It improved my speed and dribbling." Deco, former Portuguese star

"Futsal was important in helping to develop my ball control, quick thinking, passing... also for dribbling, balance, concentration." Pelé

"We need to take advantage of what Futsal has to offer – namely the lightning speed with which it is played." Luis Scolari, World Cup winning coach

As well as taking the word of some of soccer's greats, it is also very important to quantify the impact of futsal on technical development. To do this, the Football Association of Ireland undertook a study, taking four players and assessing their performance in futsal compared to 7v7 small-sided soccer. This was presented in the FAI's *Futsal Development Programme* document. The players were studied under the following headings:

- Number of successful ball controls
- Number of successful passes
- Number of successful dribbles
- Number of successful 'tricks'
- Number of goal attempts
- Number of goals scored
- Number of regained possessions.

All players had significantly more successful ball controls, passes, dribbles, goal attempts and possession regains in futsal compared to 7 v 7. Three of the four players had considerably more successful 'tricks' and goals scored. Only one player completed fewer tricks and scored fewer goals when playing futsal rather than the 7-a-side format.

Coerver® Ball Mastery

The Coerver coaching method is self-proclaimed as "the world's number 1 soccer skills teaching method" according to their official website. Although the Coerver brand details six specific aspects of the game, I would suggest that it has become most famous for their work in the areas of ball mastery and 1v1 moves. In these sections, Coerver teaches over 100 ball mastery techniques, before specifying 43 different 1v1 'moves' to enable players to take on and beat their opponents. The 43 specific moves are sub-divided into three areas - feints, stops & starts, and changes of direction. The Coerver method is openly championed by many youth soccer development experts such as Gérard Houllier and René Muelensteen.

Critics of the model will point out that the use of a formal training method to 'coach' players to play with flair is somewhat of a contradiction. The whole basis for flair and creativity is that it is unique. Nobody taught Maradona how to do the 'Maradona' move, nor did anyone teach Cruyff how to do a 'Cruyff turn' – they invented them themselves, in an environment that allowed them to. In other words, for a player to become creative with a soccer ball, he needs the environment to try different things, unique things, without pressure, the fear of failure or a prescribed set of moves. Critics will then also identify that many Coerver exercises are static practices that involve standing in queues with players waiting their turn.

Again we see there is a huge 'trade-off' between these exercises and the 'real' game. For example, while lots of 1v1 exercises will improve a player's ability to attack (and defend) a player, this eventually needs to expand to involve other players to allow for relevant decision-making. Indeed I have a colleague who will never coach dribbling in a 1v1 situation as, according to him, "A massive part of the concept of dribbling is passing. An option to pass *has* to be a part of any dribbling session. A player must then decide whether his best option is to take a player on and dribble, or whether the best option is to pass."

Nonetheless, the Coerver method, or variants of it, have their place in the development of a soccer player, particularly younger ones. The practices are heavily weighted towards technical development, and allow players lots and lots of touches and contacts with the ball. It contributes to the development of motor skills - challenging players' agility, balance, coordination and speed – all key concepts when looking to maximize the development of players prior to puberty.

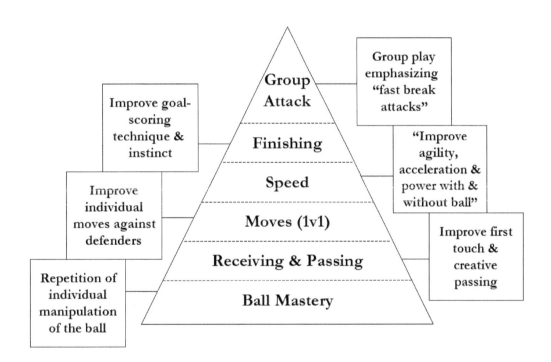

Technical Circuits

A technical circuit is as obvious as it sounds. It involves practicing lots of different types of techniques – in bite-sized chucks – in a rotational fashion. They keep players engaged as they involve the ball and activities are constantly changing. I have seen several very interesting technical circuit / carousel-type practice methods over the years. One of the most interesting ones I have seen is the Bolton Wanderers Player-Centred Technical Circuit.

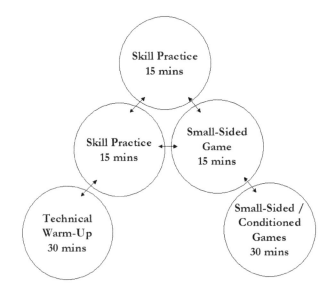

Bolton Wanderers Technical Circuit (Ages 9 – 14)

The whole group completes a warm-up that is based on ball mastery and the completion of tricks, turns, etc. Following this, the group is split in two and rotate around the following:

- Skill Practice 1 – Different variations of 1v1 exercises. The program favours the use of 1v1

- Skill Practice 2 – This is open to the interpretation of the coach, but will be a different theme than the rest of the circuit. At times, a functional practice is used

- Variants of 3v3 or 4v4 games

The group then comes back together for 30 minutes of 3v3 or 4v4 conditioned games, which are again open to the interpretation of the coach.

A technical circuit does not have to take place over an entire session, it may simply involve one part of the session, like the technical warm-up from Athletic Bilbao that follows.

Athletic Bilbao Academy Warm-Up Technical Circuit

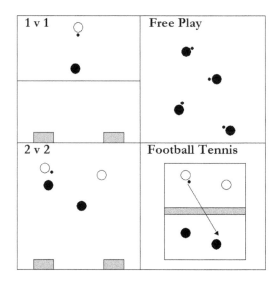

The above technical circuit was contributed to *Spanish Academy Soccer Coaching* by Athletic Bilbao academy coach, Jon Moreno Martínez. Each section lasts for five minutes and is part of the players' technically heavy warm-up – something far more productive than having players run laps of a pitch! All players rotate around the circuit completing 1 v 1 and 2 v 2 attacking and defending exercises, a soccer tennis match to practice ball control, aerial passing and heading, and a 'free-play' area where players can dribble, manipulate the ball and be creative.

Game Intelligence

Commentators and those working in soccer use the term 'game intelligence' quite frequently. They refer to Steven Gerrard for example, and the fact that, when out of possession, he turns his head (or 'checks his shoulders') a considerable number of times to assess what is going on around him. By looking, Gerrard is building a picture of what he can do once he receives possession, what to avoid, what team-mate is free, where he can drive forward, whether he needs to pass backwards, etc.

Game intelligence often refers to skills around technique, such as awareness and vision. The main premise of this type of training is to get players to think about more than just the ball. The brand *Soccer Eye-Q*, for example, calls their training model "cognitive conditioning" and uses the strap line "See more. Think quicker. Play better."

Below is a session from Wayne Harrison of *Soccer Awareness*, which is based around improving players' peripheral vision. This video is available on YouTube.[7]

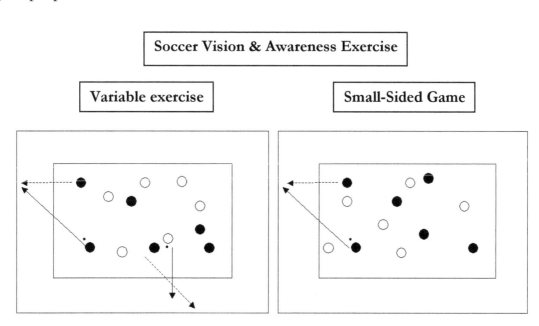

Similar to the England training exercise earlier, the group is split into two teams and start by passing the ball between them, then passing to the alternate team. Players are then tasked with identifying a player making an 'off-the-ball' run out of the area. The player in possession must see this run, then execute a pass to meet the run of the player. If this is missed, the player comes back into the grid to carry on. The premise is to play with your head up and scan for players making off-the-ball runs. The game can be progressed, as earlier, with players having to pass to alternate colors to challenge further their visual recognition.

During the small-sided game, players get a point for maintaining possession, but three points for identifying their team-mates' off-the-ball run and executing it. This allows them to prioritize a risky, goal-scoring pass, or to keep possession.

---

[7] http://www.youtube.com/watch?v=N2Yb2j-x1xg

As well as working on players' peripheral vision, the coach can also work with players on general passing and receiving skills, when to 'risk' a forward pass and when to retain possession, and also specific detail about the timing of runs, and coaching straight pass – diagonal run / diagonal pass – straight run movements.

'Testing' Technique

A number of years ago a colleague of mine got his hands on a "technical assessment template" used at the academy at Chelsea. The document presented a series of exercises that could measure players' technical proficiency; much like a multi-stage fitness (or 'bleep') test measures an athlete's aerobic capacity. Players are given a score based on their technical aptitude within these exercises. He marvelled at its notoriety, but also its simplicity. He explained the exercises to me, and it was wonderful to watch his gestures and excitement as he described each one. Although I never managed to get my hands on this document, the New York Red Bulls' website shows how their academy tests technique[8]. They focus on five techniques – dribbling, turning, receiving, passing, and shooting.

I am not convinced there is a bulletproof, scientific way to test technique however. Firstly, we tend to measure technique without any opposition, and secondly, if we were to include opposition, the variables would again be too vast to test different players within the same context. In the passing demonstration video on the 'Red Bull's' website for example, the boy involved completed the test with top marks, yet at no point was there any way of translating this test into one that measures 'skill'.

Conclusion

It is important for me to point out that although we have dismissed the certain game-like value of constant practices, they are still of use to the coach. At AC Milan, for example, their philosophy is about spending lots of time on what a recent presentation called "the basics". Therefore, and critically, although they used lots of unopposed practices (including *shadow play*, something we will look at in more detail in the following chapter), they spent a huge amount of time seeking to improve small technical details that can only be captured effectively in constant practices.

Remember then that although there are pitfalls and 'real' game compromises with any practice or technical development method, they must not simply be discarded. Some people do not like the *Coerver* method, but others including renowned youth development coaches such as Gerard Houllier and Rene Muelensteen use it extensively and swear by it. Some are not keen on *futsal* (I personally worked for an Academy manager who banned me from using futsal with an under 13 group), whereas others believe it should form the foundation of every youth development program worldwide.

As a coach you must invest some time in the practices you create, and decide what is best for your players. If your players, or some of your players, require the repetition and constant conditions of 'line-drills' - feel free to use them, but also ensure that players are active the vast majority of the time. Recognize though that, eventually, these players will need to transfer them into match conditions and more variable and random practices. Finally, consider how expert performers across disciplines and sports have based their development in deliberate practice. As summed up bluntly by the *Best Practices for Coaching Soccer in the United States* document – "No lines. No laps."

Summary

- The players' technical ability will determine their tactical performance.

---

[8] See link to website, with accompanying videos - http://www.redbullsacademy.com/training/skillschallenge.aspx

- Technical practices are unopposed – skill practices are opposed.

- A technical player can perform an action on demand. A skilful player can perform the technique under pressure.

- Skill acquisition should be the primary focus of the coach.

- Practice is one of the few aspects of talent development a coach can affect directly – unlike genetics for example.

- It takes 10,000 hours or 10 years of practice to become an expert in anything, although this is a guide, rather than a law.

- Coaches counting hours and measuring the quantity of practice rather than the quality of practice are misguided.

- Top performers invest significant hours in not just practice, but *deliberate practice*, which increases the presence of myelin in the brain.

- Any practice that you put on for your players that is anything less than an unrestricted 11v11 game will contain elements of compromise with the 'real game'.

- There are three types of soccer practices – constant, variable and random, all of which have certain strengths and shortcomings, and all of which have a compromise with the real game.

- In recent years there has been a huge shift in the coaching community away from constant, static practices.

- A coach can make practices more deliberate and more game-realistic by using the whole-part-whole method, by keeping score and using variable / random practices, rather than constant ones.

- Small-sided games, futsal, Coerver-type work, technical circuits and game intelligence sessions can all aid a player's technical development and skill acquisition.

- There are methods to measure and test technique, though results are unreliable.

- There is a place and justification for all types of practices – the coach needs to understand the compromise involved in all.

Real Coach Experience

Changing Constant for Random Practices
(Anonymous, Former Academy Coach)

A number of years ago I worked with an under-14 academy team. At this point I was at my most confident as a coach. I felt I could put on excellent sessions, even with limited time to prepare. Although my role was part-time, I poured all my energy into the role.

Little did I know that I was very much in my comfort zone. I could scatter cones around an area and the players could be put into these wonderful passing practices. Looking back, the main point I made to players prior to the exercise was to "pass and follow your pass".

During school holidays I used to hire a facility (out of my own pocket) and the players would spend two or three full days training.

One morning I put on yet another passing practice. Players were placed in a line of three, and the middle player would receive from one, and pass to the other. I progressed this to where the receiving player must make an angle to receive, check their shoulders, receive on their back foot, and then pass.

On this occasion I took a step back from the practice and noticed that the players – all good players who were generally very engaged – were flat and seemed to go through the motions. I watched my assistant coach constantly moan at the boys because the mood was flat and there was little verbal communication.

Then it hit me! They were not communicating as they had no reason to – they didn't need to! John knew he needed to receive from Robert and pass to James. Then he had to receive from James and pass to Robert – over and over again. There was no verbal communication required – they knew what to do and were just doing it. Yet the coach was barking at them! They were taking part, rather than training.

I stepped in and adapted the practice where any player could receive from any other, and pass to any player who was available. Suddenly the session took off! The atmosphere improved, the players now had to talk to complete what they were asked to do. It was challenging. They made mistakes. They were now training!

I guess that morning was my 'eureka' moment as a coach. Since then my coaching has evolved and, although I still use line drills from time to time, I do them for a reason. This reason is mainly to teach technique, or to pin down a certain aspect of the game, before quickly moving it into more game-based practices.

10

Understanding the Tactical Development of Soccer Players

"It is not a question of 4-4-2 or 4-2-1-3, it is a question of having a team which is ordered, in which the players are connected to one another, which moves together, as if it was a single player." (Arrigo Sacchi)

It is especially important, when reading this chapter, to remember the key stages in the development of youth soccer players. It is also fundamental to recall how we can use the *implicit* and *explicit* teaching methods from chapter 3. The coaching focus when working with younger players is on technique. Without this technical development and subsequent skill development, carrying out tactical work is extremely difficult.

There is a shift in focus towards tactical training as young players progress through their development, so giving complex tactical information to a 10-year-old, considering the traits of a child at this age, is not productive. See below the ages that players in some of the most renowned academies in Europe begin their tactical training. This information comes from the European Club Association's *Report on Youth Academies in Europe*.

Age Professional Clubs Begin Tactical Work

Club	Age
Ajax	12
Arsenal	14
Barcelona	8 (individual tactics) 12 (team tactics)
Bayern Munich	11
Inter Milan	8 (individual tactics) 13/14 (team tactics)
FC Levadia Tallinn	16
Dinamo Zagreb	13
Racing Club Lens	12
Standard Liege	14
Sporting Lisbon	12

Tactics Through the Age Groups

Tactics *can* be taught to younger players, but in an *implicit* manner. They can be taught without using uncontrollable jargon and without having wildly over-the-top expectations. For example, 4 v 4 or 5 v 5 games can be used to teach all players basic concepts of attacking and defending. Rotating players positionally, rather than pigeon-holing them early, will help them experience different positions.

Young players must first understand individual tactics, before moving through group or unit tactical understanding, and ultimately then – towards their mid to late-teens – team tactics.

Individual Tactics

Individual tactics are those employed by players when they are *on* or *in close proximity to the ball*. They usually relate to a player's decisions and performance when 1 v 1 against a direct opponent, both in possession (1 v 1 attacking) and out of possession (1 v 1 defending) of the soccer ball. In a wider sense, individual tactics can relate to decision-making around whether to dribble, pass, shoot, etc., how to support a teammate who is in possession, and communicating to ask for the ball.

The stronger a young player's individual tactics and decision-making, the stronger he will fit into his unit and ultimately, his team. The Grassroots coaching section of the FIFA website, although needing a significant update, summarizes these "simple principles that a player learns in order to make the best decisions during a particular passage of play".

Group Tactics

Once technique and individual soccer tactics are learnt and mastered, and as the players age, they can start to have a greater focus *around the ball*. The coach can begin to work on small group or unit tactics. The focus here is on the relationship between individuals that occupy similar spaces on the pitch. This may be the relationship between partners (for example, two centre-backs or two strikers), their unit (defence, midfield, attack) or between members of other units that affect each other (for example the full-back and winger).

The principles of cause and effect can be understood more at this age, with players able to grasp that an action they make, has an effect on those around them. Brighter players will further understand that the decisions made by others have consequences for them. This may be in terms of positioning, supporting the ball, and attempting to work out what might happen next.

Team Tactics

Team tactics is the tactical method we understand most from watching games and analysing formations, systems of play, styles of play, etc. When we discuss tactics, it is the whole team that we tend to focus on. Within team tactics, we can zoom in on both group and individual tactics, understanding that these small parts make up the overall tactical performance of the team.

Explicit tactical training sessions involving the whole team should not be completed before 12 to 14 years old. Even at that age, players will be new to this type of training so patience is needed. A young player's mind is now being asked to think beyond his own decision-making, and take into account the players around him and away from him - something that needs practice and lots of time to master.

Youth Team Tactics

In England, Holland, Germany, Italy, France and Spain – considered to be the most powerful and successful European soccer nations – they base their game formats around the same building-blocks of 7 v 7, then 9 v 9, before youth players graduate to the full 11 v 11 adult-sized game. The nations vary between playing 4 v 4 or 5 v 5 at the youngest age groups.

In Belgium, an emerging European soccer power, with a terrific recent track record in developing elite players, they vary somewhat by preferring 5 v 5 ("single diamond"), then 8 v 8 ("double diamond") and ultimately 11 v 11 approaches.

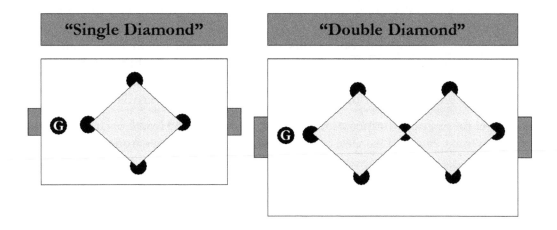

Implementing a Playing System

The Belgian FA has clearly and carefully considered a measured approach to developing their players tactically through their youth development process.

For coaches or clubs that are keen to implement a one-formation development process, consider not just the 11 v 11 formation you will implement, but also the set-ups used pre-11-a-side.

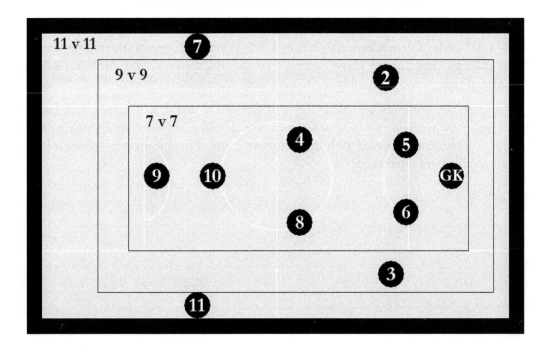

Above, we see that the 4-2-3-1 system from 7 v 7, through 9 v 9, then eventually 11-a-side is interlinked, so players are exposed to this way of playing from the earliest opportunity. Remember at 7 and 9-a-side levels, tactical learning will largely take place implicitly. In 7-a-side, although players 2, 3, 7 and 11 and not in place, players 5, 6, 4 and 8 will provide width, hence sampling the duties of these players. So numbers 5 and 6 will adopt the role of a central defender and full-backs (2 and 3), and 4 and 8 adopt the roles of central midfield players, but also provide the width of players 7 and 11.

A one-formation youth system, however, is not agreeable to everyone. There are those within the game who rightly feel it is far too restrictive and that players need to have a more rounded tactical development. When working with your players, carefully consider whether you want to expose them to various systems of play throughout their development (remember that this needs to be periodized and structured, rather than jumping episodically from one formation and style to another) or whether, like Ajax and Barcelona, you wish to focus on variables of the same system.

Thomas Tuchel for example, former youth coach at Stuttgart and Head Coach at FSV Mainz 05 at the time of writing, outlined his view in an interview for BBC 5 Live podcast *Developing the Individual*:

> "…we in our club have to take care, in my opinion, that we don't put the system over the talent and over the individual talent and skills of the youth players… If I have an excellent number 10… it is necessary that we put him there and we develop him there, no matter if the first team plays at this time with a number 10 or not."

The "Numbers Game"

Throughout this chapter we will use lots of numbers – we are after all talking about soccer tactics – whether those numbers happen to be 4-2-3-1, 4-4-2, 4-3-3, or whether they are the historical staple of 3-2-2-3 (or 'WM') or the futuristic likelihood of 4-6-0 being commonplace.

What we must realize however is that tactics are much, much more complex than a combination of numbers on a tactics board. Tactics, as so clearly explained by Jonathon Wilson in *Inverting the Pyramid*, are "a combination of formation and style" – so, they are a merging of the numbers we use to describe our formation and the style of soccer we wish to implement. In addition, tactics are a culmination of player strengths, movements and decisions.

By using the formation alone to define our tactics we are really saying very little. Contrast Barcelona's 4-3-3 under Guardiola with Chelsea's 4-3-3 under Mourinho during his first spell at the club for example. The former played with a free-flowing passing-style, the latter a more direct, functional style – and ultimately both were very successful.

For the most part, the numbers we speak about in tactics are just that – numbers. A back 4 for example is rarely now made up of four defenders. You could easily convert Barcelona's 4-3-3 into a 2-3-2-1-2 if you became obsessed with the numbers game. The question is – does it really matter what numbers are attributed?

Barcelona: 4-3-3 or 2-3-2-1-2?

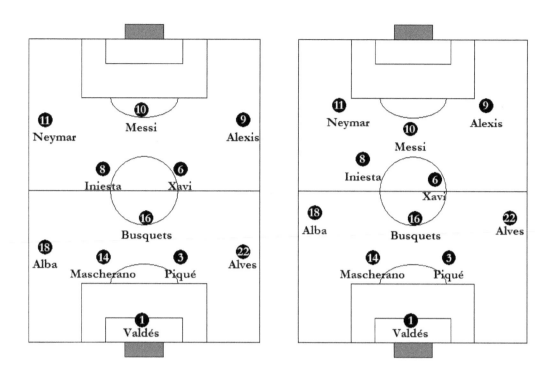

I was recently given a document called *Playing 4-3-3*, which has been attributed to Dick Bate, easily the best coach, coach educator and soccer mind I have been able to work with. He presents a thought-provoking answer to what I have called "the numbers game" visually, showing us how different interpretations of the same formation over the last decade have been used (to bring this up-to-date, and offer another variant, I have included the Barcelona one at number six):

Variants of 4-3-3 System

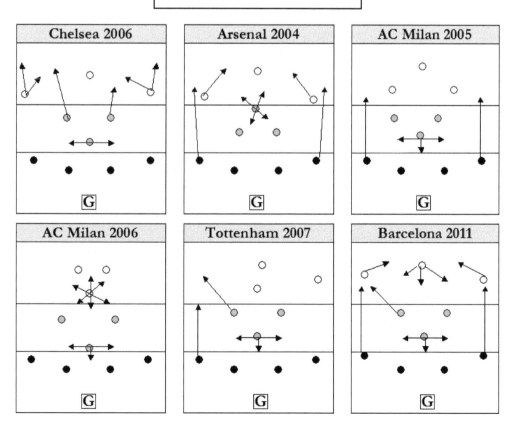

Again, some of the "4-3-3" formations above could be called something else. You may call Arsenal's 4-2-3-1 for example, or AC Milan's, a 4-4-2 Diamond Formation. Ultimately, however, *it really does not matter what numbers you use*, what matters is the style the team possesses, the players you have, and the traits, movements and decisions made by these players within that formation. It is only when we throw the shackles of the numbers game off that we can really begin to understand soccer tactics.

Principles of Play

Regardless of what formation, style or tactics a coach employs, soccer is based around the *Principles of Play*. These principles govern both the offensive and defensive parts of soccer.

Attacking

There is an argument that soccer is based around space. The team that is attacking is looking for space to exploit, while defending teams look to limit the space available to the opposition. Attacking play, as defined by the FA in its coach education literature, is about *creating, maintaining and exploiting space*. Below, we will study the five attacking principles.

1. Penetration

The first intent when a player receives the ball should be "can I score or can I create an opportunity for someone else to score?". This has become lost in lots of coaching philosophies where keeping the ball is emphasized and in some cases, overemphasized. In soccer, the overall objectives are to score goals at one end and not concede them at the other. So, when we are attacking, the first principle is to try to penetrate the defence and score. If this is not possible, or comes with an undue risk, we then look to keep possession and 'build' a scoring opportunity.

In recent decades, soccer has changed from a focus on supplying goals from wide areas through crosses, to the growing influence of 'Zone 14'. This is the term used to describe the central area outside the penalty box. In the modern game, this area has been extremely influential in the creation of goals. The concept of Zone 14 came about at the turn of the century after a John Moore's University study found that 50% of the dominant French team's goals on the way to winning both the 1998 World Cup and the 2000 European Championships came from Zone 14. In a subsequent study of ten Premier League games, Dick Bate (again!) found that "73% of all goals scored came via a possession in Zone 14".

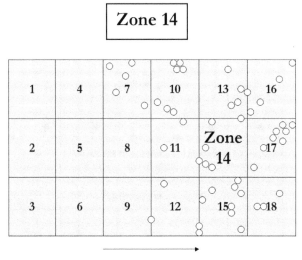

Direction of Attack

This chapter opened with a quote from Arrigo Sacchi, the famous Italian coach and tactical thinker. Sacchi has become renowned for his witty, intelligent comments on the game. His understanding of how the game is constantly evolving is best found in his quote: "As long as humanity exists something new will come along – otherwise football (soccer) dies!"

Zone 14 is the area that would be traditionally occupied by the number '10' – an attacking midfielder or 'shadow' striker. To counter the growing influence of the number 10 and the threat to their goal posed by zone 14, teams began using a designated defensive midfield player. In turn, the role of the number 10 has changed and attacking midfield players are now given lots of license to roam around zones 13, 14 and 15, away from designated markers.

The dots included on the Zone 14 diagram are a visual of the areas of the pitch where Chelsea's attacking midfield player Eden Hazard touched the ball in a Premier League game against Newcastle United in February 2014[1]. This highlights the multi-purpose and multi-positional nature of this new breed of player.

2. Support

When the first attacker (the player on the ball) is in possession, he needs the support of others around him. This support should ideally be ahead of the ball through forward runs, support to the side, and support behind the ball (should he not be able to play forward). The priority is to attack in the quickest way possible, but at times the best support may well be backwards.

3. Length, Width (and 'Pockets' of Space)

The principle of creating width and length is an effort to make the pitch 'as big as possible'. This stretches defences out making the space we can attack and exploit a lot bigger. At least one of your attacking players may play as high as possible to push defenders back. Wingers, or increasingly, full-backs, can offer width to an attack. By giving width, your team will try to draw defenders away from central areas where they are protecting the goal. Crucially then, once defenders are dragged apart, players can look to find *pockets of space* in central areas to support the ball, and ultimately penetrate the opposition and score.

4. Movement and Mobility

Movement is key when trying to create and exploit space. Off-the-ball attacking runs can include, amongst others, overlapping runs, underlapping runs, and third man runs. The intent is to destabilize and disorganize the defence. Clever runs can drag defenders out of position, allowing runners or other attackers to exploit the space that is created. Teams that play against better opposition often comment that it is the movement of players which is the most notable difference between them and more-able high level teams.

5. Improvisation

To an extent defensive play is quite straightforward and is governed by rules, and the best decision is often obvious and prescriptive. At particular times, there will be a specific method that is needed to defend. When attacking, however, there are always choices. Some may be better than others; some we will 'see' as being the best option. There are times, though, when you stand back and let attacking, creative players do their thing. If you look at any compilation video on YouTube of attacking play or great goals, the decisions made by players may not be the optimal decision, but their creative genius and improvisation means that players can see things and execute things that are unpredictable.

This unpredictability and element of surprise should be encouraged rather than coached, as improvisation needs freedom and an almost individual, artistic touch. Encourage young players to attack creatively, and allow them the safety-net of your support, and encouragement, if creative attempts are not immediately successful. One of the best attacking players I have worked with

---

[1] Source: BBC Television Match of the Day programme.

told me quite bluntly one day: "Tell me exactly what you want me to do when defending, but when I am attacking, set me free."

Defending Principles of Play

In contrast to attacking principles, defending principles of play are aimed at reducing the space available to opponents by *denying, restricting and predicting space* (FA coach education literature). Below are the five defending principles.

1. Press or Delay

When the opposition has the ball they will be looking to penetrate and score a goal. The first decision then, when defending, is whether we can put pressure on the ball immediately, or whether we need to drop off, delay the attack and reorganize. If we can get immediate pressure on the ball and regain it, that is brilliant, but it is not always possible. To delay means getting in-between attackers and the goal becomes the most important thing to protect.

2. Support

Support players are essential to effective defending. While the first defender makes the decision about whether he can press or delay, his immediate team-mates will look at *what support he needs* and *where*. This may involve making recovery runs to get back into cover positions. If the attacker evades the first defender, the second and third defenders can form a secondary barrier between the ball and goal. Likewise these support players can screen forward passes into more forward positions.

3. Balance

'Balance' players are players that are positioned on the 'weak' and less dangerous side of the attack. So, if the attack is building on the left, the attacking players on the right hand side are less of a priority. Therefore if the right-back is pressing the ball, the left-back will be 'tucked in' to add protection to the goal. If the ball is transferred to the weaker side, the defender can *travel as the ball travels* and become the first defender.

4. Compactness

A culmination of press/delay, support and balance is 'compactness'. While the attacking players use principles of length and width to stretch the defence, defenders conversely attempt to remain 'compact' to stop attackers making attempts on goal. By achieving compactness around the ball, defenders try to reduce the attempts to penetrate, cater for dangerous support players, and can negate forward runs. A useful way of teaching this is to divide the pitch into four or five vertical zones, and ask defenders to occupy three of these areas depending on where the ball is. Being compact also means reducing the space 'between the lines', blocking pockets of space that attackers will attempt to exploit. For example, the modern defensive midfielder is a specialist at defending and reducing space between the defensive and midfield lines.

5. Discipline

Defending requires a lot of discipline. There are occasions when you will need to be patient, prioritize decisions, communicate effectively and show restraint. There may be times when defending can be stressful and challenging. Any ill-discipline and rash decision-making, especially in and around the box, can lead to attackers exploiting gaps in your defence, or the concession of penalty-kicks, free-kicks, etc.

Using the Principles of Play

The flow chart below is a useful reference tool for the coach when he speaks about the *Principles of Play* and on-field decision-making. This 'Decision-Making Tree' is a slightly adapted version of a poster that is on display at the Liverpool FC Academy. It takes the player and the coach through the process of their decision-making, both in and out of possession.

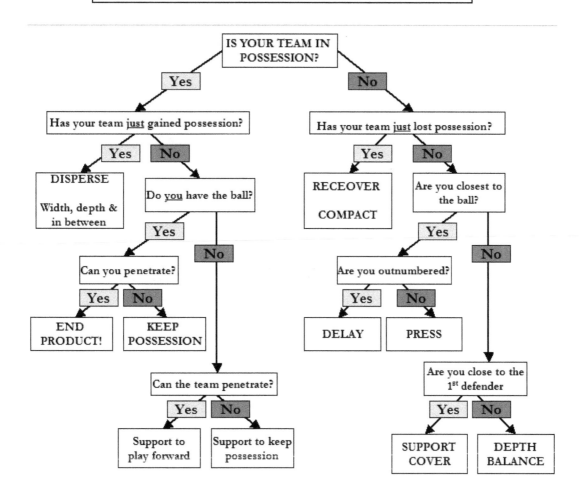

Liverpool FC Academy Decision-Making Tree

Transitions

We would be extremely short-sighted to believe that soccer has only two phases – one where you attack and one where you defend. In modern soccer there has been a huge shift in focus towards the importance of 'transitions'. These are the moments in a game when possession of the ball changes from one team to another. One team therefore has just won the ball and will try to attack; the other has just lost it and will need to reorganize defensively. The theory is that the team who can deal with transitions more effectively, is the team who will ultimately succeed.

Four Phases of the Game

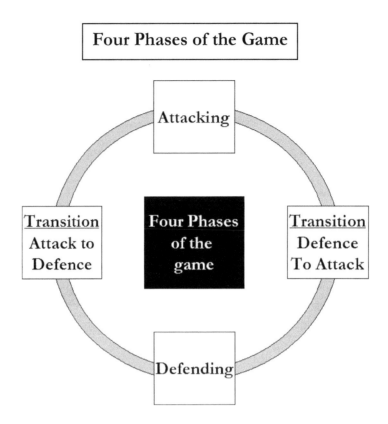

Dividing the game into "four phases" is useful and becoming more and more common as a template for coaching players. However, we must understand first of all that none of the four phases exist in isolation from each other. A key factor in attacking is ensuring you are secure at the back. Likewise, when you are out of possession, players must have a grasp on how they will attack should they regain the ball.

Such is the growing focus on *transitions* that more and more information and session plans are coming to the fore that have transitions at their core. José Mourinho is a dyed-in-the-wool advocate of training players around transitions, through a method known as 'Tactical Periodization'. Indeed it was rumoured that the coaching staff altered all Academy practices at Chelsea to include elements of transition.

Tactical Periodization

In concurrence with Juan Luis Delgado-Bordonau and Alberto Mendez-Villanueva, writers of seemingly the only English language article on the topic[2], Tactical Periodization is José Mourinho's "best kept secret". The godfather of the concept was a Portuguese university lecturer called Vitór Frade, and the concept is particularly strong in Spain and Portugal.

Basing practices on Tactical Periodization entails *involving all four periods of the game in all training exercises and working with players technically, tactically and physically* simultaneously, rather than in isolation from each other.

---

[2] At the time of writing, Xavier Tamarit's Spanish book *What is Tactical Periodization?* is being translated to English – a must read for forward-thinking soccer coaches and will be published in 2014.

This concept is useful for younger players as well as full-time professional players. Even from an early age, simply using 4 v 4 games for example, the coach can teach players the concepts of defending, attacking and quick transitions, be it implicitly through the games, or explicitly by emphasizing quick play and fast-reaction defending.

Transition from Defence to Attack

If we look first at the moment when your team wins the ball, what is their first instinct? Often coaches tell them the priority is to "keep the ball" but this actually works somewhat *against* the Principles of Play. As noted above, a player or team's first instinct on regaining the ball is whether they can score or create a goal. This, in my opinion, is one of the pitfalls of the fascination we now have with possession soccer – we misinterpret it as being what the game is about. The game is about scoring goals and defending a goal. Possession is one vehicle a team can use to score a goal, although tactics and the state of the game influence this also. Barcelona, for example, are famous now for their long passing sequences, but when the opportunity presents itself to penetrate, they invariably try to take it!

Counter-Attack

A counter-attack begins when a team wins possession of the ball and looks to attack quickly. Some teams will purposely defend deep with the intention of being well organized and looking to score on the counter-attack. It is not only purely defensive negative soccer teams that are doing this – all top-level teams are!

See below various statistics on the number of counter-attack goals scored during various tournaments:

Competition	Goals scored from Counter-Attacks
European Championships 2012	25%[3]
European Champions League 2008-2009	27%[4]
European Championships 2008 goals from open-play[5]	46%[6]
European Champions League 2007-2008	33%
Premier League Champions Chelsea 2005-2006 open-play goals	42%
European Championships 2004	48%[7]

Teams that play on the counter-attack either set up to defend as they feel inferior to the opposition, or they feel it is the optimal way of playing having analysed their own strengths and weaknesses or the strengths and weaknesses of the opposition. Teams will also use a counter-attacking tactic if they are winning games and are attempting to see out the victory. During the 2008 European Championships, only one of the 16 counter-attack goals was scored when the team was losing.

---

[3] Source: UEFA EURO 2012 Technical Report
[4] Source of both Champions League statistics: FA CPD Event on Counter-Attack by Noel Blake, England youth coach
[5] Open play goals discount the goals scored as a result of restarts (free-kicks, corner-kicks, throw-ins etc.)
[6] Source: UEFA EURO 2012 Under 17 Technical Report
[7] Source of Chelsea and EURO 2004 statistics: Dick Bate presentation *The Game in the Future*

Evolution

With Sacchi's comment in mind about the constant evolution of the game, we now see a concerted effort to defy this by developing tactics to prevent being punished by a counter-attack. You will notice from the counter-attacking statistics above that there is actually a *decrease* in the percentages of goals being scored in this way. The *UEFA Technical Report* suggests some reasons for this decline:

> "At UEFA EURO 2008, 46% of the open-play goals stemmed from fast breaks but in the interim percentages have been steadily declining in the UEFA Champions League (to 27% in the 2011/12 season). This downward trend was underlined at UEFA EURO 2012, where 25% of the open-play goals were derived from counters. This highlighted the efficiency of defensive blocks and the efficacy of counter-the-counter ploys, such as immediate pressure on the ball carrier, the use of 'tactical fouls' to break up counters, or the constant presence of four, five or six players behind the ball as a precautionary measure when a team is attacking."

Counter-Pressing

The common perception of a counter-attack in soccer is when the ball is regained in zones 1 to 9, however a counter-attack can occur from possession won back in any area of the pitch.

Teams, recognizing that winning the ball back in the opposition's half can lead to swift counter-attacking options, now use a tactic known as 'counter-pressing'. This term originated in Germany ('*gegenpressing*') and was put to particular use by Borrusia Dortmund under innovative coach Jurgen Klopp, and possibly perfected (*against* Klopp's side) by rivals Bayern Munich in a 3-0 away win in November 2013.

Rather than dropping deeper to defend, the team presses high and early with the intention of regaining possession in attacking areas. The objective is to destabilize your opponent before they have *composed* control of the ball. In *The Whitehouse Address*, a popular soccer blog from author of *The Way Forward*, Matt Whitehouse, this tactic is termed as "positive defending" as there is a proactivity to regain possession. This is opposed to the seemingly negative, reactive manner of waiting for the opposition to give you the ball back. This high, early pressure is also known as "ultra-offensive" pressing by Massimo Lucchesi in his book *Pressing*. Pep Guardiola famously worked to an eight-second rule, where his players were given eight seconds to press and win the ball. If this was not achieved, they then reverted into more organized, defensive positions.

Transition from Attack to Defence

A team is never as vulnerable as when they are in composed possession of the ball – and they lose it! Regardless of how technically able they are, players and teams will inevitably surrender possession, so an understanding of what to do in these frequent situations is a must.

Defending When Disorganized / Outnumbered

Without the ball, a coach's preference is for the team to defend in an organized manner. In other words, no player is out of position, your defenders have even numbers or, hopefully, outnumber the opposition.

There are, however, frequent occasions when your team will be disorganized upon losing possession of the ball, and will have to defend against opposition attacks. So, along with concepts of organized defending (who puts pressure on the ball, who takes up cover positions, etc.) players need to be put into situations where they learn about delaying opposition attacks, prioritize defending the goal, and how to make recovery runs to goal.

Adding Transitions to Your Practices

Any practice, certainly any opposed skill practice, can be modified to include transitions. There are two examples below to highlight this, one a skill-based possession practice, the second a small-sided game.

Possession Exercise with Transitions

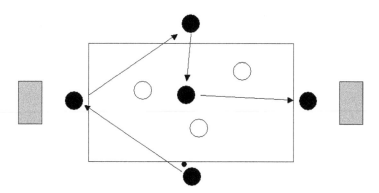

Four players (black, above) are placed on each side of the playing area. The focus is on working with a central midfield player who attempts to receive the ball, before playing a pass to a team-mate. The three white players look to stop him doing so. Once a transition takes place, and the whites win the ball, they can work together to score in either goal. This is where players need to spring into action! The whites need to counter-attack swiftly before the black team recovers. The black player nearest the goal needs to delay the attack and wait for the other black players to recover. Once the blacks win the ball back, they can counter the counter-attack and score in the other goal.

Defensive Transition – Mourinho's 39 Practices

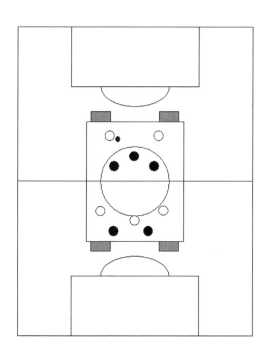

This small-sided game is set up, as shown, with 3 v 2 in the attackers' favour in each half. The defenders are forced to defend when outnumbered. The attackers are instructed to drop into the centre circle as soon as an attack as finished.

Restarts

Restarts are one of the only parts of soccer that can be scripted with any sort of accuracy. A team's moves *can* be scripted, but the variables involved in a live game mean they cannot be replicated exactly, every time. By 'restarts' we generally mean free-kicks, corner-kicks, throw-ins, kick-offs and penalty kicks, and they are sometimes known as set-plays or set-pieces. Figures for the number of goals scored directly, or indirectly, from restarts can be as high as 50% in various competitions. Although restarts can be scripted, there are still numerous variables involved in translating these plans from a tactics board onto the field of play.

The ideas involved, and ultimately the implementation of set-play routines by young players, is very much a long-term process. Younger players do not need, and will not process or understand, complicated instructions. They can be introduced to basic concepts of attacking and defending, before being assigned individual duties as they grow older. Professional teams may prepare 10 or 12 restarts prior to games, such as the three below.

The three set-plays below were leaked from the Swansea City FC changing room in preparation for their game against Liverpool in 2012. All the restarts contain a central concept or idea, a trigger that starts things off and certain individual responsibilities.

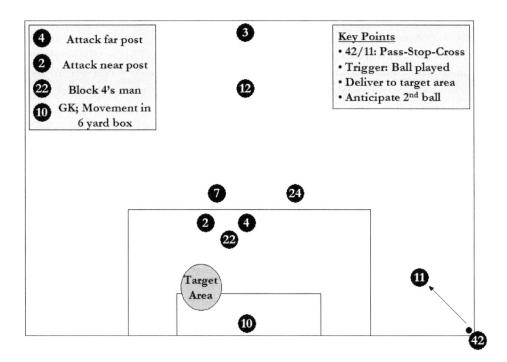

Swansea City – First Corner from the Left

- ④ Attack far post
- ② Attack near post
- ㉒ Block 4's man
- ⑩ GK; Movement in 6 yard box

Key Points
- 42/11: Pass-Stop-Cross
- Trigger: Ball played
- Deliver to target area
- Anticipate 2nd ball

Target Area

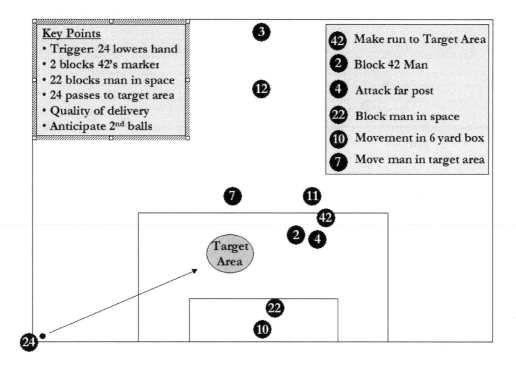

There is a constant debate around whether zonal or man-to-man defending should be prioritized when defending corner-kicks. Note how Swansea used a mixture of both, in particular to deal with the specific aerial threat of Liverpool's Andy Carroll.

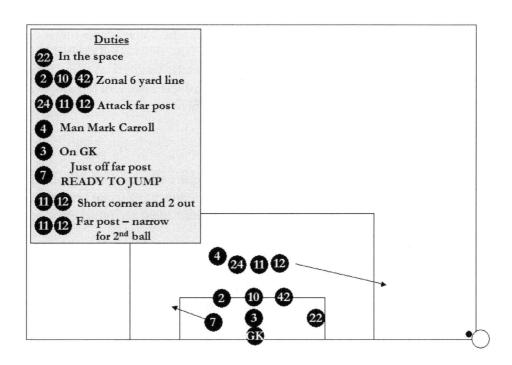

Making Technical / Skill Practices More Tactical

Traditionally coaches teach tactics through the full 11 v 11 game, or through small-sided games. Alternatively coaches may use a 'Phase of Play' or a 'Functional Practice', like below.

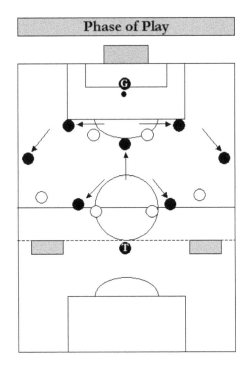
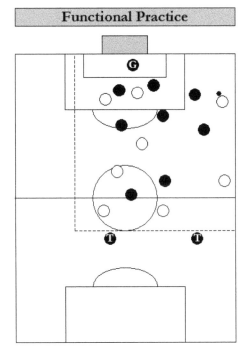

A *Phase of Play* can commonly be known as 'defence versus attack'. Two units play against two units (i.e. the black team's back 4 and midfield 3 versus the white team's midfield 4 and 2 strikers). In this example the blacks are trying to play out from the goalkeeper and the whites try to score in the big goal. It is important that the team defending the full-sized goal has a method of scoring. In this case they can score into two small goals. A target player can be used to start the practice.

A *Functional Practice*, or 'function' for short, is a scaled down version of a Phase of Play. It is best used when working around a specific topic that uses a specific area of the pitch. The pitch is 'sliced' into an area that is relevant to the topic. In the above example, the white team is attempting to attack from wide areas. The black team's right-back and right-sided midfield player are omitted, as is the white team's left-back and left-sided midfield player.

Away from these traditional practices, which can often require the space and facilities that even academy youth teams do not have access to, and with the concept of using implicit and explicit learning and deliberate practice in mind, coaches can use and adapt technical exercises in a way that develops players tactically also.

Position-Specific Technical Work

I mentioned in a previous chapter about a specific English Academy who were renowned for producing players for the professional game. Between 2006 and 2011, the number of Academy players in the club's first team had increased from 16% to 43%. They had a clear vision and philosophy about how to do this.

One of the program's cornerstones was that players would practice based around their position, especially beyond the age of 14. The club adapted *Pareto's Principle* of 80:20 to soccer. So 80% of the player's time is spent practicing the main 20% of the techniques they require to be a specialist in a particular position.

If the player was a winger, he would spend 80% of his development time doing 20% of the technical work that a winger would specialize in – for example, crossing, dribbling, shooting, etc. He would not spend time working, for example, on defensive heading, nor would he practice long passing to switch the play.

The club was immensely proud of its success in producing players, and similar to the traditional model at Ajax, they were happy to pigeon-hole players positionally, though not before twelve years old. Prior to this age players would play in a variety of positions as championed by the overwhelming majority of youth soccer development experts[8]. Players may have traits or instincts of an attacking or defensive nature, but their fixed position will not yet be determined.

The club's development philosophy document outlines their age-related approach:

> "Players from the age of U12 onwards should be learning a position; at 12 a player may play in a variety of roles within a unit however by the ages of 15 and 16 players should be working toward being an expert in a specific role... At the later age, players will have a set position and will only move one place forward, back or to the side, or will play the same position on the other side of the pitch. So, for example, a right full-back will primarily play there, or secondarily as a right winger, right-sided centre-back or as a left-back."

All players receive at least four position-specific sessions per season where the age groups are mixed and train with other players in their position.

Position-Based

When the coach is working with players in technical or skill practices, they tend to become generic squad practices. So in a possession game, for example, all players, (regardless of their position) tend to do the same thing, or are certainly asked to do the same thing. Many technical and skill-based exercises, however, can be modified to make them more tactical - making learning implicit.

Below is an example of a very popular 5 v 5 v 5 possession practice. The central players in white and grey attempt to keep possession of the ball. They can use the five black target players if required, making the practice 10 v 5.

---

[8] Therefore, as much as it is argued, a pre-teen soccer player should not already be pigeon-holed as a striker, full-back, winger, etc.

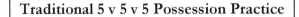

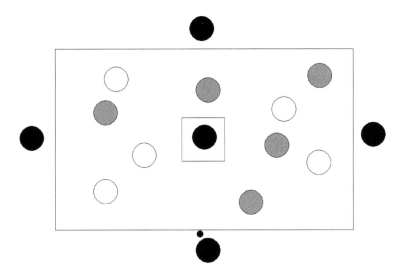

This practice can be adapted to become more position-based, like the two examples below.

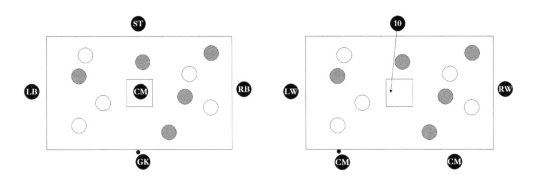

This practice places the team in black in positions they might normally find themselves in, on the pitch. So the striker and goalkeeper will receive, facing the rest of the team as they do in game situations, and the full-backs receive in wide areas. The central midfield player has a 360-degree view of the practice, as he would do in a game.

This exercise in similar with the wingers playing in wide areas, two midfield players receiving to play forward, and a number '10' looking for free spaces to receive. Centre-backs can easily be included either at the base of the playing area, or in the wide areas if the goalkeeper remains present.

Shape-Based – Shadow Play

In the previous chapter, we frowned upon the *overuse of constant, drill-line practices*. We noted that they involved little decision-making and only considered short-term learning. More value, however, can be added to a constant-type practice, by making them more tactical. Using 'shadow play', a concept particularly favoured in the tactically cultured Italian game, is a way of doing this.

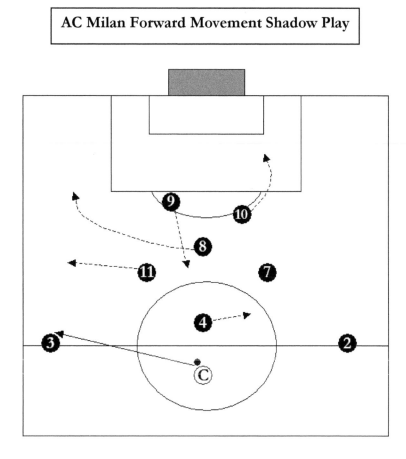

AC Milan Forward Movement Shadow Play

The exercise, above, came from a study of the Primavera team's training at AC Milan. The topic in question was 'coaching forward movement', particularly when the left-back receives the ball. In the example above, the players have predetermined movements – the 11 goes wide, and the 4 moves away from the ball. Number 8 makes a forward run into the channel, and the space left by him (and the 4) is taken by the number 9. The number 10 stays away and looks to play as far forward as possible.

Use Players in Their Position

Just like both previous examples of shadow play and position-based technical work, using players in their specific position, where possible, allows them to experience the techniques and decision-making that is required by this position. Certainly prior to 12-years-old this focus is not necessarily important, but as players grow older and become more specialist, it can be a very useful method.

Use The Pitch!

A colleague of mine who worked within the Ajax system recently spoke to me about a real 'light-bulb' moment in his coaching career. He was delivering a coaching session around dribbling and had players dribbling *across the pitch*. A senior staff member pulled him to one side after the session to offer some advice. He described to him how players use visual references when on the field of play, so it is important to *teach technical exercises in the relevant part of the pitch*. So dribbling should be coached in wide or attacking areas, and be focused towards goal; goalkeepers should practice in front of goal; centre-backs should defend and strikers should practice finishing in and around the penalty area.

Rondos

In the previous chapter we looked at the use of 'rondos', and in particular their use in the development of soccer players in Spain. The example from Chapter 9 was a rondo in an 8 v 2 situation, although noting that various numbers and arrangements can also be used.

I was always a little dubious about the impact of rondos in the development of young players – I always felt the compromise or trade-off between them and the real game made them a tad too unrealistic to base a coaching program around. In all honesty, I have seen English players use them in a pre-warm-up activity, and they seemed little more than a way of joking around and bonding before the main practice begins. A friend of mine who coached in Poland echoed the same thing.

My doubts however we washed away when I saw an excellent presentation by Kieran Smith (@kieransmith1 on Twitter) on the variety and far-reaching extent to which rondos can be utilized "with technical, tactical and positional aspects of your team's overall play".

The modern Spanish soccer team are renowned for their ability to keep possession of the ball, and do this by constantly seeking positions on the pitch that help them to outnumber their opponents. Remember, however, that it will be the players' ability to see and make live on-field decisions about where, and when, they can outnumber their opponents. This level of thinking therefore is suitable only for older players. Rondos, though, can implicitly teach younger players how to operate in situations where they outnumber opponents. Players must be technically able to perform what is required, before being able to complete it from a tactical point of view.

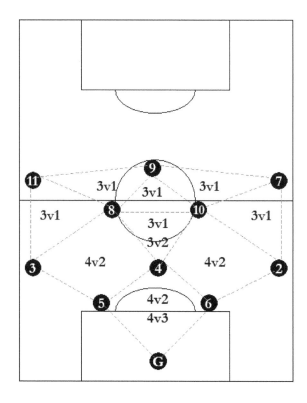

Conclusion

Let's conclude this chapter with the most important factor for coaches working with younger players, certainly pre-12 year olds. You must focus on the all-round technical development of players, or the 'individual tactics' involved in *their* game. Do not waste your, and your players', time trying to drum in concepts of positioning, tactics, set-plays, etc. It will not help youngsters develop in the long-term. Leave complex unit and team tactical development until they are old enough to understand it.

Summary

- Most top youth development academies do not begin specific tactical work until players are between 12 and 14.

- Prioritize technical development and skill acquisition before the age of 12.

- Teaching tactics can be phased, starting with individual tactics, then group tactics and ultimately, team tactics.

- Tactics can be taught implicitly from a young age, from 4 v 4 / 5 v 5 and have common traits with the 11 v 11 game.

- Tactics are not to be confused with formations or "the numbers game". Tactics are a mixture of the team's formation and style.

- The same formation can be played in countless different ways.

- Regardless of what formation, style, or tactics a coach employs, the game is based around the *Principles of Play*.

- The attacking principles of play are: penetration, support, length and depth, movement and improvisation.

- The defending principles of play are: delay, support, balance, compactness and discipline.

- Soccer has four phases – attacking, defending, the transition from attack to defence and the transition from defence to attack.

- *Tactical Periodization* is a method of involving technical, tactical and physical work simultaneously in practices. This method also involves transitions.

- Restarts are one of the only parts of soccer that can be scripted in any way.

- Traditional forms of teaching tactics come in the form of small-sided games, full 11 v 11 games, Phases of Play and Functional Practices.

- Technical exercises can also be adapted to become more tactical.

Chapter 10

Real Coach Experience

Four Phases of the Game and the Penny Dropping

(Dave Kelly, Technical Coach, North Toronto Soccer Club)

It was half-time, and my team were playing away to Wigan Athletic. I was rattling through what I had noted down on the notepad that helps me gather my thoughts during games. I used my notes as the basis for my team-talk.

The players went out for the second half and I had realized I had told them 7/8 things to improve on! I had also jumped from the movement of our strikers, to the decisions of the centre-backs on the ball. I did not offer any 'question and answer' opportunities – just my thoughts to them. I realized that the players needed a structure that they could understand and apply consistently.

I learned about the 'phases of a game' and 'tactical periodization' from an article I had read about José Mourinho. From that moment, it became embedded in everything my team and I did. The players used it to analyse their own individual and team performance, and it gave them a better understanding of how to interpret the game. Although they will have no clue what that is by name, the players understand the '4 phases of the game' as the following:

- When we have possession (attacking)

- When we don't have possession (defending)

- When we win the ball and

- When we lose the ball

The concept especially helps with the understanding of transitions and made players understand exactly what was needed every time we won and lost possession of the ball.

I began to use this method on match days to structure half-time team talks and, after a game, we analyse things in the same way. The players find the structure useful and helpful in terms of analysing the game. The stronger the team is in all four phases, the better the performance. The weaker they are in one of the areas, gives an understanding as to why we may have not performed as well, and provides a focus for future training.

11

Understanding Physical Development in Youth Soccer

"Soccer training is conditioning – conditioning is soccer training." (Raymond Verheijen, Dutch Fitness Expert and Soccer Coach)

The physical development of youth soccer players is a contentious issue. It is certainly an area where having just a little bit of knowledge can do a lot of harm.

As a younger coach, I attended a lecture on speed development. The lecturer stated the optimal way to develop speed in players is to ensure that they regularly hit their top speed. Taking that as face value, I started to regularly add repeated 60-metre sprints to training sessions. No ball, no player interaction, and ultimately very little knowledge was involved. Players were demotivated. I did not consider that soccer speed involves so much more than players' 'flat-out speed'.

The evolution of sports science in recent decades has cast the past habits of fitness components within youth soccer into question. The 'norm' for coaches would be to get players to run almost marathon-style laps of the pitch, and execute constant sprints and hill runs. Making players sick was a measure of how well and how hard they had worked. Mentally, these tasks were considered to build character and show the mental toughness of players. In reality these methods measure very little.

There can be a certain paradox when it comes to the opinions of coaches towards the fitness components of the game. Some, who may only have one or two training sessions with their team can complain that they do not have the time to concentrate on fitness work, whilst others devote far too much of their extremely limited training time to conditioning. I have yet to find a single soccer-fitness book that deals with the practicality of the game for coaches like these. This chapter then is not an A-Z of fitness – there are whole libraries that deal with that. What it will give you, however, is methods of working with players around their physical needs, but in the context of soccer.

Understanding the Game

Even with the greater knowledge uncovered thanks to sports science, poor practice and habits around fitness remain alive and well on the world's youth soccer pitches. This needs to change. First of all we need to consider the age-appropriateness of physical development, and that the fitness work that players do complete has its basis in the game of soccer. As a rule, and for player motivation, *include a ball and a soccer-task wherever possible.*

Modern soccer is far quicker than with previous generations. The physical demands on players mean that to compete they need to be quicker, stronger and fitter than their ancestors. In the previous chapter we spoke about quick counter-attacks, aggressive pressuring of opponents, and the concentration needed to make tactical decisions and maintain technical quality – even within the final moments of a game. Soccer, a game that is so often won by a single goal, a late goal, a mistake, a lack of concentration, etc., now demands that players are able to cope with its varied and random nature, even late in games.

Physical Work Completed by Elite Players

Top-level soccer players can cover around 10 – 13 kilometres during a 90-minute game of soccer. On the face of it, it may be easy to assume that we ought to produce players that can comfortably run this distance, and therefore coaches need to have this at the foundation of their physical work. This assumption, however, is highly dangerous and highly misleading. *Sending your players on a 12 kilometre run will not make them fit for soccer.*

First of all, the distance covered is not just completed by running at the same speed in the same direction, like a middle or long distance athlete would. It involves moving forwards, backwards and laterally – and in some cases a mixture of two of the three – and all at varying speeds and in random patterns! Strides can be long, short, or require interchanging feet positions. Players will also skip, jump, slide, balance, fall over, have to burst back onto their feet, or change direction – and all within a competitive environment where opposition players provide physical interference. Opponents need to be blocked, raced against, predicted and held off.

Physical Movements of Elite Soccer Players During a 90-Minute Match	
Action Performed	**Percentage of Game[1]**
Standing	18%
Walking Forward and Backward	36%
Jumping	2%
Jogging	16%
Low-Speed Running	15%
Moderate-Speed Running	10%
High-Speed Running	2%
Sprinting	1%
During a 90-minute game, players will complete around 1,400 changes of direction	

In addition to the variety of movement patterns in game-situations, we must also note that these movement patterns (and focus) can vary from position to position. A centre-back for example will not cover as much distance as a box-to-box midfield player. Attacking midfielders are not expected to be as physically strong as defenders. The goalkeeper, of course, is exceptionally different in these terms compared to his teammates.

Fitness Testing

Motivation amongst players is interesting when it comes to fitness testing. Most probably hate the thoughts of being tested, but their competitive edge means they enjoy being scored and measured against others. Other than the final score at the end of a game, players rarely get any tangible, quantitative scoring and feedback like they do with fitness tests. Results can motivate players to do better or demotivate them if scores are not considered good enough.

---

[1] Source: Sport Dimensions *How to Develop Soccer Players – Soccer Speed* presentation

Testing players' fitness is a complicated one. Lots of common tests are used for soccer players. In *Total Soccer Conditioning Volume 1 – A Ball Orientated Approach*, Justin Cresser presents the following table around fitness testing and their relevance to the game:

Fitness Test	Conditioning Parameter	Application to Soccer
Sit and Reach Test	Flexibility (hip and lower back)	Stride distance while sprinting
Overhead Squat	Flexibility (whole body)	Efficient movement while passing, receiving, shooting, etc.
T-test	Agility	Evading tackles and creating space in tight areas
40-yard Sprint	Speed	Recovering runs after losing possession
10-yard Sprint	Acceleration	1 v 1 battles
Push-up	Local Muscular Endurance (upper body, core)	Shielding, throwing
Body-Weight Squat	Local Muscular Endurance (lower body, core)	Continuous movement over course of the game
300-yard Shuttle	Anaerobic Endurance	Repeated sprint ability
1.5 Mile Run	Aerobic Endurance	Reduce onset of fatigue

Added to the above tests, others commonly used are the 'Multi-Stage Fitness Test', repeated sprint test, and the 12-minute 'Cooper Run'. I have quite a few issues with all these above tests, not because of their scientific foundations, but because of their lack of soccer specificity. The fitness components are related to the game, but I cannot help but feel that too much valuable soccer training time could be consumed with these tests, and there is a huge compromise with the real game. A 1.5 mile run for example may work on an athlete's aerobic endurance, but as yet I have never seen a soccer player run at a consistent pace for 100 meters, never mind doing so for 1,500 meters. I also take issue with a publication citing "a ball orientated approach", when none of these tests contain a ball!

The table below shows the Multi-Stage Fitness Test results of a group of players at English Academy, Ipswich Town, and was published in Soccer Conditioning by Simon Thadani. Note how the under-14 age group was the youngest group tested. It is recommended that you should not use this test with younger players.

	Under 16			Under 15		Under 14	
Player	Mid-season	Early-season	Prev. season	Mid-season	Early season	Mid-season	Early season
A	13.6	-	12.0	12.6	12.3	12.7	12.5
B	13.2	11.9	12.0	11.1	11.5	11.6	11.5
C	13.0	12.5	12.2	11.9	11.4	11.7	11.4
D	13.0	13.3	12.7	11.2	-	11.9	11.8
E	12.9	-	11.9	12.7	12.2	11.3	11.9
F	12.9	12.5	12.3	11.7	11.3	11.1	10.4
G	12.6	13.2	12.5	11.4	11.0	10.1	10.8
H	12.3	12.0	11.6	11.4	-	10.3	10.2
I	11.9	11.5	11.5	10.9	-	10.3	-
J	11.6	11.4	-	-	-	10.0	9.9
K	11.4	11.3	11.0	-	-	-	-
L	11.3	10.6	10.2	-	-	-	-

Academy Multi-Stage Fitness Results

Although the test is popular and quite straightforward to set up, the reliability of the test scores can be questioned. There are countless times where I have seen players drop out of tests mentally, rather than having reached their physical peak. I had a conversation with an ex-professional player some time back whose coach insisted that players must reach Level 13 before they were permitted to leave the test. He relayed humorously how once level 13.0 was achieved, all the players simply stopped!

Rate of Perceived Exertion (R.P.E.)

An alternative and more empowering method of measuring player fitness and exertion was devised by Gunnar Borg, who began his work in this area in the 1970s. After training or competition, the coach, or better still, the players themselves, can rate their own physical exertion. There are two scales that are commonly used. Below is a simplified 0 – 10 version of the *Borg Scale*. Although this method can be both subjective and open to manipulation, it has its uses and Borg's studies found that these ratings provide a good estimate of more scientific measures such as testing a player's heart rate. If the players rate themselves, and are in an environment to do this honestly, it can work as self-motivation to try harder, and act as an assessment measure for the coach's reference.

Borg RPE 0-10 Scale	
Rating	
0	Rest
1	Really Easy
2	Easy
3	Moderate
4	Sort of Hard
5	Hard
6	
7	
8	Really Hard
9	Really, Really Hard
10	Maximal Effort Required

A "Ball Orientated" Approach

A former colleague of mine once lambasted my under-15 squad as he did not consider them "fit enough". This was because some were physically ill after being subjected to countless repeated 60-metre sprints. These were the same players whose soccer fitness and on-field application made them the best group I have worked with! My response was, "Trust me, give them a ball, and they won't stop running and working".

If you are not a sport-scientist, and do not have access to one when working with players, I suggest you follow one rule – *absorb fitness work within your soccer sessions*. Ensure your practices are soccer practices with a fitness focus, rather than fitness sessions with a dash of soccer, as promoted by Raymond Verheijen at the beginning of this chapter.

Soccer games and soccer practices can easily be used and adapted to improve the physical performance of your players. 'Scoring' them is not as easy or as tangible as formal fitness testing, but what better way to produce soccer-fit players than by playing soccer! That way players experience the multitude of movements required, within the random, decision-making context of the game. So, rather than spending 20 minutes completing what may be largely irrelevant fitness exercises, players can become soccer-fit and develop technically, tactically and further their game understanding and decision-making, as advocated by the *Tactical Periodization* method used by Portuguese coaches José Mourinho and André Villas Boas.

Throughout much of the following pages, we will therefore look at ways of incorporating fitness and conditioning elements into your soccer sessions.

Endurance

Young players are not the same as adults. Their physical make-up is different, not just in shape and size, but in terms of muscle development and the capacity of their energy system. Young children react differently to heat and have a much more limited cardiac output. As their physical requirements are different, they therefore need a really considered physical development program.

Broadly speaking, soccer players require the use of both aerobic and anaerobic systems. Both energy systems tend to work at the same time, although one dominates over the other at any given time during exercise.

Aerobic

The intensity of aerobic exercise is low enough that the energy required to fuel the muscles can be produced from the natural oxygen intake of the body. It is when the body is exercising at a constant, comfortable state.

Below is a very simple small-sided game that looks to boost the aerobic capacity of players. Two teams play against each other, in this case the blacks and the whites, for four minutes. The grey players act as floating or target players along the outside, and play off a maximum of two touches so that the ball is in play for longer periods.

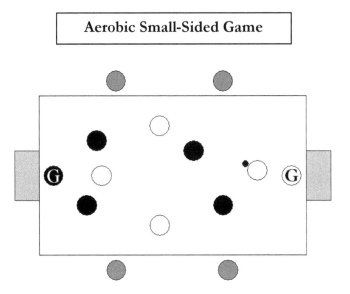

Anaerobic

Anaerobic exercise is shorter, more intense work. It is too rigorous for the heart to produce enough energy through oxygen pumped through the blood. The anaerobic system does not fully develop until after puberty. Simply playing the game includes all the fitness work that players need pre-puberty. Children *will* sprint, but may tire quicker and need longer periods of rests. Therefore shuttle runs or repeated sprints at this age are seriously discouraged as it has no physical benefits and works against the physical development of young children.

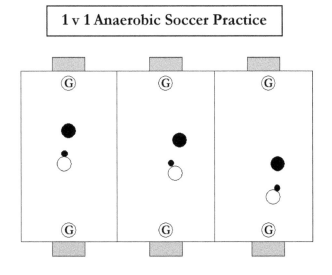

Physical Literacy

When soccer coaches speak about fitness and physical development, we tend to mean endurance. How 'fit' the players are is reflected in how long they last in a soccer game, or how breathless they are after a training session or specific practice. The longer I have worked in soccer, the more I have come to the conclusion that the most important aspect of youth player development is their ability to complete fundamental movements or how *physically literate* they are. Players need to be comfortable and capable of moving their body and manipulating the ball at the same time.

In *The Way Forward*, Matt Whitehouse points out that Borussia Dortmund, whose production line of home-grown players is ever-increasing, and includes the likes of Marco Reus, Mario Götze and Kevin Großkreutz, insist that players - by their teens - have "excellent" physical literacy.

Teaching Physical Literacy

It is essential then to focus on the physical literacy of our younger players, but not at the expense of players' fun and enjoyment. Coaches do not necessarily need to be experts, but have a conscious understanding of how we can get players moving in as many different ways as possible. These can be scripted, or better still, facilitated and left in the hands of players, as per the exercise below. It is fun, chaotic, contains a ball and allows players to take control of the activity. It may look disorganized to the outside observer, but soccer is not an organized game, nor are the movements involved. Contrast the benefits of the practice below with a straight-line warm-up where coaches dictate what movements to complete and when.

'Move and Copy' Physical Literacy Exercise

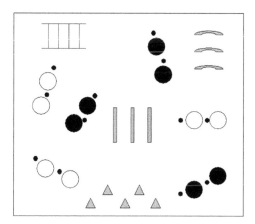

The exercise is set up as above. The size of the area is largely irrelevant – just make it big enough to cater for whatever numbers you have. Add cones, poles, hurdles, ladders, or any other obstacles randomly around the area.

The players pair up and number themselves 1 and 2. Player 1 moves randomly around the area – forwards, backwards and side-to-side or, better still, twisting turning and changing direction. Allow them to use the obstacles to run through or around. Their partner must follow and replicate the movement. The only rule is that they must be moving and they must at least attempt the movement displayed! Player 2 then leads.

This exercise can be progressed to where players are challenged to be as random as possible – even if that means they end up rolling on the ground, sliding or diving – the more creative and even bizarre the movements the better (once these are safe!). Encourage them to keep their partner guessing.

Progress this so that each player has a ball, and must dribble around the area. Player 2 then attempts to copy a skill, turn or trick displayed by Player 1.

Each 'lead' needs to only be about 30 – 45 seconds. The leader will normally execute movements they are good at. The follower then gets to sample the physical and soccer ability of their partner. To enhance these experiences, change partners regularly.

Players love this exercise, although some can be unsure of the wide parameters as they are essentially allowed to do anything. Allow them the freedom to be really creative, regardless of how messy it may all look. They are developing in a really positive way, and have taken control of their own learning.

Within 15 minutes, players will have worked on their physical literacy, warmed-up for the upcoming session and have had lots of ball manipulation work.

Early Specialization

There is a raging debate in soccer and beyond about the benefits of children specializing in *one* particular sport. Increasingly in soccer, with professional clubs operating 'pre-academy' age groups from the age of five or six, and even amateur grassroots clubs operating soccer schools to attract and recruit players at the youngest age possible, young players are often participating in soccer only, rather than indulging in a variety of sports and activities. Professional clubs in particular, operate in a very competitive recruitment environment, and are desperate to locate and sign talented young players as soon as possible, to beat off competition from rival clubs.

Early specialization, however, can lead to many long-term disadvantages around physical literacy. Children's physical experiences are essentially too narrow to develop good all-round motor skills. Other disadvantages include overuse injuries and demotivation due to the physical and sometimes mental stress of playing one sport in isolation.

Specializing in one sport from an early age then does not increase players' chances of reaching peak performance – it actually significantly reduces it. Those children who take part in a variety of sports and exercises at least until their mid-teens are more rounded athletes and are at less risk of overuse injuries[2].

Warming Up and Cooling Down

If there is one part of the soccer session that coaches obsess about – it is the warm-up. I am constantly asked for new ideas, places to get practices, and about what habits they should use with their players. This enthusiasm is great, but I always feel we worry about getting them right or wrong a little more than we should.

A warm-up should simply start with some pulse-raising activities that do not go as far as an all-out sprint. Physically, this gets the muscles warm and allows them to be stretched beyond their normal capacity. It can end with movements that are more physically demanding and contain more intensity and tempo. Once this is interspersed with some dynamic stretching you are on the right track. *Virtually any type of technical practice can be used as a warm-up*, especially variable-type practices. I would encourage any warm-up to involve a ball, some sort of team-building concept, or a way of implementing an idea you may want to focus on in the remainder of your session. By now you will know that warming-up by running laps around the pitch is especially frowned upon and offers no benefit to youth players.

---

[2] Overuse injuries occur over time (or 'micro-traumas' – as opposed to acute injuries that occur in a single moment). They occur due to repetitive forces on the same part of the body. In youth soccer, one of the most common overuse injuries is Osgood Schlatters Disease, which occurs just below the knees.

Even at younger ages, players can be introduced to the principle of warming-up. Although physically the activity does not need to be over-strenuous, it develops good early habits in players.

Pre-Match Warm-Up

We are all familiar with the pre-game warm-up routines commonly used by professional teams prior to matches. They tend to involve lots of movements with players performing exercises repetitively in straight lines. I have never quite understood this, beyond accepting that their simplicity allows players to focus in an uncomplicated manner. To maximize your time with players, and to absorb them in the game, use warm-ups that include a ball and that replicate the random movements that occur in a game.

The pre-match warm-up below is taken from the excellent work carried out by Louis Lancaster about Bayern Munich in recent years. It is worth noting how it has moved away from functional, coach-led actions to a more soccer-specific routine.

Bayern Munich Pre-Match Warm-up v. Arsenal
Champions League Last 16 Match, 19th Feb 2014

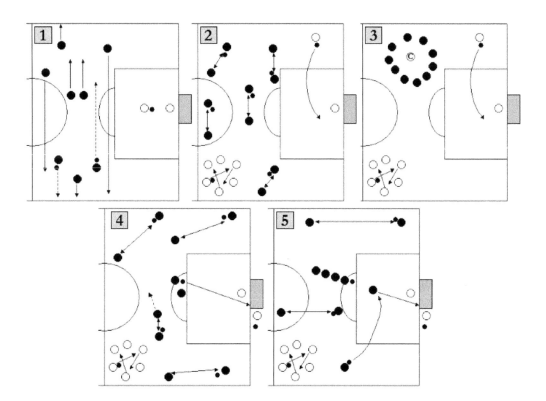

1. Players started their warm-up by jogging across the pitch. Some did so alone, others in pairs and others with a ball. *The players decided which activity to do.* The goalkeepers worked on handling.

2. Players practiced short passing over around 15 yards. The substitutes did a 2-touch rondo type exercise. The goalkeepers practiced catching crosses.

3. Players completed dynamic stretches and movements with the coach, before completing sprints. The substitutes continued the rondo and goalkeepers catching crosses.

4. Players got back into pairs and practiced longer passing. Robben completed short passes and explosive movements away. Two strikers worked on finishing with the goalkeepers.

5. Four players continued long passing. The others joined into a finishing session with Lahm crossing from the right. The fitness coach took the 10 outfield players for two final sprints.

There are a number of extremely interesting points made by Lancaster during his analysis. One was the lack of presence of a coach, other than the fitness coach who led the dynamic exercises and sprints. No other coach was involved at all which leans towards a player-centred environment. Also absent from the warm-up was the traditional possession-based exercise. This was surprising considering the possession-based nature of this Bayern Munich team[3].

Dynamic Stretching

Dynamic stretching is essentially stretching on the move. In preparation for soccer activity, these stretches replicate the movements the muscles go through in the game itself. I have listed some of the common dynamic stretches below. Dynamic stretches are far more valuable during warm-ups than static ones as they replicate the movements involved in the upcoming game or training session. These stretches will ideally be dispersed throughout a ball-orientated warm-up activity. Explanations and applications of these stretches can be found in Alan Pearson's *SAQ Soccer* or on various soccer and fitness websites.

Common Dynamic Stretches		
Ankle flicks	Russian walks	Hurdling
Various skips	Walking lunges	Walking hamstrings
Lateral running	Side lunges	High knees
Leg swings	Carioca	Butt flicks

Static Stretching

As opposed to dynamic stretching, static stretches are normally completed while standing still, sitting, or lying down. Static stretching should mainly be used in the cool-down section of your training sessions or games. Static stretching aids recovery by removing the lactic acid that builds up in the muscles during exercise.

Staggeringly, people begin to lose their flexibility from the age of 10, so it is important to include static stretches in your soccer development program. These can easily be incorporated in short, cool-down segments.

Static stretching *can* be used in warm-ups as players will often feel they need to stretch specific muscles to feel ready and prepared. There is no need for the coach to take players through the whole range of static stretches, but allow players time to do them themselves. This may be as much about their mental preparation as it will be their physical preparation.

PNF (Proprioceptive Neuromuscular Facilitation) stretching is a progression of static stretching and involves working in pairs to extend the muscles and increase flexibility and the range of

---

[3] Even though Bayern Munich did not complete the traditional possession-based game in their warm-up, the team dominated possession against Arsenal (Bayern Munich had 79% of the ball), completing 816 of their 862 passes. These statistics were however blurred by Arsenal having a player sent off in the first half. Source: *FourFourTwo Stats Zone* (powered by *Opta*)

movement in specific muscles. Ensure these stretches are completed in a controlled environment to ensure that poor approach or poor technique is not threatening to harm or injure players.

The main muscles groups specific to soccer stretching are:

Quadriceps	Hamstrings	Calves
Lower back	Groins	

Speed

In the modern game, speed has been highlighted as a major asset for players to have. In fact, many academy managers, scouts and coaches will recruit on the basis of how quick a player is. This process is highly flawed and has even seen representatives from professional clubs turn up at athletics clubs and events to specifically recruit the quickest youngsters they can find! It begs the question now as to whether we identify soccer players or athletes in the first instance. I strongly believe that recruiting players on the basis of their physical qualities alone is dangerous and merely puts limits on the talent identification process. Many players who have graced soccer have not been quick, but whose technique, game understanding and mentality have allowed them to reach the upper echelons of the game.

The focus of coaches and scouts on speed has also led to a misunderstanding of it. Speed in soccer is not just about getting from A to point B as quickly as possible. Other factors include acceleration, deceleration (what use is it to get there quickly, if you cannot slow down appropriately?), changes of direction, cruise speed, and more.

A colleague of mine, Alex Trukan, submitted the exercise below to www.coachingsoccerconditioning.com. The focus is on soccer-specific speed and contains lots of opportunities to sprint short-distances, accelerate, decelerate, change direction and, most of all, deal with a soccer ball all the while!

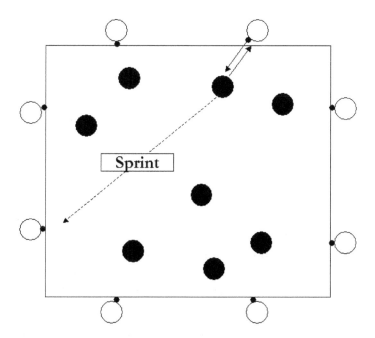

Speed Endurance and Ball Control Exercise

Sprint

Split the group in two; half actively work in the centre of the grid (blacks) and half actively rest on the outside as servers (whites). The size of the area will be appropriate to require the workers to sprint five to fifteen metres between servers.

The concept is simple. The workers sprint to the server and complete any technical exercise. This may be to exchange passes on the ground, and can progress to volleys, half-volleys, knee and volley, etc. The technical activities are entirely up to the coach (or the players). After around 45 seconds, swap the servers and the workers so the work : rest ratio is balanced.

From a physical point of view, the key aspect is the sprint to the next server. Ensure players accelerate, decelerate and change direction as appropriate. Players should not wait for a server to become free, he must remain mobile and on the lookout for a free server, much like in the game of soccer itself.

Speed Agility Quickness

Speed, Agility, Quickness training is designed to focus on the specific elements of speed to ensure that players gain a rounded development in all aspects of speed work. SAQ work contains lots of changes of direction, quicksteps, changing foot patterns and carioca.

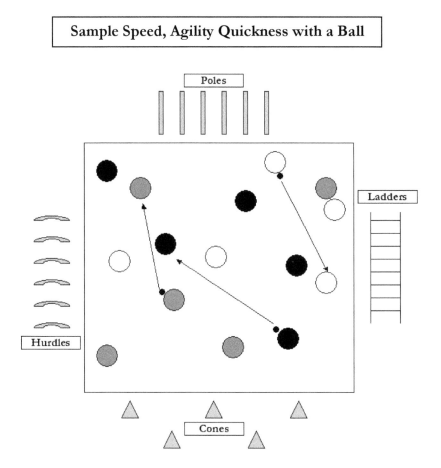

For this exercise I have set up a variable soccer practice within a square. Again, the size of the square will depend on the age and number of players you have. Three teams aim to keep the ball between them. This can be progressed to where the players must pass to a different colour, or receive from a different colour and pass to another. More details on this exercise can be found in Chapter 9.

Although I have used this particular technical exercise, in reality most technical practices can be used, especially if they are variable or random practices.

On the coach's command, one team leaves the area and completes an SAQ exercise at one of the outside stations. The coach can set specific movements, or allow the players to choose a way of navigating through the obstacle.

If you want some ideas on what SAQ movements are - relative to soccer - consult Alan Pearson's book *SAQ Soccer*.

Core Strength

There is a common misconception about core strength. Many see it as just about building a 'six-pack' stomach and therefore set about doing a countless number of sit-ups or 'crunch' type exercises. The core muscle-group however is made up of the abdominal, oblique, lower back and glute muscles. To develop a strong core, players must work around all these muscle groups. A strong six-pack must have the support of a strong back, otherwise they will not function sufficiently and will damage the back required to support it.

Core Muscles[4]		
Pelvic Floor	Transverse Abdominus	Rectus Abdominus
Internal Obliques	External Obliques	Erector Spinae
Multifidus	Gluteus Maximus	Latissimus Dorsi

A strong core helps not just the strength required to hold off players in 1 v 1 situations, but assists with balance, stability and the ability to change direction quickly and effectively.

Various exercises can be used to strengthen the core area. As advocated throughout this book, use your soccer practices for soccer. You can use core exercise handouts to your players who can complete them in their own time, away from the main sessions.

If you do want to work on soccer-strength in your sessions, I have included an example below as a way of activating the core within a soccer-specific exercise.

---

[4] This list is taken from Pro Football Support's *Core Performance for Footballers (2)*. Pro Football Support has several booklets available for free download that cover a whole range of physical development topics. Further soccer-specific core exercises can be found in the *FIFA 11+ A Complete Warm-Up Program*, which is also available as a free download online. This method, although completed without a ball, is self-proclaimed as having the ability to reduce injuries in players age 14+ by between 30 and 50%.

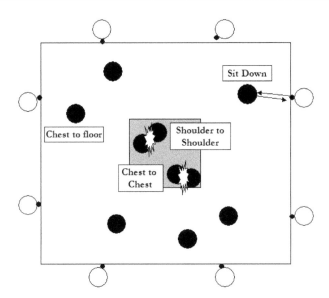

This exercise is similar to the speed one above. The black players work around the centre of the grid while the white players are involved in active rest as servers. There is also a smaller grid set up inside the main area. Like before, the players run to an available server and perform a technical exercise with the ball. Players must run back through the central square each time they complete a technical exercise.

Core strength in soccer is about activating the mid-section of the body. In the diagram above, I have included four ways of doing this:

1. Players must put their chest to the floor, before getting up quickly and completing a technical exercise with the server.

2. The players 'sit down' to complete a volley with both feet, before getting up quickly and completing the same volley standing up.

3. When players are running through the middle, they meet shoulder-to-shoulder in the air.

4. When players are running through the middle, they meet chest-to-chest in the air.

It is important to be wary of health and safety in this exercise. Change workers and servers every 30 – 45 seconds and ensure that elbows and knees are tucked in when meeting shoulder-to-shoulder or chest-to-chest. During the latter half of this exercise, players tend to focus on competition with the biggest players. It is worth pointing out that completing these exercises successfully is not about height and weight, but about activating a player's core to remain in balance upon physical contact.

Pre-Season

Pre-season is a time when many coaches focus on the fitness of their players. It is traditionally known as a gruelling time for players where they are worked consistently hard on their physical conditioning. Players may have spent weeks or even months without the same physical activity they are used to for nine months of the soccer season, and are therefore seen as in need of a strenuous period of exercise.

The Off-Season

The period between the end of the season and the commencement of pre-season is often known as the 'off-season'. This period of rest is important for players to recuperate physically from the demands of a long, demanding season. Traditionally, even amongst professional players, this period was used to indulge in eating and drinking to excess, safe in the knowledge that a gruelling pre-season program awaited, when all this excessiveness could be worked off. In the modern game this is now frowned upon and players are given off-season programs to ensure that they balance rest with the maintenance of their physical condition.

It is imperative that players are allowed this rest and recuperation time. During the off-season period it is optimal to rest completely in the early stages, before allowing players to build their activity up as the pre-season period approaches. Non-soccer exercises such as cycling and swimming can be very effective in keeping players active, but simultaneously working different muscle groups and energy systems.

Pre-Season Schedule

There is a temptation during pre-season to involve too much physical exertion, and there is certainly a temptation to use lots of exercises without the ball. Often we hear players of all ages relaying stories where they do not even see a ball for the first two weeks! If we take a step back, we will accept that any pre-season program should be designed to allow players to reach their full soccer and physical potential for the beginning of the games program. If the focus is simply on consistently tiring players out, you are going to induce fatigue amongst players before the season has even begun.

In *Soccer Conditioning*, Simon Thadani presents lots of very useful information around the appropriate use of the pre-season, and also attempts to dispel some myths that exist around soccer conditioning, most of which are evident in pre-season programs. He argues, as we do here also, that long distance running has little benefit for soccer players and advocates the reconsideration of the "no pain-no gain" mentality of many working in soccer.

On this basis, *Total Soccer Fitness For Juniors* recommends a "stair-step" approach to physical training for young players. The tendency can be to offer fitness-based sessions that are continually intense.

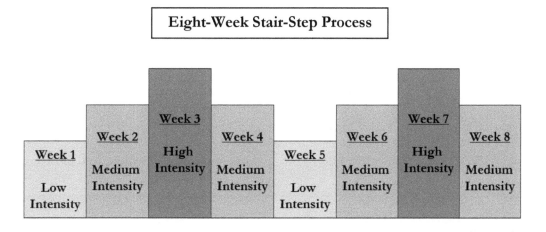

Nutrition

What your players eat is difficult to control. Let's face it, you cannot be with them 24/7 and, ultimately it will be parents and the child himself who will be making decisions around what food they consume. We may also remember that young players are young children also, so 'banning' junk food from their lifestyle is likely to ultimately backfire on you.

What you can do, and what you can control, however is the information that you provide to players and parents. We all assume that both know what good nutrition is, or should be, but do not be surprised if they don't! These are lots of good fact sheets and booklets available on nutrition that can be summarized and adapted for parents. Amongst other books, Elite Soccer Conditioning's *Soccer Nutrition* and FIFA's *Nutrition for Football – A practical guide to eating and drinking for health and performance* are available online without charge. The latter is particularly useful as it deals with young players, females, amateur, semi-professional and elite players, and also studies hydration, nutrition for players traveling, and details the effects of individual food groups.

Nutritionists will openly advertise what players eat being the ultimate difference between poor and successful performance. It is true that technical ability and tactical understanding will diminish if fitness levels do not complement them. Players consequently will not achieve their peak physical performance unless they consume the correct foods and remain hydrated.

Energy

Carbohydrate is the main food group required by soccer players. 'Carbs', once broken down and digested by the body, provide the players with the energy they need to compete in and complete a soccer game that is all-action, energetic, fast-paced and competitive. We tend to discourage players from eating fatty foods, but we must understand that a certain amount of fat also provides players with energy, and there are 'good fats' like those present in fish, olive oil and nuts. Too much fat, and certainly eating processed, fatty foods prior to exercise, can however be detrimental.

The chart below from Manchester United details relevant food groups, amounts, and the foods that contain such nutrients:

Nutrition Chart from Manchester United Soccer Schools

Nutrient	Amount to Eat	Foods
Carbohydrates	High	bread, rice, boiled, baked or mashed potatoes, pasta, noodles, breakfast cereals, oven chips, baked beans, deep pan pizza, couscous, noodles. potato cakes, crumpets, iced fingers,
Protein	Normal	lean meat, chicken, turkey, gammon, fish, beans, eggs, milk, nuts
Fat	Normal to Low	fried foods, mayonnaise, cheese, sausages, burgers, pastry, crisps, butter, margarine.
Vitamins and minerals	High	fruit, vegetables, salads
Water	High	water, fruit juice, cordials, low fat flavoured milk, fruit, vegetables

Individuals

Like any aspect of soccer development, nutrition can be very individual. It can vary in terms of player preference, parental habits, their habits, their school menu, and also social, religious and cultural differences may exist. "Each player is different, and there is no single diet that meets the needs of all players at all times." (FIFA, *Nutrition for Football*).

Below is an individual, 24-hour food diary of former Manchester United, Atlético Madrid, and Uruguay forward and captain, Diego Forlan, published in *FourFourTwo Magazine*. Forlan was renowned for his on-field energy and tireless running. The original article also features the expert analysis of elite sports nutritionist, Matt Lovell.

Diego Forlan's 24-Hour Food Diary	
Breakfast 8am	Plate of pineapple
	Brown toast
	Yogurt
	Ham and cheese omelette (occasionally)
	Fresh orange juice
Lunch 1pm	Pasta / rice
	Grilled chicken (not fried)
Snack 4pm	Fruit smoothie
	Toasted sandwich
	Cereal
Evening Meal 9pm	Fish
	Salad
	Steamed vegetables
Drink	Water

Fatigue

In any practice session, but ones based around physical development in particular, the coach must be aware of the effects of fatigue or tiredness. Younger players in particular can tire extremely quickly, and will need longer breaks. Ensure that you provide players with optimal times to rehydrate. Fatigue will affect learning (remember Maslow's Hierarchy of Needs from Chapter 3!), technical quality with the ball, tactical decision-making, and also motivation. If you are attempting to teach players something new, ensure this work is completed while players are relatively fresh physically and mentally.

Conclusion

If you, as the coach, are taking the physical development of youth players into your hands, be sure you know what you are doing! A little information can be a dangerous thing, so ensure you are well versed in whatever aspect of fitness, conditioning or testing that you are enforcing. If you are not knowledgeable enough or comfortable enough in delivering scientific fitness sessions, deliver soccer ones instead! I have seen and heard many coaches provide players with incorrect technical or tactical information – even information that exists beyond best practice and the principles of the game. In many ways these are harmless. Physical development however is not something you ought to bluff and can lead to serious consequences for players.

Summary

- Having just a little knowledge of youth physical development, can do a lot of harm.

- Sports science and soccer-specific considerations have put a lot of traditional fitness concepts into question.

- Elite soccer players cover 10 – 13 kilometres during a 90-minute game, but these movements vary and are not completed in straight lines at a consistent pace.

- All formal fitness tests, although based in science, have their flaws.

- If you are unsure about the science of fitness follow one rule – absorb fitness work within your soccer sessions.

- Soccer-based exercises can be used to develop aerobic and anaerobic endurance, physical literacy, speed, SAQ, and core strength.

- Avoid repeated shuttles with younger players – their bodies are not built for them. Complete physical literacy exercises instead.

- Specializing players early in just one sport hampers the development of all-round motor skills, can reduce motivation, and can be the cause of overuse injuries.

- Include a ball and dynamic stretches in your warm up.

- People begin to lose their flexibility from age 10 – include static stretching in your cool down to improve this and to help players recover quicker.

- Speed is important in modern soccer, but is not just about how quickly a player gets from A to B.

- Core strength is not about the '6-pack' only – it involves the abdominal, oblique, lower back, and glute muscles.

- Pre-season is no longer about working players physically over and over again. It is about preparing them for the season ahead.

- Your players' nutrition is difficult to control – do not assume players and parents know what an effective, healthy soccer diet is.

- Fatigue affects concentration, learning, technical ability and tactical decision-making.

Real Coach Experience

Let Down in the Process

(Anonymous, Former Academy Player)

Up until now this section of each chapter has been reserved for stories from coaches. This was until I met a 17-year-old former academy player whose story underlines the importance of getting physical work correct when developing players. I have paraphrased the player's side of the conversation we had.

"From the age of eight, I spent six years playing for a particular academy. I was spotted playing for my local team and joined the academy in a heartbeat! I left my local soccer club, and, on the club's advice, stopped playing other sports.

Throughout my six years there, I was always told that I was a great worker and that so long as I worked hard, I would be successful. I took the coaches at their word – after all, being told that success follows hard work is the most common thing I have heard from coaches. On the back of this, I made sure that if I did nothing else, I would run around with enthusiasm, work hard in any fitness sessions, and let my work ethic shine through.

At 14-years-old however I was released from the club. The main reason provided was that I was not technically good enough, that I struggled to control and manipulate the ball, and I was too "awkward" for the modern game.

Although being released hit me hard, I soon dusted myself down, and armed with the feedback from my former coaches, I decided to do something about it.

There was a local coach whose expertise was in individual technical development, so I sought his help. I went to his house one evening, boots in hand, expecting to be worked one-to-one with a ball. Rather than train however, he took my dad and I inside and began asking questions about my soccer background.

He traced all my sporting background and determined that my "awkwardness" was a result of not being exposed to fundamental exercises when I was younger, either in primary school or at my soccer club, and that being encouraged not to play other sports was a big mistake. He pointed out that at my age, it was difficult to develop players drastically both technically and in terms of fundamental movements.

By working with this coach I felt an improvement in my game, although the process was extremely difficult. We worked mainly on a combination of individual ball-work and SAQ exercises, using ladders, hurdles and cones to try to "quicken my feet".

I felt this coach did right by me, but still feel very sad and bitter that some simple primary school ABCs work could have been the difference between me being a professional player and the reality of essentially being left on the scrap heap. I would advise any player that is simply told to "work hard" to be aware of the need to work smart also – and be under the influence of smart coaches.

Understanding the Modern Goalkeeper

"Goalkeeping is more than line keeping and kicking the ball up front." (Ruben Sterrenburg)

The position of goalkeeper has changed and evolved greatly over the last few decades. In the modern game they are now permitted, for example, to move along the goal line on a penalty kick and take as many steps as they require with the ball in their hands. Other changes in the game like the increased movement of newer soccer balls, making the predictability of a ball's flight harder to judge, have also impacted the role of soccer's last line of defence.

Changed Forever

The early 1990s saw the greatest challenge, but also the greatest change, in the life of a goalkeeper. In 1992, the "back-pass" rule was introduced into the Laws of Association Football. For those young enough not to remember football pre-1992, it was perfectly acceptable for a goalkeeper to pick up a pass from his teammate. This was often used as the ultimate means to time-waste legally and often led to dull games, which came to a head at the World Cup: Italia 1990.

One game springs to mind from that tournament. England were leading Egypt 1-0 in Cagliari, and in the meantime - 400km away in Palermo - the Republic of Ireland and Holland merely needed a draw for both to qualify from Group F. With the scores level at 1-1, the game petered out in the closing stages leading to the Irish goalkeeper, Pat Bonner, constantly rolling the ball out to his defenders, before happily collecting the back pass to kill the game. Against Egypt in the same tournament, Bonner allegedly had the ball in his possession for a total of six minutes!

The modern game now demands that the goalkeeper becomes a player. Of course he has to be able to stop shots, catch crosses, and dominate the goal area, but now he needs to have soccer skills similar to those of outfield team-mates.

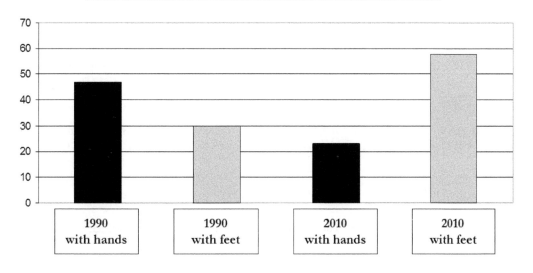

World Cup Final 1990 v World Cup Final 2010: Goalkeeper Interventions

The diagram above illustrates quite clearly how the role of the goalkeeper has changed since the back-pass rule was implemented. In the 1990 World Cup Final between West Germany[1] and Argentina (the last World Cup prior to the rule change), of the 77 balls the goalkeepers had to intervene upon, 47 were with their hands, compared to just 23 (of 81) in the 2010 final between Spain and Holland. This trend is reversed when we see that goalkeepers in 1990 used their feet 30 times, but the 2010 ones played the ball with their feet almost twice as much (58 times). Of the 25 back passes received in the 1990 final, 21 were handled whereas, as you would expect, all 29 back passes in the 2010 final were dealt with by the goalkeeper using his feet.[2]

Long-Term Goalkeeper Development

During an interview with *The Goalkeeping Conference*, Eric Steele, current goalkeeping coach for English Championship side, Derby County, and a former coach at Manchester United, was asked what topics he would cover with players every week. Steele was succinct and unequivocal in his answer: "Look to cover the following 4 areas using other departments at the Football [soccer] club – Technical, tactical, mental and physical."

His answer reveals a lot about the modern approach to coaching goalkeepers. First of all it is not just about technical training, it must be multi-disciplinary. Also, goalkeepers need to work in an integrated way with the rest of the team, rather than in isolation, far away from the main group; an approach that has traditionally been the norm.

With this in mind, and changes to goalkeeping in the modern era, we will now look at the various components of long-term goalkeeper development and explore ways of integrating them into team practices.

Psychological

The position of goalkeeper is arguably the most mentally demanding position in soccer. To do it well, players need a huge amount of self-belief, confidence and a recurring ability to recover from setbacks. There are some that argue that goalkeepers even need be a little bit "mad"!

Strikers are often forgiven for missing chances as they are 'getting in the right position' and will most likely have another chance to compensate for their error. Conversely, a costly mistake from a goalkeeper will most likely result in the concession of a goal. With this comes lots of pressure to perform to high standards consistently.

There is a video on YouTube of goalkeeper Petr Cech during a training exercise. The practice involves multiple balls, and also the coach firing tennis balls at him. During the one-minute video, the stopper must either catch or throw around 100 different balls from three different angles. Of the 100 or so he deals with, he mishandles one – quite an excellent percentage. If you watch the video, however, you will notice the reaction of the coach to this drop and is shows you exactly what pressure goalkeepers at the top level have to deal with.[3] Now you would not expect a youth coach to react in such a way, but it does highlight the huge expectations on modern goalkeepers.

Recovering from Set-Backs

Chances are that if your team's goalkeeper makes an obvious error or poor decision, they will already understand their mistake – and will feel bad enough about it! In a coaching sense, this

---

[1] Although the Berlin Wall came down in 1989, 'West' Germany competed in the World Cup Italia '90. They competed in post-war international competition as 'Germany' for the first time in the European Championships of 1992.

[2] All statistics are from FIFA's *Goalkeeping* manual, which is available to download free online.

[3] To view this video, search YouTube for "The Ultimate Goalkeeping Drill…with Petr Cech".

gives them a ready-made opportunity to self-correct which, in itself, is an excellent tool for long-term learning. When dealing with these errors, beware of adding negative comments to an already negative situation[4] - I doubt negativity will help.

Technical errors will befall any player, in any position, and in any sport. The fact that conceding a goal highlights the error further is probably punishment enough for goalkeepers. If there is an error that is less obvious – for example the goalkeeper's start position was too deep – then use this as a learning tool as the player may not be able to self-correct.

In *Coping With Negative Media Content: The Experiences of Professional Football Goalkeepers*, published by the *International Journal of Sport and Exercise Psychology*, one of the goalkeepers interviewed stated his gratitude to his coach after a particular mistake:

> "I really appreciate support from the coach, like last year when he told me that I would play regardless of the number of mistakes I made… I knew that I most likely would not make so many more mistakes. I did not make any mistakes for three games in a row. I got confidence from him – it helped."

Ironically, the work of a competent goalkeeper can tend to go largely unnoticed. When errors are made, however, they can find themselves right in the spotlight. At youth level this can be from teammates, their coach and opponents – and at professional level from supporters, rival supporters and the media. In *Coping With Negative Media Content*, research showed that goalkeepers were given specific media coverage in only two instances. The first was when they made a high-profile error; a derogatory headline and a photograph of the stricken goalkeeper normally accompanied the story. The second was to scrutinize them when they were called up to play for their national team.

Coping Strategies

Support from the coach when errors occur – and they will occur – is clearly a massive part of the support network that helps goalkeepers cope with the anxiety of the position. Also, and for the young goalkeeper in particular – the understanding and support of his peers is key. Young people, in general, value the opinion of their friends greatly, so creating a culture of support amongst all members of your squad is vital.

Goalkeepers (as well as outfield players) can be supported further by coming up with their own coping strategies when recovering from inevitable set-backs. Some may be naturally confident and self-aware, and accept errors as a major part of their job. I once heard a story about Australian International goalkeeper, Mark Schwarzer. If he made an error, he would react by symbolically walking slowly around the back of the goal. By the time he re-entered the pitch a few moments later, he would be over the mistake and ready to go again.

When Dan Gaspar (former Portuguese National Team Coach) was asked about coping strategies in an interview with www.keeperstop.com, his answer was laced with useful advice that we can pass on to young goalkeepers:

> "Once a mistake is made during the game the first thing is to understand at that moment and accept that you cannot change that mistake. Acceptance is key. You can do this by controlling your breathing. Inhale positive energy through your nose and exhale the waste out through your mouth. Shake your body and get moving again. Be dynamic and alive. You can even pick up grass and hold it until you release the mistake from your mind. You can create an imaginary wastebasket at the corner of the field. You made a mistake – mentally toss it into the wastebasket. Remember the quicker you bounce back, the more confidence your team mates will have that they can depend on you. No matter how great of a goalkeeper you are or

---

[4] I recently had an opposition coach shout to his goalkeeper: "I hope you are not catching the train home tonight, because you will probably miss that as well"!

will be, one thing is for certain, you will make mistakes and concede goals. The great ones learn and grow from the mistakes and move on."

Who else could endure a livelihood where mistakes are so cruelly punished and the best parts of your game so blatantly cast aside once an error is made? Coaches concern themselves with diagnosing whether the goalkeeper could have held the cross rather than punch it, while commentators and pundits feebly claim that a keeper should have palmed a 60 – 70mph shot on goal away to safety, rather than in front of goal. Most analysts still persist in calling Jerzy Dudek's wonder save in extra-time of the 2005 Champions League final as "lucky" even though the Polish stopper made a save, got up quickly and made himself 'big' for the rebound – something goalkeepers work on every day!

Decision-Making

A great line I recently read from an Academy goalkeeper syllabus was about advising goalkeepers on the importance of making a decision – irrespective as to whether it is right or wrong. Indecision amongst goalkeepers is considered the worst possible outcome. This adds a certain pressure on keepers, but also requires a lot of courage. A goalkeeper's decision – whether to catch or punch a cross; catch or parry a shot; distribute short; confront an onrushing striker in a 1 v 1 situation – will be made in a fraction of a second and will often be critical to preventing a goal (or not). Once a decision has been made, the goalkeeper *must live with it!*

Technical

Although goalkeepers initially struggled with the new technical demands imposed on them by the back-pass rule, twenty years later, they are now developed with the technical ability to live with this rule. So much so that indirect free-kicks for back-pass offences are a rare occurrence – in fact, a sharp 'Cruyff' turn by the goalkeeper, with a striker bearing down on them, is a far more regular occurrence.

The goalkeeper is now not just the mad one in the group, but a player, a sweeper, and the starter of attacks from his defensive third. The goalkeeper is now a soccer player. A FIFA study analysed 43 games from various competitions from September 2004 to May 2005; the interventions used are displayed below:

FIFA Study of Goalkeeper Interventions

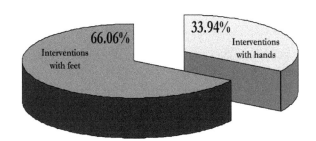

Youth goalkeepers need to be as comfortable with the ball at their feet, as they are with their hands. Below we will look at ways of incorporating both disciplines within the goalkeepers' technical program.

Although the soccer skills of the goalkeeper needs plenty of attention, there is still real importance and real value in the handling techniques required to stop shots, parry, catch or punch crosses and, of course, distribute with one's hands. They will need specific work for what is a very specialized position. There are several technical-specific goalkeeping resources available where you can learn more about the intricacies of hand position, body shape and detail around handling technique and decision-making. Andy Elleray's *Scientific Approaches to Goalkeeping in Football* is very good in this respect, as is FIFA's *Goalkeeping* manual (available free online).

Problems or Solutions?

When working with very young goalkeepers, it is easy to identify certain technical 'problems'. Coaches bemoan issues such as not being able to kick the ball far or high, and when the ball is kicked - it being intercepted near to goal by the opposition.

The easiest, most immediately successful solution may be to get an outfield player to take goal-kicks for the goalkeeper. As a long-term youth development coach, ask yourself whether that will result in the long-term improvement of the young player, or just the short-term improvement in the match result? Then consider which one is more important – your goalkeeper's long-term development or the result of a single match?

Another flawed solution may be to spend lots of time practicing long distance kicking with the goalkeeper during your training sessions. However, I am afraid that the power in a young player's legs to strike a ball with power and distance is not going to change with a single training session.

Tactical

The goalkeeper is the last line of defence. The influence of the goalkeeper in this respect means that he or she may well be the most important player on the pitch. If tactics are dependent on individual decisions, performances and in many cases, errors, the goalkeeper is a vital cog in that machine. A good goalkeeper, as the old saying goes, is worth ten extra league points a season. If their performances are not up to scratch, then tactics become largely irrelevant.

Goalkeepers are not just a part of a team's defensive tactics, they are now very much a part of a team's offensive strategy. If the goalkeeper catches the ball for example, he will use this possession to potentially counter-attack if required, or slow the game down if the team are in the lead. His tactical decision-making, as the originator of an attack, is critical. He will choose whether the attacking build-up is slow and precise by playing short, or quick and direct by playing longer up-field. What I am keen to emphasize, however, is that no goalkeeper's possession is haphazard. Distribution is linked to a tactic, with the ball rarely just distributed back into the field of play randomly.

Many teams will now use their goalkeeper as an eleventh outfield player or 'libero', with outfield players happily turning and passing to the goalkeeper who helps the team get out of trouble, keep possession, switch play and restart stuttering attacks. Teams now base their in-possession, attacking tactics on plays originating from the feet of the goalkeeper. The style of Barcelona is a case-in-point. Goalkeeper Víctor Valdés, as part of his club's ultra-possession-based philosophy, is *almost* banned from playing the ball long and turning the game into a 50-50 battle between opponents to secure the ball. Often (though not 100% of the time), the longest kick goalkeepers like Valdés will produce, is a diagonal pass to their forward-thinking full-backs stationed around the halfway line.

Using the goalkeeper as the first line of attack, and demanding that they are technically excellent is a wonderful example of football bravery. To use such calculated risk in building play from your own defensive third, especially considering the pressures of goalkeeping discussed earlier – one mistake and you are in trouble – is admirable. A world-class goalkeeper will now be the most rounded player at the club, able to compete technically with their outfield counterparts, but excel when it comes to their handling.

Goalkeeper Role at Set-Plays

Goalkeepers are keen to dominate their goal area and penalty box. It is, after all, their domain. Their disinterest in scoring goals or being a flamboyant dribbler, means the goalkeeper lives and dies by what happens in and around his goal, and will judge himself heavily on the number of goals conceded. As a result, young goalkeepers need to be influenced to have pride and accept responsibility in protecting their goal, and have other players help them do so.

The goalkeeper's role at set-plays or restarts is crucial. He should be prepared, not only to get his positioning and decision-making correct, but also the positioning of others and ensure that they help him stave off the attack. I like to encourage goalkeepers to be a part of the decision-making process with regards to how the team sets up their defensive set-plays. Some, for example, prefer to take control of the goal and not use any zonal markers at goalposts. Others will want one post or both posts covered. Allow the players to take this responsibility. It is empowering, player-centred, and encourages goalkeepers to take responsibility for their decisions.

I am often asked questions around setting up a defensive wall at free-kicks. The first diagram below is from *The Modern Goalkeeper* presentation from Neil Cooper, where he suggests the numbers involved in a defensive wall in a particular area of the attacking third.

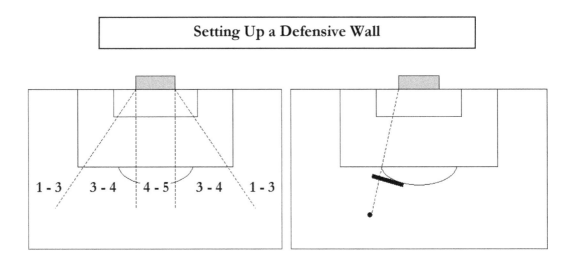

The second diagram shows the setup of a defensive wall. Traditionally, goalkeepers would line up the outside of their wall in a line between the near post and the ball. Given, however, the increased movement of the modern soccer ball, and the more unpredictable nature of whether left or right footers will take free-kicks from different sides, goalkeepers will now set up the wall with one player placed outside the line of the post and ball.

Physical

Physically, the demands on goalkeepers are different than the demands on outfield players. Like their outfield counterparts, goalkeepers still need a base level of aerobic fitness, but their actions and physical traits are notably different.

The Height Debate

There is probably no better place to begin, when examining the physical attributes of a keeper, than with their height. If height is *the* significant factor in producing players for the position, what implications does that have for the youth coach?

During a recent conversation with goalkeeper coach specialist, Rob Parker, he commented: "Coaching keepers at a young age is a true lottery. For many their success can depend on whether they will grow tall enough to cover the necessary ground that is required, as well as be able to move efficiently in the body they are given."

As we have discussed in previous chapters, the soccer fraternity is moving away from judging and assessing players merely based on size and strength. We noted that players who display these physical features from a young age often stand out and cosmetically appear to be the best player, but as they grow older, other players start to match them physically and they begin to lose their advantage.

There seems to be very little change when it comes to measuring a goalkeeper's ability and potential based on their height and size. In the professional game, it is rare to find a goalkeeper that is not among the tallest in their squads. The below statistics have come from David Nield's article *The Average Goalkeeper Height*.

Average Goalkeeper Height Across Three Major Leagues (2010)	
League	**Average GK Height**
Premier League (England)	1.92 meters (6 foot 3)
La Liga (Spain)	1.87 meters (6 foot 1)
Major League Soccer (USA)	1.89 meters (6 foot 2)

Each year the *International Federation of Football History and Statistics* (IFFHS) compiles a list of the world's best players. From the winners of the goalkeeper award since 1987, only German stopper Andreas Köpke and Belgian Jean-Marie Pfaff (out of the 13 winners) were less than six feet tall. Again, the table below of the top five goalkeepers of 2013 shows that the smallest, Víctor Valdés, is the shortest by some way, but still stands at six foot.

IFFHS The World's Best Goalkeeper 2013	
Goalkeeper	**Height**
Manuel Neuer	1.93 meters (6 foot 4)
Gianluigi Buffon	1.91 meters (6 foot 3)
Petr Cech	1.97 meters (6 foot 5 ½)
Thibaut Courtois	1.98 meters (6 foot 6)
Víctor Valdés	1.83 meters (6 foot)

Physical Exertion of a Goalkeeper

In 2008, a study of 69 Premier League goalkeepers found that they covered an average of just over 5.5 kilometres during a 90-minute match, over four kilometres of which was spent walking. This distance, however, was regularly interrupted with short, intensive bursts of energy – making use primarily of the anaerobic energy system that we discussed in the previous chapter. Logic would then suggest that coaches match the game-related requirements of the goalkeeping position, and specific goalkeeper training should involve intensive bursts of work, followed by sufficient periods of rest.

Anyone who has seen a specific goalkeeping session will know that they provide the participants with quite a workout. The force with which goalkeepers hit the ground after a dive, before getting back up quickly to make a secondary save, means that their strength, power and core stability is constantly being worked and tested. Periods of rest are therefore vital to maintain the quality of work being completed. Remember, also, from the previous chapter that young children's anaerobic energy systems are not yet fully developed, and they will tire quicker, so shorter bursts of work and fewer repetitions, followed by longer active rest periods is important.

Along with strength, power, core stability and anaerobic fitness, goalkeepers also need to be quick and agile. In the previous chapter we discussed the use of Speed, Agility, Quickness in soccer training – something that is also imperative for goalkeepers. Although the use of pre-positioned SAQ equipment is valuable, Andy Elleray argues that "multi-directional movement drills or acceleration speed drills are more important" given that goalkeeping is not performed in straight lines.

Communication

Goalkeepers are often judged on how loud they are and how well they communicate. There is an expectation on them to "be the eyes, ears and mouth of the defence" (*5 Simple Rules for Young Goalkeepers and Their Coaches*). They have a positional advantage on the field in that they can see the whole pitch and the 'big picture'. This may help them recognize what is happening, or predict what may happen next. The notion of the goalkeeper dominating 'his' or 'her' penalty area stems from not just his 'stature' and presence, but also his ability to dominate verbally. This may be to warn teammates of dangerous opponents, 'squeeze' his defenders higher up the pitch, organize team mates at set plays, or to claim the ball ("keepers!").

An ex-colleague of mine was excellent when it came to developing communication in young goalkeepers. In match situations he would initially ask them to speak – it did not matter what they said initially – just get used to using their voices. As they progressed and got older, he would then start to demand more concise and precise information be used.

The Youth Goalkeeper

There is something especially innocent and heart-warming about a young child that wants to be a goalkeeper. Unlike the majority of 8-year-olds, he does not crave scoring a goal or dribbling at speed beyond numerous defenders. He wants to prevent scoring. He wants to be the last line of defence and jump, dive, and fall like his TV hero Tim Howard or Iker Casillas.

Like all youth soccer player development, the youth goalkeeper will travel through the age and development-related: Long-Term Player Development. Just as with outfield players, young goalkeepers will go through numerous stages that begin with experiencing the game and physical literacy before 10 years of age, through the "golden age of learning" and puberty-related consequences, before entering stages of refinement and game-understanding towards the end of their teens.

In fact, the development of the goalkeeper can be much later than outfield players. It is rare, for example, at the top end of soccer that a teenage goalkeeper will become a team's first choice. Goalkeepers also tend to play for longer, with goalkeepers frequently playing in the professional game in their 40s. In many ways a teenage goalkeeper needs to be more patient when searching for professional opportunities, and be willing to spend some time as second or third choice to more experienced goalkeepers. The importance and maturity required to dominate games and the requirement to be mentally strong in the face of adversity requires this maturation.

Specialization

Goalkeeping can be seen as a hybrid of general soccer and of other sports. It is a position where the value of hand-eye coordination is imperative for success. Encouraging your young goalkeepers to play a variety of other hand-based sports may be very useful in the long-term. Sports such as handball, basketball and rugby can provide goalkeepers with lots of specific hand-eye and catching practice that will benefit them greatly. During these sports, players will also be required to perform techniques around catching and throwing in an *opposed environment*, thus inducing further *deliberate practice* into their development.

Integrating Goalkeepers Into Team Practices

With the breadth of the goalkeeper's role, from 'line-keeper' to first attacker, it has become more and more important that our youth goalkeepers are developed with their specialist position in mind, and with the technical skills that allow them to act like an outfield player.

Traditionally, team coaches watched the goalkeepers and goalkeeper coach walk into the corner of the pitch for three-quarters of the practice, and either rejoin the team to allow outfield players some shooting practice, or when a small-sided game was beginning. This, in itself, is no longer good enough. One-to-one technical coaching from a specialist coach remains an important aspect of goalkeeper development. It is, after all, a soccer position like no other on the pitch, where focused, specialist work is crucial.

Coaches now, however, need to be more creative, and work with their goalkeepers as a part of the team too. They are after all, your team's first attacker. The modern goalkeeper is also a passing option and reliever of pressure, as well as a shot-stopper.

The implications therefore for coaches working with goalkeepers are considerable. It remains important that they receive specific work in handling and footwork exercises as per the traditional norm. This will generally be through one-to-one sessions or small-group sessions with a specific technical goalkeeping coach[5].

Modern goalkeepers must also be absorbed in the technical work that outfield players undertake. Passing and receiving exercises are especially important, as are ball manipulation exercises aimed at making them more comfortable with the ball at their feet, especially from a young age.

A recent conversation with an Academy goalkeeper coach highlighted this new pressure that the club's number one, and his mentor, is under. He explained:

> "We have produced several goalkeepers now that have made it through to the first team over the past few years. The most common negative feedback I get relates to their ability with the ball at their feet. As a result of this we had to completely re-write our goalkeeping curriculum to ensure that a) we improve their feet and eat into this criticism from above, but b) also ensure that we continue producing goalkeepers that are good enough with their hands for that level. Getting the balance between both is critical."

As a result of this, more and more professional goalkeeper coaches are now actively leaving their goalkeepers to spend more time getting involved in squad practices, rather than taking them for one-to-one or small group work. Depending on the philosophy of the individual club and individual coaching program, the ratio of handling to passing and receiving work may be 50:50.

Involving keepers in ball manipulation work is also becoming increasingly important. These 'one ball, one player' exercises, which may evolve into 1v1 work, allows the myelination process to help a goalkeeper develop their natural footwork whilst encouraging confidence and habit with a ball at their feet, under pressure. They can then be comfortable enough to perform that Cruyff turn with a striker haring down on them. They may need to perform this 'get out of trouble' manoeuvre only a handful of times in their career, but crucially, they will be able to complete it. By learning the complicated things, the routine tasks they are asked to complete in game situations will come as second nature.

---

[5] For a variety of technical detail and practice sessions around one-to-one goalkeeping exercises, it is worth downloading FIFA's manual *Goalkeeping*. The 200+ page document contains lots of information around lots of techniques around handling, diving, punching and positional play.

Below, I have offered a variety of practices that can be easily adapted to involve the needs of the goalkeeper.

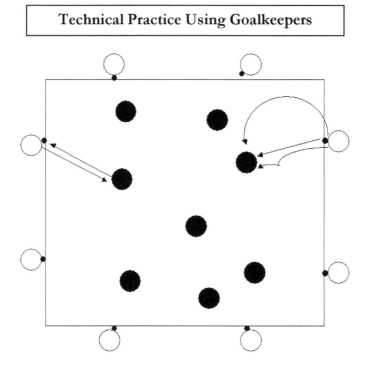

This technical or physical practice can be adapted to include specific goalkeeper work also. The ball can be served to outfield players to include one or two touch passes, volleys, headers, etc. Goalkeepers can be fed differently to allow them to practice their handling on the ground, to the mid-body, chest, aerial catches, or even saves and punches.

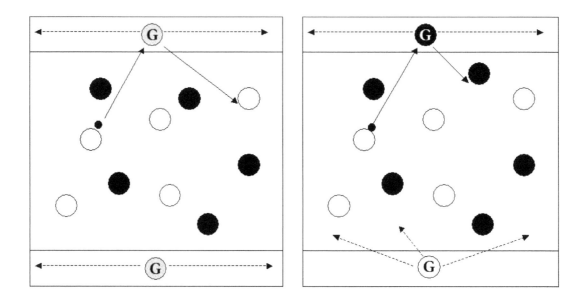

This exercise can be set up to help with developing possession-based elements of both outfield players and the role of the goalkeepers. It also includes both handling and footwork.

In the first game, the blacks play against the whites. They attempt to score by combining and playing passes into the goalkeeper's feet or hands. The goalkeeper can support the play by moving throughout his channelled off area. Once they score a goal playing one way, they keep possession and attack in the other direction. The goalkeeper whom the team is not attacking can be used as an option to retain possession, and build up the attack.

This exercise can be progressed to become a more directional practice, with one goalkeeper playing for the black team and one goalkeeper playing for the whites.

Once in possession, the goalkeeper can be encouraged to join in the attacks along with his team-mates.

This gives him practice with his feet in opposed, pressurized situations, to help him acquire the skill needed to compete with outfield players.

Coming for Crosses Small-Sided Games for Goalkeepers

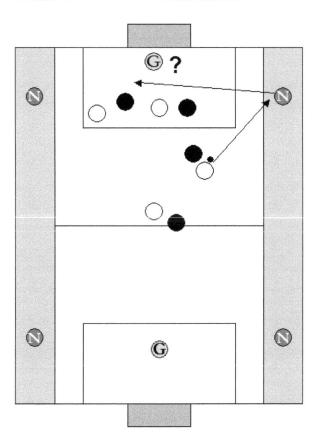

This small-sided game can again be used for outfield players, but with an extra focus on the goalkeepers involved.

Four neutral players are placed in outside channels and are tasked with crossing the ball into the penalty area once they receive possession. Mix the traits of the neutral players so that some crosses in-swing, and others out-swing. Of course, this session could be used to work on the crossing of wide players, the finishing of strikers, or the defending capabilities of the defending team.

The emphasis here, however, is on the goalkeepers and their decision-making and technical proficiency when coming to catch or punch crosses. This, of course, may be linked with the role of defenders and a goalkeeper's communication skills.

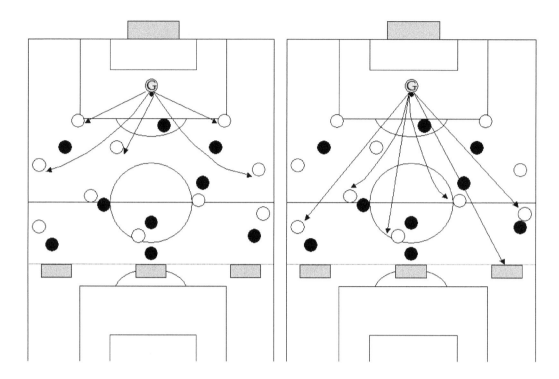

The phase of play above would be best used for players beyond the age of 14. It can be adapted for younger goalkeepers, in terms of a technical exercise, but they may not fully understand the tactical elements of the practice. Nor may they be physically able to complete the technical elements required for the longer passes.

In the first diagram, the goalkeeper is making decisions about whether to pass short to his back four, or defensive midfielder. The goalkeeper's decision will be largely influenced by the decisions of the opposition. The technical elements around the weight of pass, direction and movements of the receivers are important, as is the movement of the goalkeeper to receive a return pass if necessary.

The second diagram shows the goalkeeper distributing over longer distances. The technical requirements involved are for more advanced (older) youth players. Again, decisions will be based on the opposition. If the goalkeeper can score in one of the goals, this will cause opponents to drop off and allow more space to play shorter passes. Playing passes safe-side to any receiver needs to be considered.

Planning

Like with outfield players, appropriate planning is important when developing goalkeepers. Planning sessions around your goalkeeper's needs are essential. They should not be expected to improve and develop when placed in random sessions. Sessions should be periodized and not episodic, as we discussed in chapter 8.

Session Planning

Most goalkeeping planning documents I have seen contain a multitude of goalkeeper-specific work that takes place on a regular basis. The *Goalkeeper Development Program* from English Academy Doncaster Rovers demands that the following take place in every goalkeeper-related session:

1. A warm-up involving footwork and ball-familiarity exercises

2. As many touches of the ball as possible

3. Attention to the improvement of basic techniques and skills

4. Where appropriate, the application of these basic techniques and skills in game-related practices

5. A debriefing at the end of the session to cover the coaching points

6. A cool-down involving flexibility exercises

Syllabus

Below is an age-appropriate syllabus taken from a club in the English Championship. Note the progression from the outcomes required as the player grows older. Remember, however, that these are outcomes. For example, a six-year-old is not expected to have all these attributes, but will work towards them progressively.

Technical	5 – 11 Years Old Outcomes
Ball Manipulation	Be able to control the ball with a maximum of three touches. Good use of dominant foot and hand
Distribution	Short passes over 10 – 15 metres Ability to take goal-kicks over a distance of 20 – 30 metres Kick out of hands to reach halfway line (relative to pitch size) Throw the ball underarm and overarm over short distances
Handling	'set' position 'W' and 'M' hand positions Straight and bent leg pick ups Using body as second barrier Forward scoop Protecting the ball
Diving / Saves	Collapse dive off the knees, both sides Short mid-height thrown serve Hands protect the ball, head over it Decisions around whether to catch or parry Reactions to parries and dropped catches Step and save, both sides, low and mid-height
Crossing	Confident start positions Into and down the line of the ball Knee up to protect themselves Take off using both legs
Shot-Stopping	Into and down the line of the ball

	Basic angles
	Reacting to second balls
Positioning	Positive distances from the ball
	Getting into positions to receive back passes
	Positioning for crosses
Set-Plays	Being alert
	Start position
	Communication
Footwork	Forward skip
	Combinations of footwork movement
	Slalom
Communication	Basic use of terms

Technical	12 – 16 Years Old Outcomes
Ball Manipulation	Work all parts of feet and body
	Control back passes with one touch or maximum two touches
	Ability to use both feet
Distribution	Short passing to defenders
	Reach half-way line from long goal-kicks
	Long wide passes to team-mates in their own half
	Develop the half-volley
	Throw the ball underarm
	Throw the ball overarm to players 20-20 yards away, with pace
	Javelin throw
	Throw in front of receiving player
	Just two bounces into receiving player
Handling	Using 'W' and 'M' technique
	Catch served volleys and drives 60 – 75% of the time
	Correct decision on whether to catch or 'parry' 70% of the time
	Use of ball once caught
	Bent knee pick-up with both legs
	Using parts of the body as a second barrier
Diving / Saves	Collapse dive off the knees, on both sides
	Short mid-height thrown serve
	Forward scoop, hands protect the ball, head over ball

	Reaction to parries or dropped catches	
	Step and save on both low and mid saves	
	Develop top hand saves	
	Make bigger saves at mid-height	
	Taking the save outside the line of the shot	
	Parrying into safe areas	
	Attack the save aggressively	
	Higher tempo	
Crossing	'Aggressive' start positions	
	Getting into the line and down the line of the cross	
	Using high knee to protect themselves	
	Taking off using both legs	
	Improve decision-making on when to come for crosses	
	Develop technique of punching	
	Technique of going to ground after catching a cross	
Shot-Stopping	Into and down the line of the ball	
	Improve positioning and angles	
	React to second balls	
	Improve distance on parried shots, hitting 'safe' areas	
	Improve reactions to close-range shots	
	Improve decisions in 1 v 1 situations	
Positioning	Adjustments in relation to ball being in attacking, middle of defensive thirds	
	Understanding the position of defenders in relation to goalkeeper and the ball	
	Be in position to help defenders give back passes and demand the ball	
Set-Plays	Improve start position, relative to the position of the ball	
	Be alert and aware of players around them	
	Provide players with relevant information	
	Take charge and show leadership	
	Aware of defender responsibilities whether defending man-to-man or zonally	
	Making decisions	
	Organizing a defensive wall	
Footwork	Refine footwork from pre-12 years old	
Communication	Advanced use of terms in the right context	

Conclusion

The role of the goalkeeper has changed significantly since the early 1990s, and so has the evolution of how they train and practice. Goalkeepers still require traditional one-to-one coaching around technique, shot-stopping, positioning, etc. but the modern goalkeeper is now required to have the distribution and foot skills of his outfield counterparts.

There is a requirement to understand, like Ruben Sterrenburg suggested at the beginning of the chapter, that in order to develop a well-rounded goalkeeper, coaches need to expect more from them than to just stand between the goalposts, make saves, and them simply thump the ball up-field. Youth goalkeepers need to be treated as specialists, but within the team, and their specific work needs to be considered *within* your team practice sessions.

The *FA Youth Module 2 Learner Resource* booklet suggests ten ways in which to work with your goalkeepers, which neatly sums up what this chapter has discussed.

1. Organize practices to include the goalkeeper, rather than considering them merely as an "afterthought".

2. Provide them with objectives that are specific to them.

3. Allow them the scope to make their own decisions.

4. Give them the chance to work on their specific technical needs and work on their game understanding.

5. Ensure what you ask of them is realistic.

6. Make sure that they are "active" in practices – rather than a passive bystander until the outfield players require them.

7. Allow them to work on their communication and relationships with other players.

8. Provide them with the same technical assistance that you would for outfield players.

9. "Devise practices specific for the keepers".

10. Give your players confidence and treat mistakes with sensitivity.

At what age a young player becomes a goalkeeper is debateable, as lots of factors will influence whether he will ultimately stay in that position throughout his time in soccer. It would be easy, at eight-years-old, to select the biggest player to play in goal, but ultimately we do not know whether they will become physically or mentally able to fulfil this early desire and promise to play between the posts.

There is a growing school of thought that, pre-puberty, there should not be a specialist goalkeeper in your squad at all – that coaches ought to rotate this job to assist with the all-round development of all players. Whatever our decision we need to ensure that they are developed technically, like outfield players are, so they can compete as a soccer player first, then fulfil the tactical requirements of being the last line of defence *and* the first line of attack.

Summary

*   There have been numerous changes to the position of goalkeeper, none more so than the introduction of the "back pass" rule in 1992.

*   Statistics show that a goalkeeper will now use his feet more than his hands.

*   Youth goalkeepers should work towards a long-term development model.

*   Psychologically, goalkeepers need to be mentally strong, resilient and recover from set-backs, with positive help from the coach.

- Technically, goalkeepers should be as comfortable with the ball at their feet as they are with their hands.

- Tactically, goalkeepers are the last line of defence, but increasingly also the first line of attack.

- Although there are exceptions, adult goalkeepers tend to be well over six feet tall. Youth coaches, however, need to be careful about selecting players based on height.

- There is an expectation that goalkeepers should be the ears and mouth of the defence.

- Other sports that are based on handling, or hand-eye coordination, can be helpful in the development of young goalkeepers.

- It is important to fully integrate goalkeepers into your practices.

- To integrate and produce goalkeepers sufficiently, planning is required for the short (session planning), medium (syllabus) and long term.

- The "outcomes" put in place for youth goalkeepers should allow them to develop towards, rather than be judged against, adult criteria.

Real Coach Experience

Goalkeeper or Midfielder?

(Greg Thurstans, UEFA A Licence Outfield and Goalkeeper Coach, English Independent Schools Under-16s)

I had been regularly coaching the England Independent Schools Under-16 Goalkeeper and started to realise just how significant the goalkeeper's role in initiating play has become. This was the first goalkeeper I had seen, even during my time at the Academy of Premier League club Crystal Palace and observing a variety of elite level senior goalkeepers, who distributed the ball like a play-making holding midfield player!

He could play with both feet from the ground, in his hands and his throwing was also exceptional. The most impressive thing however was that his pass completion rate was always over 90%. When you consider that from most goal-kicks, where the ball lands is often a 50-50 between both teams, this is particularly special. Another key feature was his decision-making of when to distribute the ball, and ensuring that the player he had given the ball to was always supported from behind and would therefore not lose possession.

After speaking with him I discovered that he had played as a central midfielder, as well as a goalkeeper, until the age of 14.

I believe the goalkeeper of the future will certainly need these abilities as the game evolves and should be involved in outfield play as much as possible in their youth development program. This will allow maximum access to a variety of distribution methods, opposed as well as unopposed, and clever game-relevant decision-making. The list of these types of goalkeepers is ever-increasing with the likes of Edwin van der Sar, Pepe Reina, Victor Valdés among the best. The recent outstanding performance form Claudio Bravo of Chile against England is another great example of a goalkeeper who can dictate and initiate play.

I will never forget this young goalkeeper! He is now the model of the youth goalkeeper I am aiming to produce.

13

Understanding Talent Identification and Assessment of Players

"At 16, we could play Scholsey for only 20 minutes a game. He couldn't run. He was a little one. Had asthma. No strength. No power. No athleticism. No endurance. 'You've got a bleeding dwarf', I remember somebody saying to Brian Kidd [the youth team coach]. 'You will eat your words', said Kiddo. If Scholsey had been at a lesser club, they would have got rid of him and he would probably not be in the game now. We stuck with Scholsey, a wonderful technician." (Sir Alex Ferguson on former Manchester United midfielder, Paul Scholes)

In Chapter 1 we spoke about the frailties of the 'win at all costs' mentality in youth soccer. We noted how a pure focus on winning at a young age means that the long-term development of our players is over-looked for short-term victories.

On the back of this, what if I told you that the way coaches' view and select players is completely flawed? What if I told you that this flaw is prevalent not just at a local level, but is reflected right at the top of international soccer? And what if I told you this was because of your birthday?

Relative Age Effect

To ensure clarity around age-groupings in soccer, we must note that in England, the soccer year runs in line with the school year. Therefore, players are grouped by age on a September to August basis, whereas across international competition, players are grouped by calendar year, from January to December.

Birth bias, or 'Relative Age Effect' is based on a player's date of birth and is created when there is a cut-off point in age group banding. For example, using the calendar year system, you may have players that are born in January competing in the same group as those born in December of the same year. The January-born will often then be selected ahead of any December counterpart as he is more physically, emotionally and socially developed. Such is the impact of relative age, I have had several conversations with parents who were actively aiming to conceive a child that is born within the early part of the soccer year!

Let's start by looking at the impact of Relative Age Effect in soccer with a story…

RAE in Action

Whilst running a soccer program that aimed to get ex-Academy players back into the professional game, I arranged a trial game against a local professional team. Most of the players were in the under-16 age bracket, apart from a handful who were either late starters to the program and therefore slightly older, or younger players who were excelling. I made no secret to anyone that although the players playing were being assessed against their suitability to join the program, the potential of a strong individual performance might get them noticed by the professional team.

As the first half was drawing to a close, I was approached by an opposition staff-member who was particularly interested in one of the centre-backs on my team. The usual questions followed: What is his background? What kind of personality does he have? Where does he live? Do you think he could play at a higher level? Etc., etc.

The boy in question however was not under-16, but an under-17 player. The very second the professional team heard this they were no longer interested. Not at all – no further discussion. His birth date was August 28th – he was four days off still being an under-16 – the correct age they were looking for! *Four days.* Those measly four days robbed him of a shot back at a professional club. Had he been conceived a handful of days later, he would have had his shot.

You may have a vision of the above story as happening on a very local level, with the opinion and small-mindedness of one coach blocking the pathway of a clearly talented player, but one just slightly on the wrong side of a dividing line. The pattern however is much, much bigger.

RAE in Elite Soccer

In May 2009, data was taken from almost 2,500 players from English Premier League Academies. These are essentially the 'best' young players in the country – allegedly. The study showed that well over half of them were born between September and December – 57% of these academy players were born during one-third of the year. A mere 14% were players with 'summer' birthdays. This stat was compounded in a discussion I had with a local academy staff member who had belatedly discovered that there was a "50-50 split" between the September to December boys and the rest.

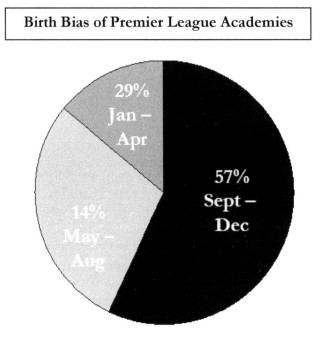

Birth Bias of Premier League Academies

The above data comes from a presentation by the *FA's National Development Manager for Youth and Mini-Soccer*, Nick Levett. His presentation went on to outline similar trends across local, non-professional youth soccer in various competition structures across England. In and around 50% of all players were born between September and December. In one particular under-13 league, 41% of players were September to November babies.

These statistics tell us that, from top to bottom, we are still selecting players based on size, and discarding talent that simply has not come to the fore yet.

Relative Age Effect Across European Soccer

TEAM	1st M	2nd M	3rd M	4th M	5th M	6th M	7th M	8th M	9th M	10th M	11th M	12th M	1st Q	4th Q
England	21	15	11	5	5	3	4	6	8	8	5	3	50%	17%
Spain	8	4	6	11	7	4	4	1	0	2	2	1	36%	10%
Germany	18	17	17	6	13	7	9	7	5	2	2	0	50%	4%
France	9	3	6	5	5	3	4	0	0	4	1	1	44%	14%
Italy	14	12	10	7	6	5	6	9	5	1	0	2	47%	4%
Holland	14	5	11	6	8	7	1	12	14	6	5	2	37%	16%
Portugal	8	15	10	13	9	3	1	5	3	2	3	0	37%	7%
Sweden	6	8	3	5	7	4	4	1	0	2	2	1	47%	3%
Denmark	14	10	9	4	15	10	7	7	6	6	0	2	37%	9%
Belgium	15	10	12	13	9	10	9	6	5	3	3	4	37%	10%
TOTAL	**16%**	**14%**	**12%**	**10%**	**11%**	**7%**	**6%**	**7%**	**6%**	**5%**	**3%**	**2%**	**43%**	**9%**

The data above comes from a study of international teams in 2005 and is presented on the *Beautiful Game* website. If you had a random selection of 100 people, even those with lots in common, you would expect that their birth distribution across the four quarters of the year would not veer too far from 25% each. If we study the final columns in the above table however, we find that European national teams have a *minimum* of 37% from the first quarter, and in the cases of both England and Germany, half of their players had their birthday in the first quarter of the year. In no country represented above has any nation (incidentally the most developed soccer nations in Europe) a representative figure of anywhere near 25% from the last quarter of the year.

The detail in the graph below comes from Steve Laurence, author of the *Wikipedia* page about Relative Age Effect. It shows the distribution of ages across UEFA international tournaments (white) against the percentage of births in the same month (black). Once again we see that the first four months are over-represented, and the last four are under-represented.

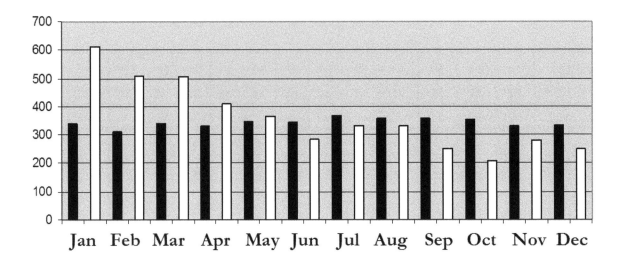

The *Relative Age Effect* is not merely a European problem – there are studies available online from all over the world. The fact that youth players are being selected based on this bias has had implications the world over. In 2005, Mexico won the FIFA Under-17 World Cup. Of their 20-man squad, 19 were born in the first six months of the selection year, and zero players had a birthday in the final three months. In the same tournament, the Brazilian squad only had one player born in the final three months.

"The Cream Rises to the Top"

There are those who will point to Xabi Alonso for example (November birthday) and suggest "the cream will always rise to the top". If players are good enough then nothing will stop them reaching their peak performance. The cream however *will not* reach the top if they are disengaged in the process before it has even started, as presented brilliantly by Robert Horn and Michelle Okumura in their article *It's Time to Eliminate the Relative Age Effect in American Soccer*.

The article outlines that "older" players between 5 and 10-years-old, who are typically bigger physically, and typically more experienced as a result, succeed in try-outs 70-80% of the time, whereas their younger counterparts fail this first try-out 70-80% of the time. As time passes, the divide increases even further. The older players experience more and better coaching, play at a higher level for longer, whereas the younger ones spiral towards possible drop-out from the sport.

Whilst believing they are identifying talent early, coaches and selectors have essentially judged the whole sporting future of a child who is yet to reach double-figures in age, and all the while they are measured against peers that are too far removed from each other age-wise.

It is important, however, that we address one key thing. The phenomenon of RAE is a social one, created by society depending on where the man-made age-divide line is drawn. Whether you are born in January or December will have no impact on genetics in terms of ultimate size, weight or bulk. The issue comes when players born months apart are *measured against each other and judged on that basis*.

Solutions?

Quoting research is fine, but solutions are better. As a lone coach, you may feel that a worldwide soccer problem is far too big for you to challenge independently. Well you *can* affect it.

A coach can start by knowing the birthdays of his players. If we frequently measure our players in terms of their technical ability, tactical nous, physical capabilities and so on, surely we can also factor relative age into the context of our players' performance? By not understanding the age difference within your squad, you may well be measuring players against each other who are up to 12 months apart. In fact, in *The Gold Mine Effect*, Rasmus Ankersen argues that there, "can be as much as three years' development difference between children born in the space of one year". Ankersen goes on to consider how a physically developed 11-year-old could reflect that of an "average" 14-year-old, but so could a late-developing 17-year-old!

By understanding the consequences of your players' relative age, your judgments about them can reflect this. Maybe you do not throw away your small, end-of-year born player quite so readily. It is possible that he is struggling in games now, but just maybe, with some time and patience, he can start to influence games – if he is afforded the opportunity. Maybe a late-developer can spend some playing time with a year-group below, or a physically dominant one playing up.

This drags us right back to Chapter 1 where we advocated that results in youth soccer are of secondary importance to development. Are you willing to put the long-term development of your players above the instant results of your team? If you are, prove it! All coaches claim to know their players inside out – now is your chance to put that to the test. They may just simply need more time.

It may take well into the early 20s for late-borns to catch up with their early-born counterparts – if they are even still involved in the game due to the high dropout rate. Steve Lawrence cites Gareth Bale and Andros Townsend as examples of players who needed lots of time and patience before flourishing once they hit adulthood; players who eventually 'caught up' with their older peers.

Tottenham Hotspur

It is interesting that Lawrence should mention Andros Townsend, the England and Tottenham Hotspur winger who seemed to burst onto the scene in 2013, as if from nowhere. In the *Real Coach Experience* at the end of a chapter, we see the North London Premier League Academy is again featured as a model of good practice in terms of the RAE.

In an interview with John McDermott, the Academy Manager at Tottenham, the Guardian newspaper published several of the techniques used by the club to combat the impact of relative age. Rather than split players according to their soccer age, the club bands them according to their chronological age at seven, eight, nine and ten. Once their birthday arrives, they are moved up an age group, giving players the experience of being the youngest and the oldest in their respective groups – all in the same year.

He also referred to the use of the loan-system once players enter the adult rankings at Tottenham, noting eight names (including Townsend and current first team players Kyle Walker and Danny Rose), all of whom have summer birthdays. Using the loan system to give younger players experience and the chance to learn their trade in adult soccer, but at a lower level, has allowed players that vital extra time to develop and remain in the game into their early twenties. Interestingly, in Lawrence's opinion, Manchester United starlet Adnan Januzaj (an early born) will be surpassed by his peers by 22. That may be worth a watch as he develops…

Talent Selector or Talent Identifier?

In a very interesting article from www.soccerwire.com, author John O'Sullivan poses the question as to whether youth coaches across sport are "talent identifiers" or "talent selectors". He defines each with a very thought-provoking paragraph:

> "Talent selection is the culling of players with the *current* ability to participate and be successful in events taking place in the near future. Talent identification, on the other hand, is the *prediction of future performance* based upon an evaluation of current physical, technical, tactical and psychological qualities. Talent selection is pretty simple; talent identification is an art. One yields great results today; the other builds elite athletes and winning teams for the future".

Once more, he observes that coaches who fall into the 'talent selection' category choose players based on how big, strong and quick they are[1], as the late developing players are once again left to the side. He then points out a statistic that 70% of these children leave organized sports by the time they enter their teens! That is a lot of potential talent that is going to waste.

Youth soccer coaches that fall into the 'talent identification' category, however, have a far more long-term outlook and attempt to look to analyse the unearthed *potential* in a young player. In the *Deutschland Fussball Bund's* (German FA) *Talent Identification* document, they call this "train[ing] for the long run". This identification requires more skill, time, effort and foresight – but it's worth it.

When we think of a talent scout, we think of a thoughtful man going to a game attempting to find that hidden gem – that player with something special that nobody else can see. Seeing what most cannot see does not happen because it is easy. It doesn't happen by watching the biggest 12-year-old power around a small-sided field barging his peers into oblivion – and then selecting him. It requires an eye that looks beyond instantaneous impact. The *Real Coach Experience* section at the end of this chapter shows how this outlook can have a potentially life-changing impact on a young player.

The short-term vision of scouts, coaches and selectors mean they can literally miss the *potential* of others. For example, your 10-year-old may have a wonderful sense of space, or have a clever, creative mindset, but this does not come to the fore as he is physically not fully able to compete – yet. If the coach looks towards the long-term, he may be able to see past any initial impact and further into the potential of the player. So, in a way the 'eye' of a selector can both find *and* dismiss potential.

Identifying Potential

As frequently noted throughout this book – and its importance seems to grow and grow –soccer is an ever-changing, fast-flowing, fluent game, making the identification of potential difficult. In *Sports Talent – How to Identify and Develop Outstanding Athletes*, Jim Brown outlines two complications in measuring soccer talent early by quoting Tom Hart (former Director of Coach Education for US Youth Soccer) and Dave Simeona (US National Team Staff Coach) that reflect the unpredictability of the game:

1. Soccer is fluent and changes constantly. A player's potential may change over several years, or even from game to game. Hart also acknowledges the Relative Age Effect flaw.

2. Those measuring talent may not have the objectiveness or foresight to accurately predict the potential of young players.

Although the beginning of Brown's chapter offers useful information, and acknowledges *Relative Age Effect*, my heart dropped when he went on to insist that physical factors "at any age" are the first indicators of talent in soccer. Let's get this right - here and now - if we measure talent in youth soccer based on "How fast can a player run? How high can she jump? How quick is he? How strong?" we will allow RAE to win, and potentially lose out on 75% of the natural talent that needs to be harnessed rather than dismissed.

The methods required to identify potential are the same as the long-term development process that we spoke about in previous chapters. We can base the identification process around technical, tactical, physical, psychological and lifestyle considerations – understanding that all factors are needed and can be improved upon.

You will not find a single youth soccer player who is already the end product. If he were then he would already be a superstar. It is a coach's responsibility not to bemoan his deficiencies, but to work with the player to get the best out of him.

---

[1] Data collected from 11 to 14-year-olds involved with Coerver Coaching, showed that the majority of those born early in the year are statistically heavier, taller and quicker.

As noted previously, the famous Ajax Youth Academy uses the *TIPS Model* – Technique, Insight, Personality and Speed. At this level, identified players must have potential within three of these four qualities. Logically, to dismiss a player who has TIP, but not Speed, would clearly be foolish, likewise if he had TPS and not Insight.

Below is a simple, yet useful player scouting form used at an English Academy, that twists the famous Ajax model into a "SPIT" Assessment. Again, players must show a pedigree in three of the four criteria.

<table>
<tr><td colspan="6" align="center">**Academy SPIT Assessment**</td></tr>
</table>

	Below Average	Average	Above Average	Good	Excellent
SPEED					
PERSONALITY					
INSIGHT					
TECHNIQUE					
COMMENTS:					
RECOMMENDATION	A	B	C	D
	Offer Trial	Dev. Centre	Continue Monitor	Not up to Standard

Assessing Players

In the following section, we will look at how we, as coaches, assess players and provide them with feedback on their performance – their strengths, areas for improvement, and the targets that are set for them. We will do this, as usual, by offering examples from professional academy schemes. Before we begin however, I must start with a disclaimer.

Be very aware and careful when assessing players formally, especially at an early age. During this process it is human tendency, from the coach and the player and parent, to hone in on the negative. Think back to your school report – the focus went straight to the 'F' rather than the 'A'. Use the following section to carefully choose your methods of assessment so that they are *appropriate for the players you work with.*

Formative Assessment

Once part of your program, players can be regularly assessed in two ways, either of which, if neglected, can leave gaps and question marks in terms of their development. These types of assessments are used regularly in education and can be used in soccer.

The form of assessment most familiar to coaches is regular, informal feedback provided throughout the season – this, in education, is known as *formative assessment*. It may be a point made at the end of a game, or a reinforced point that is made throughout the training process. This formative assessment is important as it offers players frequent feedback and a short-term focus on their development.

This feedback, however, can tend to be abused. Coaches may become over-zealous in offering too much feedback, or changing the focus of the feedback from game to game, or session to session. As this feedback is more informal and unrecorded, players, especially younger ones, may not absorb the information fully or correctly – or they may just simply forget! When offering this type of feedback, ensure that it is backed up and revisited to give players a measure of their improvement.

Summative Assessment

Summative assessment is a more formal process. These assessments will have designated times, and certainly in professional academies, would be documented and designed to track the long-term development of players. These will typically take place every six or twelve weeks. The regular formative feedback that players are given must be present within a formal assessment – there should not be anything surprising in there! An old manager of mine insisted that no matter what, nothing 'new' should come out on assessment evening – players and parents should already have a grasp of their progress through formative feedback.

Problems can occur at these times if criticism is involved. To stave off any potential confrontation with parents, ensure they are kept up-to-date with the soccer progress of their child, that 'new' criticism is avoided and that negative comments are made as 'areas for improvement' rather than 'weaknesses'. Crucially, a good coach will provide players with clues or ways to improve a certain aspect. If you are criticizing, ensure you can back it up with potential solutions. If they simply disagree with you, then that is a matter of opinion – and you are the impartial, expertly knowledgeable coach!

How to Devise a Player Assessment

One of the greatest issues with summative assessment is *how to do it*. I have seen my fair share of these documents, and all are based around the *Long-Term Player Development Model* – and will acknowledge technical, tactical, physical, psychological and social feedback (although the social corner remains somewhat neglected). How the clubs format and utilize these assessments are, however, all slightly different. Some attempt to offer tangible, quantitative 'scores' for performance, whereas others offer a narrative. Some attempt to do both.

Tangible Assessments

I am not entirely convinced about tangible scoring in soccer. For any of you who play the *Football Manager* computer simulator, you will be familiar with the player information screen where each player attribute is given a score out of 20. Without consulting the various versions of the game, we can assume Lionel Messi would score 20 for dribbling, but maybe seven or eight for heading.

In school you will get an A or B grade in a maths test based on how many correct answers you achieve. But what determines whether you are an 'A' at dribbling? Or shooting? Or defending? Is your number 11 the best dribbler in the team and therefore worth an 'A'? Or do we say that Cristiano Ronaldo is an 'A' and measure the player off this? Maybe we should measure it against the best player at that age regionally or nationally? Also, if an under-12 is given an 'A' grade, where is the incentive to improve? If at under-13 he receives a 'B', does that mean he has regressed? If you decide to use these tangible, score-based assessments, ensure that everyone – coaches, players and parents – understand what the measure is. Also, let's face it, these grades are generally objective and may vary from opinion to opinion.

1 = Excellent 2 = Very Good 3 = Standard Expected

4 = Improvement Needed 5 = Vast Improvement Needed

Physical Attributes	Score	Technical Attributes	Score
Strength		Passing – Short	
Power		Passing – Long	
Speed		Defending – Individual	
Agility		Defending - Team	
Aerobic Endurance		Crossing	
Psychological Attributes		Attacking Heading	
Confidence		Communication	
Concentration		Dribbling	
Commitment		Running with ball	
Decision-Making		Running off the ball	
Mental Toughness		Shooting	
Tactical Attributes		Performance	
Understanding the state of the game		Coaching Sessions	
Ability to act to change in shape		Match Play	
Areas for Improvements / Targets			
1.			
2.			
3.			

Narrative Assessments

On the other hand, narrative assessments focus less on hypothetically scoring players, but on offering information in a narrative or conversational manner. I have seen some (and written some) that are packed with narrative detail about the player's strengths and the areas for improvement required for the player to get better. It is important in this instance that there are certain foci involved. Some that I have seen, like the one below, are far more concise and to the point. No scores, no long paragraphs, just succinct information about what is required for the player to improve.

Academy 'Narrative' Assessment	

Technical	1. Try to improve receiving on either foot
	2. Try to improve your passing
Tactical	1. Work on where and how to support effectively
	2. Think about how you can create space for others
Physical	1. Continue to develop agility, balance, and coordination
Psychological	1. Be prepared to play in a position you are asked
Social	1. Try to make five positive comments to team-mates in every match / training session

Mixing Tangible and Narrative Assessments

Most academy assessments I have seen mix both tangible and narrative methods of assessment. This allows for both a score to be used as a reference point, but also allows for context and elaboration of scores and points. See below a goalkeeper-specific assessment form used in an English Championship Academy.

Academy Goalkeeper Assessment Template

0 = Not recorded   1 = Below average   2 = Average

3 = Good   4 = Very Good   5 = Excellent

PHYSICAL	COMMENT	Grade 1 - 5
Height		
Speed off mark / quick feet		
Agility		
Presence		
Strength/Power (to deal with set plays/crosses with bodies around them)		
TECHNICAL		**Grade 1 - 5**
Basic handling		
Shot stopping: - Left side		
- Right side		
Punching		
Right or left footed		
Dealing with back pass		
Short Passing		
Long Passing		
Throwing – Short		
Long		
MENTAL		**Grade 1 - 5**
Concentration		
Composure		
Bravery		
Ability to perform after a mistake		
DECISION-MAKING		**Grade 1 - 5**
Crosses: When to catch / punch		
Balls between defence and GK		
Shots: When to catch / divert		
UNDERSTANDING		**Grade 1 - 5**
Communication		
Support		
Organization		

Player-Centred Assessments

Any academy soccer player will tell you how stressful assessment times can be. These are often occasions when players find out if they are being released from a professional club, or retained for another season or two. These events therefore need to be handled with a huge amount of sensitivity. I fully recommend anyone involved in this process to read *Every Boy's Dream* by Chris Green – a book that documents several horror stories in how players have been dealt with, including one coach who proudly termed releasing a player as "binning" them.

A great way to make these times more player-centred is to involve *them* in the process.

'Self assessment' is widely recommended by experts in education. Using guided self-assessment with younger players can be very beneficial as they are judging themselves, rather than being judged by others. They can be encouraged to focus mainly on their strengths so that the 'A's' in their report are focused on more than the 'F's'. *No child playing soccer, a sport that they love, wants to be told that they are failing at it.*

Self-assessment is a learning process in itself and requires players to become more analytical of their own progress. It is a way of improving player understanding by allowing them to critically evaluate their own performance. It also gives the coach an invaluable insight into the opinion of their players, and can reveal much about their confidence and self-esteem. Some players are exceptionally harsh on themselves, whereas others are more generous. It is important to point out, however, that their scores cannot be 'wrong' – it is an opinion, just like the coach's.

Profile Wheels

The use of profile wheels, like the one below, can be useful when athletes self-assess, or indeed the coach wants an alternative, more visual way to present feedback to the player. The wheel can be shaded based on a score out of 10 for that particular point. What you will most likely be left with is some segments of the wheel shaded to a high score of nine or ten, some with a poor score of one to three, and others that fall into the middle categories. The resulting visual clearly indicates a player's strengths and areas for development.

Profile wheels can be adapted and used in a number of ways. For example, five separate wheels can be used – one for each of the five assessment criteria – technical, tactical, physical, social, and psychological. The wheel below for example, which is taken from *The Sport in Mind* website, is based exclusively around the psychological corner.

> **Sample Profile Wheel Self-Assessment – Psychological and Emotional**

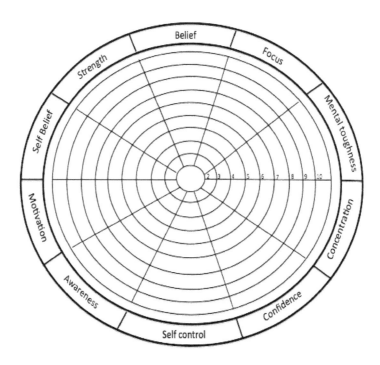

Alternatively, a single overall wheel can be used containing two of the more important traits which can be represented in each segment, one from each of the five areas, should you want there to be a specific focus.

Peer Assessment

Peer assessment can also be a very useful tool for players and coaches. We spoke previously about the power the peer group holds with young players and how the opinion of friends can carry lots of weight. The coach's impartial, possibly more analytical input and control in this process is important for the validity of peer assessment.

The assessment form below is a tangible assessment that involves both peer and self-assessment. The player being scored is a 17-year-old Academy left-back.

Assessment Template to Include Self and Peer Assessment

Technical	Player	Peer	Coach
Receiving	C	B	B
Short Passing	B	B	B
Long Passing	A	B	A
Ball Manipulation	C	C	B
Dribbling	C	D	C
Finishing	B	C	B
Running with the Ball	B	D	B
Heading	B	C	B-C
Tackling	D	C	C
Team Work			
Professionalism	B	B	B
Work-rate	B	C	B
Positional Awareness	B	B	B
Attacking Play	B	B	B
Defending Play	C	C	C

Mental			
Commitment	B	B	A
Confidence	C	B	A
Concentration	B	C	B
Communication	B	C	B
Emotional Control	B	C	A
Decision-making	B	C	A
Willingness to Learn	A	B	A

A = Excellent B = Good C = Satisfactory D = Area for Improvement

Conclusion

To fulfil the role of a development coach, we need to focus on the long-term process. We need to move away from selecting the older, physically-developed players in a quest for instant results, becoming 'talent identifiers' rather than 'talent selectors'. Talent, as described by Ankersen, is not "static" or something that "you have or you don't". It is fluid, changes and depends much on the development of the child, and the influences around him. Soccer coaches play a huge part in this development and guidance of talent. As succinctly put by the FA's Nick Levett, "Talent identification is about the future, not today".

Player development is a long-term process and there is overwhelming data that proves the widespread selection-bias towards early born players within the same age band. Once players are part of the development-program that you are in charge of, using review methods, assessments, and target-setting with them is extremely important as an aid to help players reach their potential. Keeping parents involved in this process, rather than apart from it, is important too. In the next chapter, we will have a more in-depth look at how we can understand the often-strained relationship between coaches and parents.

Summary

- Players selected based on physical attributes has led to a bias towards those born earlier in the year.

- Data from across soccer shows that Relative Age Effect is extremely common.

- RAE is a social, not a physical construct and impacts only when players are measured against each other and judged on that basis.

- There "can be as much as three years' development difference between children born in the space of one year.

- Statistically, early-born players are bigger, heavier and quicker.

- Late-born players need time, patience and to be allowed the opportunity to develop to stop them dropping out of the game.

- Are you a 'talent identifier' or 'talent selector'?

- You will not find a single youth soccer player who is already the end product.

- Use the Long-Term Development Model to assess players.

- Be careful when assessing players, especially at a young age.

- Across soccer, player feedback is given in formative and summative ways.

- Formal player assessment tends to mix tangible scoring methods with narrative-type feedback and targets.

- Profile wheels can be used as a more visual method of providing feedback.

- Methods of self-assessment and peer assessment can make assessments more player-centred, and increase critical thinking.

- No child playing soccer, a sport that they love, wants to be told that they are failing at it.

Real Coach Experience

Giving the Little One A Chance

(Dan Barton, Under-13 Coach, London)

I am a full-time coach for The Football Association, working specifically in the skills program, coaching in schools and supporting grassroots coaches in London. I also coach my son's under-13 grassroots team.

In the past five years, six players from our team have progressed and been signed by academies at Tottenham Hotspur, Watford and Barnet.

The most recent one is an especially interesting story. When the player joined us (let's call him 'Mark') aged ten, he was the smallest kid in any team in the league. He was the size of most under-8s. He had left another team because the coach didn't give him much game time. He often only came on for the last few minutes of a match when the win was already secured.

He had a late August birthday, making him the youngest in the team and the youngest in his school year-group. If he had been born ten days later, he would have been in the age group below. So while he was expected to play with and against boys 11 months older than him, he was barred from playing with those a matter of days younger than him!

Although physically small, he was the most intelligent player I had ever seen for his age. In many ways he resembled an adult when he played the game. His positioning and decision-making were exceptional, and with more game-time, these traits started to have an impact on games.

He started attending one of the Development Centres operated by Tottenham Hotspur and was soon invited along to the elite shadow squad. He spent over a year in that group and was beginning to think he was not going to get a chance at playing for the academy proper. I suggested to his dad that he approached the lead coach for the foundation stage, Gary Broadhurst, to ask for an honest assessment of his potential. Within a month he was registered with the academy squad.

He has just signed a two-year extension until the end of the under-15 season. He is still the smallest player by far but Tottenham pick and choose games for him. Some weeks he plays for his age group at under-13, other weeks he plays for the year group below. He is an individual, within a program that is tolerant of individual needs.

He now has a real chance of achieving his potential, whereas had he persevered with his original club, he may well not be playing the game at all!

14
Understanding Parents

"We need a parental cultural revolution. If we could just get them to shut the f**k up and let their children enjoy themselves, you would be staggered at the difference it would make." (Gary Lineker)

The greatest shame I find about youth soccer is the often-strained relationship between coaches and parents. Let me make one thing clear from the start however – I do not believe that there are issues with *every* parent in youth soccer. I have met some wonderfully helpful, engaging parents throughout the years. I suppose, unfortunately, when we as coaches have to deal with a problem from even just one parent, it can cloud our opinion of a whole group. Not all parents give coaches problems but the small percentage that do can make the coach's job extremely difficult.

In most coach mentoring schemes I have been involved in, it appears that one of, if not the greatest problem that coaches encounter are parent-related. This can be down to a huge variety of reasons including, but not exclusive to: match results, playing time, training methods, perceived bias towards certain other players, playing positions – the list goes on I am sure. I even once had a parent complain to club directors that the coach of their son's under-10 team was "too quiet". As if being quiet, calculated, and letting their children play was less desirable that being loud, brash and barking blow-by-blow instructions.

In an article in the *New Statesman*, ex-England international and respected pundit Gary Lineker left the reader in doubt as to his feelings on the negative role of parents in youth soccer. Along with the quote at the beginning of the chapter, Lineker had this to add:

> "This madness is only exacerbated by the maniacal parents on the touchline spouting nonsense at their children. The competitive nature of most mums and dads is astounding. The fear they instill in our promising but sensitive Johnny is utterly depressing.

> Having four boys myself, I have stood on the sidelines of countless games, spanning many years. Oh, the drivel I have heard, the abuse I have witnessed, the damage I have seen done. Promising young players barked at by clueless dad. 'Don't mess with it there.' 'Just kick it.' 'Stop f**king about.' I could go on. I have seen a father pick his son up by the scruff of the neck and yell in his face: 'You'll never make it playing that crap'."

Culture

I am a firm believer that the touchline problems we face in youth soccer are deep-rooted ones. Because a parent may have played soccer, or is a fan that watches the game on television, it is common to find so-called "armchair experts" on the touchline of our youth soccer games. At times people are happy to give their opinion very vocally, but would not dare to put themselves in a position to implement those opinions. I suppose it is like our view of politics. I may disagree with the policies of presidents or prime ministers, but should I sit in their decision-making seats I would not know where to start!

There is a culture around soccer that I have not known in other sports. I have never seen parents at a swimming gala, for example, do anything other than watch and hope their child does their best. I have never seen a dad walk up and down the pool commentating over every stroke or kick of the leg. I have never seen a mum challenge a swimming coach before, during, or after a race. Nor in other team sports have I witnessed the level of open touchline involvement in a game.

I am certain that the culture of what we see on television influences certain people heavily. Soccer games live on the edge. Every refereeing decision is questioned, whether correct or not. The tactics employed by the coach are constantly criticized and players are often abused verbally from the touchlines.

What a depressing thought it is that this behaviour is replicated on local soccer pitches the world over – and by logical, grown adults too. I once saw an under-11 goalkeeper in tears a mere seven minutes into a 7-a-side game. It turned out his grandmother behind the goal was openly blaming him as their team conceded a goal! It would almost be funny if the issue were not so heart breaking.

Creating your Culture

You, as coach and part of a wider club, have the ability to change this culture in youth soccer. There is a wonderful *Real Coach Experience* from Steve Phythian at the end of this chapter. He gives us a wonderful example of how to work *with* parents and sort out potential problems or confrontation before they even begin.

Steve tells us of a parents' evening he organized at the beginning of the season to outline fully what his methods and intentions were for the players. He bravely made himself accountable for anything he committed to, but did not live up to, openly telling parents that if he, as the coach, veered from what he promised then they were fully entitled to call him on it.

He only managed to get the parents on board by dissolving issues from which confrontation often appears – all players would get equal playing time; he would rotate them positionally; he expected parents to behave on match day and not 'coach from the touchline'. I suspect that if the parents did not like the culture he was implementing, the advice would have been to find a different team. These simple messages mean that there is little room for future arguments.

Expectations

The matrix below comes from Auckland's *Central United Football Club*. It is designed to display the expectations of all relevant parties at the soccer club. It is a very simple and succinct way of outlining to all involved the responsibilities and expectations of each other.

Expectations Matrix				

Expects from:	Player ⬇	Parent ⬇	Coach ⬇	Club ⬇
Player	Competition Friendship Commitment Focus	Fun Friends Well-being	Engaged Punctual Enjoy Open Mind	Listen to Coach Pay Fees Represent Club High Standards
Parent	Support Not Pushy Equal Opportunity Encouragement	Support Encouragement Mediator Community	Supportive No Interfering Communication Respect	Support Club Pay fees Respect Program Respect Coaches
Coach	Feedback Engaging Chance to Play Fun & Enjoyable	Positive Committed Knowledgeable Communication	Communicate Equal Values Motivated High Standards	Expert Teaching High Standards Communication Pathway
Club	Belonging Philosophy Organized Investment	Friendly Safe & Secure Be Organized Pathway	Respect Rules / Regulations Support	Safe Environment Sound Policies Transparent Opportunity

Codes of Conduct

The most familiar form of managing expectations within a soccer club environment is with the employment of codes of conduct. A code of conduct is the set of rules and responsibilities for each of the parties concerned. Below I have included examples of various Codes of Conduct from National Associations and professional Academies for the relevant parties – parents, coaches, players and the club itself.

English School's Football Association

Code of Conduct for Parents, Peers and Supporters

PARENTS

- Attendance at a game is a privilege.

- Respect decisions made by the match officials.

- Be a good role model by positively supporting teams in every way possible and be generous with praise.

- Become aware of the competition rules and keep winning in its proper place.

- Respect other spectators, coaches and participants.

- Be a fan not a fanatic.

- Recognize and respect the performances of players in both teams, not just the team that you are supporting.

- Accept victory modestly and defeat graciously, remembering that the team you are supporting will be judged by your reactions.

- Do not 'boo' anyone.

- Stand or sit in the place that you have been allocated for the match.

- Do not interfere with instructions given by the teacher/coach in charge of the team.

- Remember that nearly all those who control school soccer matches are volunteers, giving of their time freely and without any financial reward in most cases – respect them for this.

Scottish Football Association

Code of Conduct Template for Coaches

COACHES

- Place safety and well-being of the player above the development of performance.

- Be aware of the SFA's and the Club's Child & Vulnerable Adult Protection Policy and Procedures.

- Ensure that coaching sessions are enjoyable, well-structured and focus on developing skills, decision making and a general understanding of the game.

- Develop an appropriate working relationship with players based on mutual trust and respect.

- Encourage players to accept responsibility for their own behaviour and performance.

- Ensure that sessions and games are appropriate for the age, maturity, experience and ability of the individual.

- Must consistently display high standards of appearance and behaviour.

- Know where to find appropriate first-aid.

- Hold a current membership list and have a register available at all activities.

By registering as a coach with (insert name of club) I agree to abide by these principles. I support the Club in its undertakings and encourage the Club to take any necessary disciplinary actions, where warranted, of any coaches, players, parents and or spectators for repeated or serious breaches of these Codes of Conduct.

English Academy

Players Code of Conduct

PLAYERS

- Ensure that you inform your coach of any non-attendance.

- Come to games and training properly prepared. This should include eating and drinking correctly.

- Adhere to the nutritional guidelines set down by the club.

- Always dress appropriately and remember that you are representing the Club.

- Dyed or inappropriately cut hair is not allowed given that you are representing the Academy.

- Ensure that your boots are clean and in good condition.

- Black boots should be worn.

- Please ensure you bring both a pair of studded and moulded boots with you to games.

- All players are required to act within the spirit of good sportsmanship and abide by the 'Laws of the Game'.

- The decisions of the match officials should be respected.

- Violent and foul play will not be tolerated.

- Shake hands with opponents and match officials after the game.

- Players should always arrive early for games and training.

- Chewing gum is not allowed.

- No jewellery should be worn.

- Each player must bring with him a towel and change of clothing to every game.
- The medical staff must be informed of any form of medication being taken.

Bristol Rovers Academy
Club Code of Conduct

1. A safe environment in which players can learn and develop without fear of abuse.

2. Medical screening, treatment, monitoring, advice and support.

3. A coaching and training program appropriate to the needs and ability to each individual.

4. Opportunities to play in high quality Academy games.

5. A profiling and feedback program that will help each individual to reach his maximum potential.

6. An environment that will not tolerate any form of racial discrimination.

7. An environment that ensures players are treated equally and with the same respect, regardless of their ability.

8. Guidelines to the student and parents/guardians on the best ways for them to contribute to the Student's soccer and personal development.

9. Educational support (in conjunction with the Student's school) to ensure the continued academic and personal development of the Student.

10. To adhere to the rules laid down for the operation of an Academy.

The transparency of Codes of Conduct, once they are enforced, and indeed the *Expectations Matrix* used by *Central United*, allows all involved an understanding of what is expected – it is there in black and white. They are 'go-to' documents if there are any issues that develop. Such foundations are implemented as a strategy, not only to ensure that rules and standards are imposed, but also to avoid any future miscommunication or confrontation.

Conflict Resolution

In a document developed by the *Wholistic Stress Control Institute*, ten ways of resolving conflict are outlined. I have adapted these ten methods and applied them to soccer. There is no way this chapter or any library of books can prepare a coach for a confrontation that may occur[1] with a parent, but maybe these methods will help.

---

[1] I will never forget a mum cornering me after a training session one evening saying that her son should get a contract as he was "like Ronaldo" to the embarrassment of both the 15-year-old son and indeed myself. Sure, he was a tricky attack-minded player, but his wider development needs meant he needed certain other things added to his game. The player was on board – mum certainly was not!

Ten Strategies to Resolve Conflict

Strategy	Applied to Soccer Coaches
1. If you are angry – walk away	Meeting fire with fire when speaking to parents is a recipe for disaster. If there is a conflict brewing and you feel as if you are getting angry, arrange to meet the parent after the next session or game – that way things may be calmer and more rational.
2. "Attack the problem, not the person"	The central issue in any confrontation with a parent is *the problem*. If the argument is about what position their son is playing, then get to the bottom of *that* problem. Insults around how qualified or experienced the parent may be to make a judgment, for example, are not useful.
3. Be assertive rather than aggressive	Never get aggressive with parents – it is simply not worth it. Soccer can be an emotional game, but remember a key trait of the modern coach is that of emotional control. If aggression is met with aggression, nobody wins, not least the young player caught in the middle.
4. "Focus on the issue, not your position about the issue"	The issue brought to you by a parent may not be especially relevant to you – it may even seem unimportant. Regardless, it is your role to get to the bottom of the issue and identify a way forward.
5. Accept that opinions differ	We know in soccer that opinions can vary greatly from person to person. This can happen with parents also. Your position may not always be fully right, nor might the parents be completely wrong.
6. Compromise, not competition	Try not to let a disagreement turn into a competition where there needs to be a winner. The only winner should be the young player and this may mean that compromise is best.
7. Never assume you know what the other person is feeling	The root cause of many confrontations is making assumptions about the feelings of the opponents, or their motivations.
8. Listen – and thank them for listening to you	In any argument the worst feeling is when the opponent does not listen to you. If parents have a point to make,

Strategy	Applied to Soccer Coaches
	listen and take it. They know their child a lot better than you so just maybe what they have to say could be useful.
9. "Stay in the present"	If a problem is being "attacked" then stick with that problem. Dragging up past instances will not help, but only extend the disagreement. The only thing you can change is the future – by addressing present issues.
10. "Build 'power with', not 'power over' others"	There can certainly be occasions where there can be a power battle between coaches and parents. As coach, you want everyone to know that you are in charge, but at what expense? Remember, as a leader you want people to follow you. Having parents onside, with you holding the perceived power, helps strike a very useful balance.

When we expect there to be conflict in a situation, we get it! How many times have you pre-empted an argument with your partner or boss, and actually played out a make-believe argument in your head? The company manager reprimands you for something, and you have a ready-made retort in your mind. You are arguing with someone in your own head, when no real argument may even be on the cards!

Misinterpretation

When devising the content of this chapter, I spoke to a friend of mine who is the chairman of a local youth soccer club. I asked him if I could confidentially have a look at any documents he had that recorded conflicts between parents and coaches. He told me he did, but often found them difficult to decipher. He showed me the following extract from a recent confrontation. For the purpose of this book, I have left out the names of both the coach and the parent involved.

COACH	PARENT
Last Sunday after the game, Redmond's father approached me looking very annoyed. I do not know his name. In front of the opposition coaches whom I was speaking to, he challenged me about the position Redmond was being asked to play (right-back). Although he has no knowledge of football [soccer] he insisted that because Redmond had played as a striker at another club, that he should do so here too. I made it clear to him that Redmond will play where I tell him to and if he didn't like it he could feel free to find a new club. I will not have a parent dictate to me where I position my players under any circumstance.	Last weekend I approached Coach -- --- after the game against -------. He was in a discussion with some other coaches so I loitered so as not to disturb them. Although I made it clear I was waiting he must have let me stand there for 10 minutes. As Redmond is relatively new to the team I wanted to make ------- aware that he had played as a striker at his old club, and could play there with several of the team's attackers currently injured or away. ------- got very aggressive and insisted that he would decide on team selection. I got the feeling he was doing it to impress his coach friends. I really didn't want it to get this far. I was just trying to help and show that Redmond would be happy to play anywhere for the team.

Here we have two accounts of the same event – one from the coach and one from the parent. Both seemed to have a grasp of the timeline and key issue involved, but it could be argued that both misinterpreted each other. The coach thought the parent was annoyed, but the parent was annoyed for being ignored for ten minutes. The parent wanted to give the coach some information that might help the team, but the coach saw this as a threat to his authority.

Stuck in the Middle

We must remember that, in the midst of potential conflict and the differing opinions of coaches and parents, there is a young player that is quite likely to be stuck in the middle of it all. Whether you are a coach or a parent (or both) you will have certain aspirations for your child in terms of his soccer performance.

Have we ever considered what the child wants? In the above account from parent and coach, what might have been the stance of the player? I have a vision of little Redmond standing nervously between two adults he looks up to, arguing over something that may not even be an issue for him. Maybe, just maybe, he would have said: "I don't mind where I play, I just want to play and enjoy myself". Argument over.

The visual below comes from a Twitter post from the *Dorset County Football Association*. Members of the organization asked a group of under-14 players to prioritize why they played soccer. The box on top represents what they prioritized; the one on the bottom is their lowest concern. Ultra-competitive adults may find this very surprising and very upsetting.

Why Young Players Play Soccer

Soccer is fun

I like playing as part of a team

Trying my hardest is more important than winning

It keeps me fit

I like to meet new people

My friends play soccer

I want to be a professional player

I like to win trophies

I want to win the league

The results of the exercise show that youth players will prioritize having fun and playing with their friends over winning leagues (it does not, of course, mean that they do not like winning – it is just further down their list of priorities). This type of opinion is prevalent in research the world over. I would suggest that both coaches and parents specifically consider the position of the player before arguing on their behalf. You are both significant role models for them – don't stick them in the middle of your opinions and grievances.

"Be an Incredible Soccer Parent"

In a series of blog posts, Dan Abrahams, the author of *Soccer Brain* and *Soccer Tough,* outlines his vision of how parents can assist their young soccer players. In *Be an Incredible Soccer Parent,* Abrahams offers three rules:

1. Fun first

When young players stop enjoying soccer and having fun, they will stop learning. A parent should ensure their child continues to love the game. That means no undue pressure is placed on them and young players should not be treated as mini-adults.

2. Facilitate, don't coach

The players already have a coach! One of the most common stresses for a young player is when his game is dissected on the way home in the car. Often, these instructions can work against the message from the coach. Asking questions rather than making statements about their game is more beneficial.

3. Give them space

If it hasn't gone well for the child in a game or training session, it is ok to give them some silent time.

One-Two Magazine published a variation of the following document to highlight the position of young soccer players as being those who are stuck almost voiceless between adults making decisions on their behalf. When you step back and read it, it is both clever, and also quite sad. If we listen, or at the very least take into account, the position and feelings of the youth player, we may well learn something.

A Player's Message to Parents

Thanks for coming to support me today.

As my friends and I play I want you to remember a few things:

- Please congratulate and applaud both teams and keep your voice down.

- I am here to have fun. Please encourage me and applaud all the players, no matter who we play for.

- You are here representing me: please do not embarrass me by being negative, shouting or swearing.

- Please do not stand too close to the pitch as this can distract me from my game and I cannot concentrate properly.

- The Referees are also young so please do not question their decisions, our coaches will give me help if needed.

- Please do not coach me from the side, my coach is here to teach me and too many instructions confuse me.

- I think doing my best and learning to play is more important than winning. There will be no scores recorded so don't ask me the score but ask me if I have had fun.

- Praise me for good skills, discipline, sportsmanship and effort; these are the things that make me a winner.

- Do not criticize my mistakes, I will be scared to try things again. Mistakes will make me a better player because I can learn from them.

- Please do challenge in a polite way any spectators who behave badly and in the wrong way. Tell them that we do not want negative behaviour.

- I hope to make you proud of me – please make me proud of you.

I have seen the following poem a number of times, (written slightly differently each time) in various different literatures, on websites and in social media. I believe that it was originally quoted in John Wooden's *A Lifetime of Observations and Reflections On and Off the Court*. It might be a great tool to use with the parents involved at your soccer club.

A Parent Talks to His Child Before the First Game

This is your first game, my child. I hope you win.

I hope you win for your sake, not mine.

Because winning's nice. It's a good feeling.

Like the whole world is yours.

But, it passes, this feeling.

And what lasts is what you've learned.

And what you learn about is life.

Winning is fun. Sure. But winning is not the point.

Wanting to win is the point.

Not giving up is the point.

Never being satisfied with what you've done is the point.

Never letting up is the point.

Never letting anyone down is the point.

Play to win. Sure. But lose like a champion.

It's not winning that counts.

What counts is trying.

Conclusion

Ultimately it is important to help yourself, as a coach, to manage any conflict or issue with parents. There is really great work going on across youth soccer to bring some sort of balance and perspective to the role of individual people and groups within clubs. The role of the soccer parent is a huge one. They are one of, if not *the* biggest influences in a child's upbringing and are integral in most cases to their child's participation with your team. How you relate to, and manage, the expectations of this group will be vital for your work with the team – and also your sanity.

To finish, the players at local English club, East Hull Saints, created the sign below to remind those attending games of the perspective we desire.

```
┌─────────────────────────────────────────┐
│              ATTENTION                    │
│          Parents & Spectators             │
├─────────────────────────────────────────┤
│           PLEASE REMEMBER                 │
│                                           │
│           These are children              │
│                                           │
│            This is a game                 │
│                                           │
│          Coaches are volunteers           │
│                                           │
│           Referees are human              │
│                                           │
│      This is not the Premier League!      │
│                                           │
│                                           │
│    We want an environment that assists in │
│                                           │
│    the development of our young players.  │
│                                           │
│             Let them play!                │
│                                           │
└─────────────────────────────────────────┘
```

Summary

- Not all parents give coaches problems, but the small percentage that do can make the coach's role extremely difficult.

- The problems we face with parents in youth soccer are deep-rooted ones.

- You, as coach and part of a wider club, have the ability to change this culture in youth soccer.

- An *Expectation Matrix* or *Code of Conduct* can allow transparency for everyone involved and reduce conflict before it begins.

- The *Wholistic Stress Control Institute* outlines ten ways of resolving conflict that can help in our resolutions with parents.

- When we expect conflict – we get it! This can lead to miscommunication and misinterpretation.

- Within coach-parent confrontation, there is always a child stuck in the middle.

- Young players prioritize having fun over winning leagues – remember that!

- Follow Dan Abrahams' three rules of becoming an incredible soccer parent.

- How you relate to, and manage, the expectations of this group will be vital for your work with the team – and also your sanity!

Real Coach Experience

Working With Parents

(Steve Phythian, UEFA A License, Patcham United F.C. Under 10s)

A number of years ago I took on a volunteer coaching role with Patcham United, a Charter Standard club in Brighton, England. I had no connection with the club and was alerted to their need for a coach by a friend of mine who worked with the parent of one of the players.

Because I was new to the club and none of the parents knew me, I felt it was of prime importance to hold a parents' meeting to introduce myself and to set out what I intended to do for their children.

I arranged the chairs in a circle, rather than theatre style. I felt this was important to help show that I did not consider myself to be more important or to put myself in the position of 'presenter'. I feel it helped to indicate that we were all part of a team.

Before beginning, I invited interruptions or questions at any time so that they could clarify anything, before working to a pre-prepared script of issues. They were:

About Me

- Background / Experience / Qualifications.
- Why I was coming to the club (especially as I had no familial connection).

My Philosophy

- Player and *person* development.
- Game style and rotation of positions.
- Equal average playing time.
- Appeal to different 'learning styles'.
- Long-Term Player Development Principles.
- Rules and spirit of the game – appropriate behaviour.

Practices

- What they would look like and *would not* look like.
- Multi skills including tag games to promote physical dexterity.
- Small-sided practices, not always 'big' games.

Parents

- Guidelines around pitch-side behaviour.
- Things to ask their sons if they were not at the game (not the score first!).
- Helping players to understand and commit to Codes of Conduct.
- Asked them not to coach from the sidelines.
- Recognize and praise good play from both teams.

At the end, I asked for any questions. I told them that if they could ask questions in the group everyone would benefit, but that I understood if they preferred to speak to me privately.

Finally, I had prepared a handout which bullet pointed, on one side of A4, everything I had talked about. I said that if I was doing something different, or was not doing what I had said I would, they should challenge me during the season.

15
Look in the Mirror First

"Success is no accident. It is hard work, perseverance, learning, study, sacrifice and most of all, love of what you are doing or learning to do." (Pelé)

This book opened with the above quote from soccer legend Pelé. Before we delved into any detail around communication, psychology or skill acquisition, we noted from the Brazilian that learning and work is the cornerstone of successful soccer - and this applies to coaching also.

The greatest piece of information I have received on my coaching journey was not about tactical periodization, player physical development, or deliberate practice. It didn't come from Dick Bate, Pep Guardiola or John Wooden. Such was its meaninglessness at the time, I have even forgotten who told me. I merely remember that it was at a coaching event, but remain unsure whether it was a tutor or fellow candidate who uttered the words.

After I had coached what I felt was a disappointing session, I proceeded to blame the players, fatigue and pressure of assessment for my poor performance in this private chat. My accomplice responded quite boldly, "Ray," he said, "look in the mirror first."

At the time his statement made little impact other than to annoy me. I took it as a cheap dig when I was at a low ebb (hence I guess why I don't remember him!). Little did I know that, as I developed as a coach, this statement would come back to me and I would learn to understand its true meaning.

Years later I was mentoring a young coach and was observing him deliver a practice to a group of 14-year-olds. He was getting more and more frustrated that his practice was not going to plan, and proceeded to moan and show annoyance at the players. The "look in the mirror first" statement rushed to the forefront of my mind. The practice after all, like all practices, was a product of what the coach had put in place. Its flaws in terms of preparation, organization, area sizes and coach communication were obvious to me as an observer, but the guy in the middle could not see it. By blaming everyone and everything else for the flaws, he was simply passing the buck from himself to his players - and had completely no idea he was doing so. My advice to him was a direct quote, although said far more tactfully, "look in the mirror first".

You may have noticed throughout this book that I rarely, if ever, blame the players for my below par performance. I now regularly step back from practices that are going poorly, and give more thought to negative issues around my teams. I now realize that I have the power and control over what is happening.

In the past, I have had arguments with a player (and was totally inflexible with him) before learning a parent of his was actually terminally ill. I have demanded more effort and less laziness during practices that were not especially engaging in the first place. I have produced poor tactical plans, but blamed individual errors on the field of play for the strategy's downfall. I have probably made all the mistakes a coach can make.

The difference now, however, is that I look in the mirror first. I now consider whether it is something I have said, or done, that has caused the effect. Sure, sometimes it is not my fault - but I have noticed that invariably it is.

How to Look

I would like to leave you with two resources that you can use as a coach to help you look in the mirror. These can help you become more self-aware and analytical in your work, and will help you assess your own performance. Both documents are from English Premier League clubs.

The first is from Manchester United's Soccer School. The program uses this template to analyse their coaches' performances around 23 measures across four areas – planning, knowledge, management and coaching style. Each point is given a score out of five (one being poor and five being excellent).

The second from Chelsea's Development Centre Program are rules around the way coaches should behave, coach, and work with their young players, something they call "The Chelsea Way". Again, use these documents as you see fit – use them precisely, or adapt as necessary.

<table>
<tr><td colspan="2">**Manchester United Soccer Schools**
Coach Development Sheet</td></tr>
</table>

A. PLANNING & PREPARATION		Comments
Appearance	1 2 3 4 5	
Session Plan	1 2 3 4 5	
Organization Space	1 2 3 4 5	
Organization of players	1 2 3 4 5	
Use of MUSS Equipment	1 2 3 4 5	
Welfare & Safety of Players	1 2 3 4 5	
Registration of Players	1 2 3 4 5	
B. SUBJECT / TOPIC KNOWLEDGE		
Warm-up session	1 2 3 4 5	
Technical detail demonstrated and taught	1 2 3 4 5	
Skill practice progression	1 2 3 4 5	
Coaching in small-sided games	1 2 3 4 5	
Evidence of progressing to needs of players	1 2 3 4 5	
C. MANAGEMENT OF GROUP		
Coaching position	1 2 3 4 5	
Questions – right way, right time, right question	1 2 3 4 5	
Communication with group	1 2 3 4 5	
Control of group	1 2 3 4 5	
Rapport with group	1 2 3 4 5	
Encourages player-led learning	1 2 3 4 5	
D. COACHING STYLES USED		
Guided Discovery	1 2 3 4 5	
Command	1 2 3 4 5	
Question & Answer	1 2 3 4 5	
Positive environment created?	1 2 3 4 5	
Adaptability to session plan	1 2 3 4 5	

"The Chelsea Way"	
Start and end each session with fun	Lots of 1v1s against different types of opponents (quick, strong, skilful, etc)
Ensure you have a ball to each player	Inspire with your session, your personality, and your enthusiasm
Simple organization and lay out	Encourage attacking football
Simple rules and communication	Encourage hard work
No bus queues of players waiting	Occasionally set a homework task
Develop individuals, not teams	Ask questions, give choice on techniques
Realism (attack and defend the goals)	

Conclusion

When I began preparing and writing this book, I had no idea how long it was going to get. I had some idea of what I really, really wanted to say, but was not sure what other information I wanted to add.

The best books I have read about soccer, teaching, or coaching have not *told* me what to do. I did not accept every word and change my entire method of working. The best books I have read plant ideas, change habits, and influence further learning. I sincerely hope that *Making the Ball Roll* has helped you do this also.

Deliberate Soccer Practice: 50 Passing & Possession Football Exercises to Improve Decision-Making by Ray Power

Aimed at football coaches of all levels, but with a particular emphasis on coaches who work with youth players, *50 Passing & Possession Football Exercises to Improve Decision-Making* is comprised of 20 Technical Practices and 30 Possession Practices. They are carefully designed to be adaptable to suit the needs of the players you work with; to challenge them and give them decisions to make. The sessions look to make soccer complex and realistically difficult – no passing in queues from one cone to the next with no interference. Crucially, the exercises offer a means to accelerate player development effectively and enjoyably.

Part of the *Deliberate Soccer Practice* series.

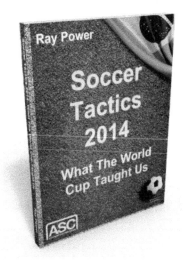

Soccer Tactics 2014: What The World Cup Taught Us by Ray Power

Soccer Tactics 2014 analyses the intricacies of modern international systems, through the lens of matches in Brazil. Covering formations, game plans, key playing positions, and individuals who bring football tactics to life - the book offers analysis and insights for soccer coaches, football players, and fans the world over.

Whether it is Tiki-Taka, counter-attacking, or David defending heroically to defeat Goliath - this book sheds light on where football tactics currently stand… and where they are going.

Includes analysis of group matches, the knock out stages, and the final.

Soccer Tough: Simple Football Psychology Techniques to Improve Your Game by Dan Abrahams

"Take a minute to slip into the mind of one of the world's greatest soccer players and imagine a stadium around you. Picture a performance under the lights and mentally play the perfect game."

Technique, speed and tactical execution are crucial components of winning soccer, but it is mental toughness that marks out the very best players – the ability to play when pressure is highest, the opposition is strongest, and fear is greatest. Top players and coaches understand the importance of sport psychology in soccer but how do you actually train your mind to become the best player you can be? Soccer Tough demystifies this crucial side of the game and offers practical techniques that will enable soccer players of all abilities to actively develop focus, energy, and confidence. Soccer Tough will help banish the fear, mistakes, and mental limits that holds players back.

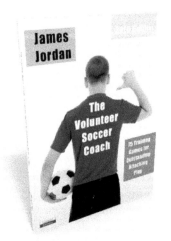

The Volunteer Soccer Coach: 75 Training Games for Outstanding Attacking Play by James Jordan

Are you a volunteer soccer coach with a full time job outside football? Then this book is for you! Minimizing jargon and looking to maximize the limited contact time you have with your players, The Volunteer Soccer Coach is a must-read practical book for coaches of all levels.

Utilising a game-based approach to soccer – where individuals actually play games rather than growing old in semi-static drills – author James Jordan offers 75 cutting-edge exercises across 15 detailed session plans which help players develop an attacking mindset, improve their skills, and, most of all, nurture a love for soccer.

Through his approach, James has won six High School State Championships and one Classic 1 Boys' Club Championship over the past decade.

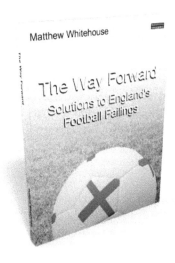

The Way Forward: Solutions to England's Football Failings
by Matthew Whitehouse

In his acclaimed book, The Way Forward, football coach Matthew Whitehouse examines the causes of English football's decline and offers a number of areas where change and improvement need to be implemented immediately. With a keen focus and passion for youth development and improved coaching he explains that no single fix can overcome current difficulties and that a multi-pronged strategy is needed. If we wish to improve the standards of players in England then we must address the issues in schools, the grassroots, and academies, as well as looking at the constraints of the Premier League and English FA.

Scientific Approaches to Goalkeeping in Football: A practical perspective on the most unique position in sport
by Andy Elleray

Do you coach goalkeepers and want to help them realise their fullest potential? Are you a goalkeeper looking to reach the top of your game? Then search no further and dive into this dedicated goalkeeping resource. Written by goalkeeping guru Andy Elleray this book offers a fresh and innovative approach to goalkeeping in football. With a particular emphasis on the development of young goalkeepers, it sheds light on training, player development, match performances, and player analysis. Utilising his own experiences Andy shows the reader various approaches, systems and exercises that will enable goalkeepers to train effectively and appropriately to bring out the very best in them.

The Modern Soccer Coach: Position-Specific Training by Gary Curneen

Aimed at football coaches of all levels, and players of all ages and abilities, The Modern Soccer Coach: Position-Specific Training seeks to identify, develop, and enhance the skills and functions of the modern soccer player whatever their position and role on the pitch.

This book offers unique insight into how to develop an elite program that can both improve players and win games. Filled with practical no-nonsense explanations, focused player drills, and more than 40 illustrated soccer templates, this book will help you – the modern coach - to create a coaching environment that will take your players to the next level.

The Footballer's Journey: real-world advice on becoming and remaining a professional footballer
by Dean Caslake and Guy Branston

Many youngsters dream of becoming a professional footballer. But football is a highly competitive world where only a handful will succeed. Many aspiring soccer players don't know exactly what to expect, or what is required, to make the transition from the amateur world to the 'bright lights' in front of thousands of fans. The Footballer's Journey maps out the footballer's path with candid insight and no-nonsense advice. It examines the reality of becoming a footballer including the odds of 'making it', how academies really work, the importance of attitude and mindset, and even the value of having a backup plan if things don't quite work out.

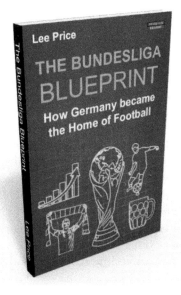

The Bundesliga Blueprint: How Germany became the Home of Football by Lee Price

In this entertaining, fascinating, and superbly-researched book, sportswriter Lee Price explores German football's 10-year plan. A plan that forced clubs to invest in youth, limit the number of foreign players in teams, build success without debt, and much more. The Bundesliga Blueprint details how German fans part-own and shape their clubs, how football is affordable, and the value of beer and a good sausage on match days. The book includes interviews from Michael Ballack, Jens Nowotny and Christoph Kramer, and the movers-and-shakers behind Germany's leading clubs including Schalke, Dortmund, and Paderborn.

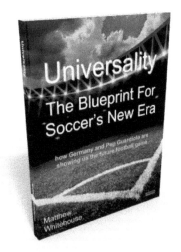

Universality | The Blueprint for Soccer's New Era: How Germany and Pep Guardiola are showing us the Future Football Game by Matthew Whitehouse

The game of soccer is constantly in flux; new ideas, philosophies and tactics mould the present and shape the future. In this book, Matthew Whitehouse – acclaimed author of The Way Forward: Solutions to England's Football Failings - looks in-depth at the past decade of the game, taking the reader on a journey into football's evolution. Examining the key changes that have occurred since the turn of the century, right up to the present, the book looks at the evolution of tactics, coaching, and position-specific play. They have led us to this moment: to the rise of universality. Universality | The Blueprint For Soccer's New Era is a voyage into football, as well as a lesson for coaches, players and fans who seek to know and anticipate where the game of the future is heading.

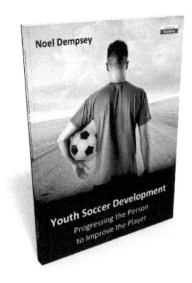

Youth Soccer Development: Progressing the Person to Improve the Player by Noel Dempsey

In "Youth Soccer Development", football coach Noel Dempsey examines where coaching has come from and where it is heading. Offering insights into how English football has developed, coaching methods, 'talent' in youngsters, and how a player's entire environment needs to be considered in coaching programmes - this book offers many touchpoints for coaches who want to advance their thinking and their coaching. Leaving specific onfield drills and exercises to other books, "Youth Soccer Development" digs deep into 'nature versus nature', players' core beliefs, confidence, motivation, and much more. Advocating that to improve the player, you must improve the person, Dempsey puts forward a case for coaches to be realistic with their players, ensure that they work positively across all facets of their lives - especially education - and to instil a mindset that leads to players being the best person they can be.

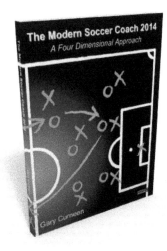

The Modern Soccer Coach by Gary Curneen

Aimed at Soccer coaches of all levels and with players of all ages and abilities The Modern Soccer Coach 2014 identifies the areas that must be targeted by coaches who want to maximize a team's potential – the Technical, Tactical, Physical, and Mental sides to the game. See how the game has changed and what areas determine success in the game today. Learn what sets coaches like Mourinho, Klopp, Rodgers, and Guardiola apart from the rest. Philosophies and training methods from the most forward thinking coaches in the game today are presented, along with guidelines on creating a modern environment for readers' teams. This book is not about old school methodologies – it is about creating a culture of excellence that gets the very best from players. Contains more than 30 illustrated exercises that focus on tactical, technical, mental, and physical elements of the game.

Lightning Source UK Ltd.
Milton Keynes UK
UKHW050319031218
333245UK00011B/85/P